Jacobean Poetry and Prose

Rhetoric, Representation and the Popular Imagination

Edited by
Clive Bloom

D1825732

MACMILLAN
PRESS

First published 1988

Published by
THE MACMILLAN PRESS LTD
Houndmills, Basingstoke, Hampshire RG21 2XS
and London
Companies and representatives
throughout the world

Typeset by Wessex Typesetters
(Division of The Eastern Press Ltd)
Frome, Somerset

Printed in Hong Kong

British Library Cataloguing in Publication Data
Jacobean poetry and prose: rhetoric, representation and the popular imagination.
—(Insights).
1. English literature—Early modern, 1500–1700—History and criticism
I. Bloom, Clive   II. Series
820'.9   PR421
ISBN 0–333–44394–2 (hc)
ISBN 0–333–46538–5 (pbk)

Contents

Preface and Acknowledgements

This volume presents eleven essays on the Jacobean period, plus an Introduction. Each essay combines, in a clear and understandable way, contemporary literary theory and sound practical criticism. Subjects covered include the poetry of John Donne, the theology and impact of the Book of Common Prayer, the politics of Jacobean theatre, the works of Thomas Nashe, the popular fictions and ballads of the period and the theory and practice of poetic production and artistic ideology. The book combines a comprehensive range of literary approaches (Marxist, feminist, post-structuralist) in order to investigate selected aspects of the richly diverse culture of the early seventeenth century. Also included is a select bibliography for further reading.

Thanks are due to Brian Docherty for his vigilance and support, to Bob Lee, Darryll Grantley and John Simons for last-minute aid, and to Graham Eyre for his expert advice.

C. B.

Notes on the Contributors

Clive Bloom is Coordinator of American Studies at Middlesex Polytechnic. He is General Editor of the Insights series and the author of books on literary criticism, Romanticism and popular culture.

Helen Carr has taught at the University of Essex and at Thames Polytechnic. She is an editor of the feminist arts magazine *Women's Review* and has published articles on American and English literature.

Malcolm Evans teaches at the Polytechnic of North London. He is the author of *Signifying Nothing: Truth's True Contents in Shakespeare's Texts* and a contributor to *Alternative Shakespeares*.

Sylvia Freedman is a practising solicitor, and the author of *Poor Penelope: Lady Penelope Rich, an Elizabethan Woman* and the play *The Voyage Home* about Virginia Woolf.

Robert Giddings is the editor of two forthcoming volumes in the Insights series, *Literature and Imperialism* and *Literature and the Media*.

Darryll Grantley lectures at the University of Kent on English and American literature. He has written several articles on the medieval and Renaissance periods.

Stephen Knight is the Robert Wallace Chair of English at the University of Melbourne, Australia. His many publications include work on medieval literature, Chaucer and crime fiction.

Valerie Pitt recently retired as head of Humanities at Thames Polytechnic. She has written on a variety of subjects and is a lay member of the Synod of the Church of England.

Neil Rhodes lectures at St Andrew's University, Scotland. He is the author of *Elizabethan Grotesque* and editor of *John Donne:*

Selected Prose and is currently working on a book about eloquence in Renaissance literature.

Mary Shakeshaft is a Principal Lecturer in English at Middlesex Polytechnic. Her research interests cover Shakespeare, Renaissance poetry, religious poetry and children's literature.

John Simons is currently Lecturer in English Literature at King Alfred's College, Winchester. Having recently finished an edition of Henry Porter's *Two Angry Women of Abingdon* in collaboration with M. Jardine, he is now working on a book about Shakespeare and Milton.

William Zunder is a Renaissance specialist at Hull University. He has published *The Poetry of John Donne* and is completing a study of Marlowe.

1

Introduction: Authority, Text and the Jacobean Mind

CLIVE BLOOM

The Jacobean period lies uneasily between a mythicised Elizabethan golden age, seen to mark a 'flowering' of Englishness, and an equally mythicised era of struggle between king and Parliament. As such, it is the victim of mythicists and propagandists from Elizabeth's reign and the seventeenth century and of the romanticised view of history presented by Walter Scott and Hollywood. Indeed, the tendency to see an age as symbolic of mythic struggle was inherent in both Tudor and Stuart England. Milton was the last great propagandist–apologist of one strand of this cultural fixation with the 'pregnancy' of an age and with its potential for a hypothesised millennial future. On all levels the Jacobean age can be seen in this way as a short hiatus before the coming self-destruction of the Civil War, a period of decadence, of a vulgarising of humanistic values – of a mounting political, artistic and cultural hysteria.

Certainly, commentators at the time from Shakespeare, Donne and Webster to James I and his bishops brought evidence that this was so. However, the period also witnessed many great dramatists and poets, philosophers and theologians, alchemists, 'scientists' and discoverers at their peak. Indeed, it might be said that the Jacobean period was *the* great period of English literature and thought – the moment when the medieval gave way to the modern. Douglas Bush, in his *English Literature in the Earlier Seventeenth Century*, points out that,

While all ages are ages of transition, there are some in which disruptive and creative forces reach maturity and combine to speed up the normal process of change. In the history of England, as in that of Europe at large, the seventeenth century is probably the most conspicuous modern example, unless we except our own age, of such acceleration. In 1600 the educated Englishman's mind and world were more than half medieval; by 1660 they were more than half modern. . . . But this process of change did not begin or end in the years 1600–60, and it took place against a background of continuity and compromise. We encounter the clash and the fusion of old and new on every side, in science and religion, politics and economics, law and literature, music and architecture. It is the impact of modernism upon medievalism that gives the age its peculiar character. Yet the forces of 'modernism' were themselves generally as old as the forces of conservative tradition and it was in the name of conservative tradition that the great rebellion in politics and religion was conducted.[1]

On one side the decadence of the Jacobean period, a period rich in all aspects of intellectual life, is the culmination of Elizabethanism, while on the other that intellectual life represents itself as striving forward in order to *return* to a lost golden age of traditions, ruralism, hierarchy, absolutism and feudalism. These yearnings were themselves part of the ideology of the period, which saw itself as precariously balanced between an older stable order of harmony between aristocrat and peasant and the new threat posed by an expanding, increasingly alienated urban society of merchants and artisans. On this view, 'Jacobean' designates not just a period but an ideology that had its roots in Elizabethan England and lasted until 1660. Milton was the last 'Jacobean' and *Paradise Lost* the last 'Jacobean' text.

There is no better place to find the tension of the age than in the literature of the period – a literature that was so diverse and profuse and so full of the tensions between the old and the modern that it gave the world the ideological concept of *English literature*: England's greatest form of imperial conquest, English culture. This is a literature which records a revolutionary struggle for cultural control; the language is that of *King Lear*, *Hamlet*, *Macbeth*, the Authorised Version of the Bible (the King James version), the Book of Common Prayer, *The Compleat Angler* and *Paradise Lost*. British colonial power took with it the prestige of an English literature which embodied the rights and *authority* of 'Anglo–Saxon' Englishness everywhere. In the literary and intellectual struggles of the time, all of which are recorded in texts, an evangelical cultural tradition was formed which needed no 'rediscovery' by Rupert Brooke or T. S. Eliot: Jacobean literature is the cultural base of eighteenth-century squires and Victorian moral reformers, of high Toryism and nonconformist liberalism. The most important text of any age in a Christian country is the Bible. In the Jacobean period the theological arena (which was always the political arena) saw the production of the most influential English book ever produced: the Authorised or King James's version of the Bible. In its production can be seen the struggles of a period which conceived of itself in a dangerous and terrifying flux leading all too clearly to chaos. The goal of the translators was a return to an older and quite clear *authority*, but a return achieved by the most modern means. In this lay an attempt to circumvent change by change itself – a 'newer' yet closer translation of the foundation of the state. How was this to happen? By the rigorous application of 'literary theory': of translation, of exegesis, of hermeneutics. The need to base authority on text did not come back until the twentieth century, and post-structuralist debates from Barthes to Derrida are a 'return' to the methods employed by seventeenth-century theologians and linguists trying to understand the process of signification. The authority of 'text' was a political issue in the seventeenth century, and the debates surrounding it had social consequences unparalleled since and now confined to an academic arena that is only haphazardly political and rarely interventionist. In the seventeenth century textuality was socialised and public and as such had ramifications that offered to shake the social fabric.

Hence it was that, following a chance remark of John Reynolds, President of Corpus Christi, at the Hampton Court Conference of 1604, a full-scale 'revision' of the theocratic centre of the state machine was set in motion – a new and more authentic version of the Bible in English was to be produced. Reynolds, we are told, 'moved his Majestie, that there might bee a newe translation of the Bible, because those which were allowed in the raignes of Henrie the eight, and Edward the sixt, were corrupt and not aunswerable to the truth of the Originall'.[2]

Reynolds, a Puritan, was calling for a return not to the period of the Tudor texts, which he declared to be 'corrupt', but beyond them to their origins in Greek and Hebrew, a call endorsed by James, himself a noted theological debater, who had produced a

'Paraphrase upon the Revelation of St John'. For Reynolds the Jacobean period was to be a return to a Hebraic purity and a Greek classicism untainted by Tudor corruption and Tudor decadence – the *Word* would finally be restored. In order to ground political authority, an abstract authority that was independent but linked needed to be found. The Word had that authority – in English (for the English as the chosen people in their 'Zion') it doubled its authorial hold. James saw this clearly, declaring 'that no marginall notes should be added, having found in them which are annexed to the Geneva translation (which he sawe in a Bible given him by an English lady) some notes very partiall, untrue, seditious, and savouring too much of dangerous and trayterous conceits'.

To achieve clarity of expression (lack of political ambiguity?) a number of learned committees were set up to check, debate, translate and rethink the Bible's language. Rules were drawn up, of which these are an example:

The ordinary Bible read in the Church, commonly called the *Bishops Bible*, to be followed, and as little altered as the truth of the original will permit. . . .

When a Word hath divers Significations, that to be kept which hath been most commonly used by the most of the Ancient Fathers, being agreeable to the Propiety of the Place and the Analogy of the Faith. . . .

No Marginal Notes at all to be affixed, but only for the Explanation of the *Hebrew* or *Greek* Words, which cannot without some circumlocution, so briefly and fitly be express'd in the Text. . . .

As any one Company hath dispatched any one Book in this Manner they shall send it to the rest, to be consider'd of seriously and judiciously, for his Majesty is very careful in this Point. . . .

When any Place of special Obscurity is doubted of Letters to be directed, by Authority, to send to any Learned Man in the Land, for his Judgement of such a Place.[3]

These are the rules of textual experts, of literary analysts and of professional intellectuals aware of their political affiliations and the nuance of a phrase or word in the hands of the seditious. By

1607 the process was under way: by 1618 the English delegates at the Synod of Dort could report,

> after each section had finished its task twelve delegates . . . met together and reviewed and revised the whole work. . . . The rules laid down for the translators were of this kind: In the first place caution was given that an entirely new version was not to be furnished, but an old version, long received by the Church, to be purged from all blemishes and faults; to this end there was to be no departure from the ancient translation, unless the truth of the original text or emphasis demanded.[4]

Modern techniques were employed to return to a 'purged' Bible, a purified document that would link for all time English fidelity to truth and Hebrew revelation, the Englishman to the ancient Hebrew prophets, the seventeenth-century commonwealth to Zion ('there should be one more exact Translation of the Scriptures in the English Tongue'). The mission of the Hebrew prophets was to be fulfilled by the Englishman of the seventeenth century. Milton, for one, felt this only too clearly, for the wayward children of Israel were to him the backsliding English of the Caroline period. Milton was the prophet of the authority of the word because he was the prophet of English rights and of a search for the second coming of an English Christ.

In the Preface to the finished translation a clear statement of divine authority is mediated via an equally clear statement about monarchical authority. The Preface is dedicated to James, the man and the symbol.

TO THE MOST HIGH AND MIGHTY PRINCE
JAMES
BY THE GRACE OF GOD
KING OF GREAT BRITAIN, FRANCE, AND IRELAND
DEFENDER OF THE FAITH, &c.
The Translators of the Bible Wish Grace, Mercy, and Peace
through JESUS CHRIST our Lord

There follows a paean of praise both to authority and to Englishness; to the myth of a divine monarch and a people with a divine mission:

Great and manifold were the blessings, most dread Sovereign, which Almighty God, the Father of all mercies, bestowed upon us the people of *England*, when first he sent Your Majesty's Royal Person to rule and reign over us. For whereas it was the expectation of many, who wished not well unto our *Sion*, that upon the setting of that bright *Occidental Star*, Queen *Elizabeth* of most happy memory, some thick and palpable clouds of darkness would so have overshadowed this Land, that men should have been in doubt which way they were to walk; and that it should hardly be known, who was to direct the unsettled State; the appearance of Your Majesty, as of the *Sun* in his strength, instantly dispelled those supposed and surmised mists, and gave unto all that were well affected exceeding cause of comfort; especially when we beheld the Government established in Your Highness, and hopeful Seed, by an undoubted Title, and this also accompanied with peace and tranquillity at home and abroad.

Here is a mythic and monumental propaganda of God and state. God sends James, like Christ, to save the English in their 'Sion'. Like 'the *Sun*', James's presence dispels corruption and 'darkness'. His authorial presence restores 'Government' and 'peace and tranquillity' to an 'unsettled State'. His title – unlike Elizabeth's, no longer disputed but 'undoubted' – is a guarantee of success to the faith and zeal of the people and the theologians toiling on their behalf, for James stands as the 'immediate Author of their true happiness'. Like God the father, James is a 'tender loving father', like Christ the Son he comes down from heaven as the 'Sun' in place of Elizabeth's 'Occidental Star'. God's word, the word of English authority, is set to fulfil its mission. James manifests 'zeal' in promoting 'the Truth' abroad in the farthest parts of Christendom, and the proto-capitalist English merchant ethic fuses with God's holy Word:

But among all our joys, there was no one that more filled our hearts, than the blessed continuance of the preaching of God's sacred Word among us; which is that inestimable treasure, which excelleth all the riches of earth; because the fruit thereof extendeth itself, not only to the time spent in this transitory world, but directeth and disposeth men unto that eternal happiness which is above in heaven.

The Bible becomes the treasure house of the state; the state becomes the patriarchal and beneficent James – his civil authority apotheosised in an ideology of divinity which is Hebrew, imperial Roman and English. If, ultimately, James could not say, 'L'état c'est moi', and the textual 'laws' could not be enforced, it was because the text was fractured and was itself representative of a tension between the old and the new, not merely a return but a departure – a true modern text, fragmented, contractidory, political and ultimately problematic. Its 'authority' was the result of an age both complacent and neurotic, an age whose neuroses were public before they were private and private only because they were public.

NOTES

1. Douglas Bush, *English Literature in the Earlier Seventeenth Century, 1600–1660* (Oxford: Clarendon Press, 1962) p. 1.
2. Quoted from J. Isaacs, 'The Authorized Version and After', in *The Bible in its Ancient and English Versions*, ed. H. Wheeler Robinson (Oxford: Clarendon Press, 1940) pp. 196–7.
3. Ibid., pp. 199–200.
4. Ibid., p. 201.

2

Open and Closed Books: a Semiotic Approach to the History of Elizabethan and Jacobean Popular Romance

JOHN SIMONS

It is over ten years now since R. H. Hilton pointed out some of the inconsistencies and problems in the arguments of historians who, in dealing with early English society, eschew the word 'class' and prefer instead some less politically charged term such as 'status'.[1] More recently, R. S. Neale has provided a detailed analysis of similar tendencies.[2] Yet many involved in the teaching of literature, especially the inter-disciplinary area of literature and history, still avoid theories of cultural development which understand literary texts as the products of societies which are divided along class lines, and may even go so far as to penalise students who wish to employ such theories in their own work. However, although this essay starts from a pluralist position, it is not intended as a piece of sustained raillery against what seem to me illiberal tendencies in the teaching of literature, nor as a polemical analysis of the issues involved. Rather, these introductory remarks are necessary because in my account of some Jacobean popular fiction I shall treat early-seventeenth-century England as a society in the process of transforming itself through the dynamic interplay of conflicting class interests, and its literature as both product and reflection of that struggle.

From the point of view of its cultural production, the English Renaissance seems most frequently to have been treated, in academic contexts, as if Peter Laslett's model of a 'one-class society' held good.[3] This is not to say that scholars and critics working in the field necessarily subscribe consciously to Laslett's schema, but rather to suggest that the concentration on a supposedly coherent canon of texts produced by (or, more accurately, for) the ruling elite tends to censor out the rich and varied popular culture of the town and countryside and to imply that it has no voice worth listening to. The drama may be an anomalous case since it possesses the curious property of being, as Raymond Williams has pointed out, 'linguistically co-extensive with the whole range of its society', but even here the familiar picture of the play which appeals to the lord of the gallery, the gallant on the stage and the groundling in the pit will not bear too much inspection.[4] Furthermore, the general ideology of English studies as it affects Renaissance drama has frequently led to a focus on issues such as magistracy and order to the neglect of that unique feature which ought to be the main focus of dramatic studies, and to the forcing of an heterogeneous form into the ill-fitting mould constructed by a model which homogenises early modern society.[5]

The practical result of such an approach to the Renaissance is the relative unavailability of popular texts, and I must apologise in advance for the obscurity of the material which I discuss below, but I believe that as scholars, particularly those who are professionally involved in the teaching of English literature, become more genuinely committed to the idea of an interdisciplinary English Studies and the structure of English in higher education changes accordingly, the materials for easier access to early popular culture will gradually become available. It is, of course, hardly surprising that this neglect has taken place. First, English as a 'subject' has traditionally concerned itself with the evaluation of what is perceived as 'best' in the range of literary production, an aesthetic judgement which places itself neatly on top of a process of political selection, conscious or not, resulting in the identification of a canon which represents the cultural interests of dominant social groups. Secondly, for the Renaissance at least, a challenge to this process of canonisation constitutes a breach of the protocols of periodisation which distinguish the methods of literary-historical criticism and, therefore, a disruption of the vision of smooth and harmonious social development which accompanies it. The student brought up on a notion of the Renaissance which runs from Sidney and Spenser to Milton via Donne will, when faced with popular literature, be struck by the challenge which this literature presents, in its world view, to any model of continuous development. Historical and artistic development is by no means the quasi-evolutionary, natural process which traditional literary criticism would have us accept, and Renaissance popular literature presents a world view which exposes development as discontinuous, being often close to that of the late Middle Ages and sometimes to that of the radicals of the 1640s.

The point of this essay is to explore some of the features of this world view through the mechanisms which reproduce it in Elizabethan and Jacobean popular romance. I shall consistently argue that this fiction operates in a space cleared by a tension between an urban middle class, which constituted the reading public of the texts and which was increasingly gaining economic power, and an aristocracy or court which retained ideological hegemony and, consequently, control over important state institutions.

Though the term 'Renaissance' traditionally describes a period of literary production which, in England, stretches between the mid-sixteenth and the mid-seventeenth centuries, the fierce Protestantism and patriotism which characterise much of its popular fiction leads me to the view that the Reformation was the culturally crucial event in the lives of the majority of those who were involved in the production or consumption of literary texts, and that the 'Renaissance' was a phenomenon which touched a minority of the cultural elite. Given the development of the Renaissance in the European context, the term has, in any case, always felt rather awkward when applied to England, and even critics who prefer to stick by it ought to account for the fact that, pragmatically speaking, Chaucer might be said to be the first English Petrarchan.

In the late sixteenth and early seventeenth centuries popular fiction came in a variety of kinds. The following list is far from complete but gives some idea of the scope of an area of literature which has suffered general critical neglect: euphuistic tales, Italianate novellas, picaresque novellas, Greek romances, Peninsular romances (based upon Spanish and Portuguese originals), retellings of classical myth, low-life pamphlets. I propose to concentrate on the genre of adventurous romance, which tells of chivalric questing and has its origins in the complex of romance inherited from the Middle Ages. This was easily available to the Elizabethan and Jacobean author through the numerous printings of these long narrative poems, which were published throughout the sixteenth century.[6] The Jacobean modifications of these texts fully illustrate the particular class-consciousness of their audience and may be viewed not only synchronically, in their relationship with other kinds of contemporary text, but also diachronically, through the modifications which they make to their source material.

That these texts do constitute the expression of a class-consciousness which challenges that of the culturally dominant group may be gauged from the fact that, if modern critics have neglected them, they fared little better in their own day. Writers whose work now constitutes the corpus from which we construct the 'Renaissance' leave us in no doubt that they understand the socio-political implications of texts which they rejected as either immoral or bad art or both:

> the fantasticall dreames of those exiled abbie-lubbers, from whose idle pens proceeded those worne out impressions of the feyned no where acts, of Arthur of the rounde table, Arthur of little Brittaine, sir Tristram, Hewon of Burdeaux, the Squire of low degree, the foure sons of Amon, with infinite others.[7]

Sidney, perhaps the best example of 'Renaissance man' that England produced, saw some of the qualities of romance but also saw through to the appropriate social context of such work: 'honest King Arthur, will never displease a soldier'.[8] But, in spite of these humanistic strictures, coming as they did from a world almost wholly dissociated from that of the literate middle-class audience, the romances continued as a vehicle for that audience's presentation to itself of its life and its ideology.

The popular romance with which this essay will be concerned takes up the basic narrative structure of Middle English romance virtually intact but uses it to articulate material which, among other things, displays an advanced consciousness of the practical problems of knightly questing and, in the most developed examples, carries out a wholesale displacement of chivalric motifs and the ideology which generated them in favour of the mercantile–Protestant ideology of the seventeenth-century audience, a displacement exemplified especially by an aggressive patriotism and the increasingly important role given to 'common' characters and utilitarian concerns.

The body of popular material may be profitably analysed through a socio-historical approach which reads the texts through the constant relation of their formal features to the political and economic life of their consumers, the trading mechanisms of the book industry and the increasing literacy rate of a middle-class public broadly defined as urban, having connections with a trade organisation either as artisan or merchant/master and, psychologically, of entrepreneurial disposition.[9] However, this approach has been worked out elsewhere, and for this essay I propose an approach through literary theory taking my model from the text semiotics of Umberto Eco.

I intend to adopt, in a limited and somewhat simplified form, Eco's distinction between 'open' and 'closed' work as a convenient expression of the processes by which Elizabethan and Jacobean popular romance was generated out of Middle English material and to show how, in spite of structural similarities, the Jacobean works constitute a peculiarly original body of literature.[10] I have some doubts about Eco's general theory of semiotics in so far as it appears to permit a degrading of the importance of the social foundations of signifying activity, but, if I may be allowed to strain at the camel and swallow the gnat, I shall extrapolate the open–closed pairing as a convenient device for the description of a particular aspect of literary production.

In Eco's scheme an 'open' text is 'a paramount instance of a syntactic–semantico-pragmatic device whose foreseen interpretation is part of its generative process',[11] one which 'outlines a "closed" project of its Model Reader as a component of its structural strategy'.[12] In other words, 'open' texts are those which posit a foreseen interpretation through the operation of a controlled range of social and literary codes. These codes will be determined in their interpretational aspects by the integration of a particularised Model Reader into the text itself. Trenchantly put, an 'open' text encloses its own reader. Opposed to this is the 'closed' text which is 'open to every possible interpretation' precisely, and paradoxically, because of its lack of an integral Model Reader, one whose function in the production of textual significance is not predetermined by the careful control of literary devices.[13] Practically, Eco's model of 'open' textuality appears to be more or less conterminous with the conventional canon of 'great' literature, but I wish to argue that, if it is used to help map the relationship between literary history and social development, it can be a powerful device to challenge and extend that canon. Through it this relationship may be seen as one in which the 'open' work of one era is subjected to progressive 'closure' as the social conditions which guarantee the 'correct' reading of its codes change and dissolve and that texts which are thus 'closed' may then be 'opened' as new texts by being read in contexts where codes other than those of the original work are dominant. I wish to analyse this process diachronically, tracing the development of romance from the late Middle Ages to the early seventeenth century, but Eco points out the synchronic dimension of an analogous movement:

> Finally, an ideological bias can lead a critical reader to make a given text say more than it apparently says, that is, to find out what in that text is ideologically presupposed, untold. In this movement from the ideological subcodes of the interpreter to the ideological subcodes tentatively attributed to the author . . . even the most closed texts are surgically 'opened'.[14]

The romances of the thirteenth and fourteenth centuries may be read, in the medieval context, as 'open' in that they undoubtedly contain the idea of their Model Reader.[15] They include, for example, an abundance of authorial interventions designed to structure the emotional response of the audience and to key it into the modes of chivalric ideology as it is articulated in the structure of romance narrative. This articulation is itself a convention operative as a directive and limiting device. H. R. Jauss has provided a valuable analysis of romance, concluding with a pithy statement of its social function which might be taken to refer to the Model Reader and his or her progressive 'disappearance' from the text:

> The later function as an entertainment for the private reader is preceded by the original function of the initiation into courtly life and courtly love: 'the legitimate quest for a terrestial happiness regulated by a social discipline and a life-style'.[16]

Jauss's stress on the courtly aspects of romance is a caveat against scholars who see romance as 'popular' in a general sense. My essay rejects such views and, though it acknowledges the formal distinctions, especially at the level of diction, between many of the Middle English romances and unambiguously courtly work such as *Troilus and Criseyde*, it will treat the Model Reader of romance as someone at least on the fringes of courtly life and sufficiently interested in its *mores* to be capable of understanding the often-lengthy descriptions of knightly behaviour to be found in the poems. In the medieval world the question of the Model Reader would not perhaps have set the problem which it does for the contemporary author. The lack of a widely diversified reading public and the limited access to written literature must have virtually guaranteed authorial predictions of potential interpretation. The ideological hold of the Church and the relative lack of a political discourse independent of theology helped to stabilise a matrix of possible meaning and to limit the proliferation of aberrant codes which might have led to the subversive use of the text within the literate group. Julia Kristeva puts it from a semiotic viewpoint:

> The second half of the Middle Ages (thirteenth–fifteenth centuries) is a transitional period for European culture: the thought of the sign replaced that of the symbol. . . .
> The symbol assumes the symbolised (universals) as not reducible to the symbolisings (the marks). The mythic thought which turns in the orbit of the symbol and which manifests itself in the epic, popular tales, *chansons de geste* etc. operates with symbolic units which are units of restriction in relation to the symbolised universals (heroism, courage, nobility, fear, treachery, etc.). The function of the symbol in its vertical dimension (universals–marks) is thus a function of restriction.[17]

In the context of this essay this is important in that the symbols meaningful in medieval systems of thought became progressively drained of their claim to universal significance as the feudal system which provided an economic and political validation and enforcement of the claims gave way to early forms of absolutism and capitalism. Hitherto 'open' texts became 'closed' as the society of their Model Reader crumbled away, and this removal of a structuring element enabled the middle-class readers of the Elizabethan and Jacobean period to reopen the texts, reading their symbols as signs and utilising them for the semiosis, the encoding in signifying practice, of a new class-consciousness.

The romances themselves had long been popular as printed

books, but the increasing obscurity of the medieval texts cried out for modernisation. The elusive Samuel Rowlands realised this in 1609 when introducing his version of *Guy of Warwick*, in some ways the most celebrated and typical of the Middle English narratives: 'Guy of Warwick . . . the neglecting of whose worthy memory, hath induced my more willing than able Muse, to revive the deeds of this dust-consumed champion'.[18] In most cases, though, this process was more substantial than a mere 'translation' of the text into contemporary English: it involved a major reorganisation of the text in such a way as to make present a new, middle-class Model Reader. Another way of putting this is to say that texts are made meaningful not only by their internal structures but also by the conditions of their production. The reader is, thus, not just a producer of meaning in the text but also a feature of that text functioning as an internal limitation. As such, readers provide the link between the text as self-referential verbal artefact and the text as social and ideological 'message'. The internal and external textual worlds are charged with meaning by a range of codes, and the terms of these codes are each subject to historical development and modification which, in the terms of literary theory, will distinctively take the form of 'closure'.

To demonstrate some of the points I have tried to make above and to give concrete examples of this theory of literary development I intend now to concentrate attention on some works by the popular author Henry Robarts. Robarts is typical of Elizabethan and Jacobean popular writers in that virtually nothing is known about his life and in that he wrote in a variety of genres, one of which was romance.[19] I shall use his fiction as an exemplary paradigm of the processes outlined above, but before preceding to an analysis it is worth pausing to look at some of his other work.

Robarts' non-fictional output, which mainly comprises encomiastic verse and journalism, shows him to have been at the centre of the cultural life of his class, subscribing to its ideology and broadcasting it through his writing. His verses and pamphlets are almost all propagandistic praise of English sailors and advertisements of patriotic fervour for the imperialism embryonic in the semi-piratical adventuring then being undertaken by such figures as Sir Francis Drake.[20] It is worth looking at these works as they make explicit the concerns of the middle-class ideology which are only implicit in the prose fiction. In his prefatory remarks to the *Friendly Farewell, Given by a Welwiller to the Right*

Worshipful Sir Frauncis Drake Knight (1585),[21] Robarts clearly
identifies himself as a citizen, with interests and abilities distinct
from those of a higher class, who will praise Drake when others
have omitted to do so:

> Seeing none of the learned sort have undertaken to write
> according to custome, I being the unworthyest, yet the most
> willing, was lothe good Knight that you should depart oure
> Englishe coastes without some remembery to be published in
> prayse both to your worshippe, and the rest of your Gentlemen
> followers in this your noble exploit.

The whole tone of the *Farewell* is patriotic and the poem is filled
with an awareness that exploits such as Drake's bring not only
ideological and political advantage but also material wealth.
Drake's actual status as a knight may be invoked as part of the
displaced subcode of chivalric glory, but the mercantile perspective,
that his martial abilities are of material value, is never forgotten.
Here is a passage taken from another of Robarts' poems in praise
of Drake; *The Trumpet of Fame* (1595):

> Tis Englands honour that you have in hand
> Then think thereof, if you do love our land.
> The gaine is yours, if millions home you bring,
> The courage take, to gaine so sweete a thing.
> The time calls on, which causeth me to end,
> Wherefore to God, I do you all commend,
> For whome all subjects that do love our Queene,
> Shall truly pray, to send you safe againe,
> And for my part, I wish you alwaies health,
> With quick returne, and so much store of wealth,
> That Phillips regions may not be more stored,
> With Pearle, Iewels, and the purest gold.

Through this kind of verse and his journalistic pamphlets Robarts
is sketching out the concerns which are developed in his fiction,
especially the connection between the chivalric values of bravery,
glory and honour, and patriotism and mercantile success. It is out
of this complex and the displacement of the former group of
virtues into the latter that the Model Reader for Robarts' romance
is created.

Robarts is typical of the popular-romance writer of his time in that he shows a full consciousness of the part which he and his class have to play in the development of early modern society. Robarts particularly has a grasp of the material bases of imperialism. Even so he does not, at first, articulate a purely middle-class ideology: he still conceives the adventures which he describes in terms of a chivalric code which is only partially transformed. While his hero is the 'closed' product of the medieval world, Robarts has not properly 'opened' him by the location of virtue directly in mercantile activity.[22] This is not merely a question of grafting a new ideology onto an old structure but also one of understanding that structure and ideology are necessarily integral in the literary text. To 'open' a 'closed' text is a process of reading which can only be achieved by the structural reorganisation of the text in question.

The relative non-specialisation of the idea of literature in the late sixteenth century means that in his patriotic verse Robarts draws a very thin line between journalistic accounts of real life and the romantic narrative of travel and return on which he mainly draws for his prose fiction.[23] This lack of a clear division between the fictional and the journalistic operates at both the structural and the stylistic levels and may be clearly seen at work in other non-fictional works by Robarts. In *Newes from the Levane Sea*, for example, the activities of English sailors are described in a manner derived directly from romance.[24] It is clear that Robarts conceived of himself as a member of a class which was importantly involved in national enterprise, and to reproduce this he turned to the transformations of romance, which could both express the ideology and describe the experience of that class. Robarts' claims for the importance of the urban middle class are made explicit in the prefatory verse to the pamphlet *Lancaster his Allarums* (1595):

> heere cavallers of high esteeme,
> that Londiners contemne
> may know what worthy mindes they bear
> and serve like valiant men. . . .
>
> If London-merchants dare to doe,
> such actions as he did:

Then why should not their acts be tolde,
why should his fame be hid.[25]

A journalistic account of one expedition is thus used in a wider
context to authenticate the claims of the metropolis and its
inhabitants to heroic status. These claims are made in such direct
and generally pervasive terms as to encourage the critic to read
Robarts' fiction as a material product of the ideology specifically
promoted in his journalism.

We may pass over Robarts' first venture into fiction, a moralistic
tale called *A Defiance to Fortune*, as this is highly derivative of the
style of Robert Greene, and move onto the much more interesting
Historie of Pheander the Mayden Knight, which first appeared in
1595, had reached a fourth edition by 1617, and was still in print
in 1661. *Pheander* is a clumsy book which manipulates romance
conventions into an uneasy combination with a decayed euphuism.
The text is highly moralistic, but what is especially interesting
here is Robarts' use of the motif of disguise, which shows the
process of 'opening' clearly at work. Pheander begins the story as
Prince Dionisius and he is love-struck by the Princess Nutania. In
Middle English romance it is common to find a hero pining for
the love of a lady of higher status, but Dionisius is a prince (and
knows it, unlike the typical foundling of medieval narrative) and
has no need to feel a pariah. On the very simplest level a love
affair between two social equals does not suit the demands of a
conventionally conceived romance mode, but, more interestingly,
the ideological sub-codes of the new Model Reader who is implied
by Robarts' text effect a deformation of the expected narrative. To
solve the problem of status Robarts had to look no further than
Guy of Warwick to find a situation in which a junior knight strives
for the love of a social superior and finally wins it through
chivalric accomplishments. In the 'open' period of the Middle
English text this situation can be seen as easily fitted into a
narrative code which articulates, as its sustaining fiction, the *mores*
of the 'courtly love' ethic, but, as chivalric activity become less
and less valuable as a courtly practice, this narrative possibility is
progressively 'closed'. Robarts takes up this closure and, by
deforming the text, is able to throw emphasis onto the class of the
participants and not on the action itself.

Robarts adopts the strategy of having his protagonist disguise
himself as a merchant in order to undertake the questing journey

mandatory in romance. The prince clearly believes that this disguise will enable him to win some favour with Nutania and will certainly not militate against the display of chivalric prowess should the opportunity arise. Even so, when the chance comes, he is knighted before he begins any military adventures. This clearly exemplifies Robarts' relatively underdeveloped ability fully to reorganise the mode of romance, for, though he shows the merchant class with the potential for chivalric action, its members must, formally at least, take on the trappings of another class before embarking upon it.

Pheander is victorious in battle, but his decision to disguise himself as a merchant has another interesting consequence in that, though he has displayed enough valour in battle to make any hero feel confident of winning the lady's hand, he is now only an elevated bourgeois and, as such, not at all suitable to be a princess's husband. The initial reversal of expectations now comes full circle as Nutania wonders whether it is proper to marry a merchant:

> let each estate frame themselves in love to their equals, so shall they sooner obtaine their desire and their loves in more tranquility to be maintained. Thou knowest thy birth how base it is, and though for thy vertues as it pleased my princely father to advance thee who cannot of his princely nature but reward the deserts of the well-deserving. If for his good to thee thou seeke to rob him of his child, therein thou showest a very ungrateful mind, and layest open to the World thy base condition.

Thus, in spite of Pheander's virtues as both trader and knight, the success or failure of his suit will be determined ultimately by his class. He succeeds when he reveals his true identity: 'if thou couldst not love Pheander being a Marchant, for ignobling thy noble house, yet as I am the Prince of Numedia, vouchsafe me thy liking, by whom thy honour can in no way be disparaged'. While it is clear that Robarts is developing romance in such a way as to remove it from the orbit of the aristocracy, his technique has not sufficiently matured to transform romance totally into citizen realism. The central events of *Pheander* show Robarts working out an 'open' poetics for romance as the ideological sub-codes and formal innovations of his method construct within the text itself a

Model Reader of a kind inimical to the original medieval poems.

Robarts' next work, *Honour's Conquest* (1598), is a foray into legendary history. The text we have appears originally to have constituted the second volume out of three, but forms a self-contained romance. In *Honour's Conquest* Robarts again appears to be drawing on the Middle English *Guy of Warwick* to provide a structural model and uses the travels of his hero to exalt the virtues of piety and patriotism. I have already suggested that in Robarts the line between fiction and non-fiction is slim, and, just as his pamphlets prepare the gound for the developing ideology of his romances, so, in this work, he uses history as an authenticating device. As W. R. Davies says, Robarts tried to 'incorporate virtue into an actual historical personage, Edward of Lancaster, and to use the apparent historicity of the events he recorded as a further goad to "the end of all thy reading", "to attaine true vertue"'.[26] Thus, the patriotic romance takes on an educational function, with an end drawn from a different paradigm from that of medieval romance, becoming a product of the paraphernalia of middle-class utilitarianism.

As will be expected, the text is constantly concerned with the mercantile possibilities of the narrative, and an interesting example of this occurs when Edward's supplies run low while he is crossing the desert. He sees a camel train and the merchants gladly replenish his stocks. As the train moves on, it is attacked by Tartars. At first the merchants are amazed, but Edward mobilises them and they bravely drive off their assailants. When Edward has returned from the pursuit the merchants reward him with jewels.

This sort of incident would not be out of place in a Middle English romance, but the treatment which Robarts gives it shows his 'opening' of a plain heroic adventure in order to produce an exact textualising of his Model Reader's ideology. First we should note the obvious: a group of merchants are employed as characters. Immediately their virtue is apparent as they help Edward without question. More subtle is Robarts' conception of the logistical problems of a knightly quest and the recognition that support for the request for material aid can only come from the merchants, a position analogous to that which he takes in some of the patriotic verse described above. As the knight himself is dependent on the merchant, so he becomes a more sympathetic and interesting figure to the popular audience, for whom 'pure' chivalry may have appeared irrelevant or even ludicrous.

Secondly, the merchants' class does not prevent them from being courageous. This too is consistent with the views expressed in Robarts' pamphlets. However, they cannot immediately organise their own defence: it is the example and leadership of Edward, the representative of another class, which enables them to do this. The effect is as if the merchants were drawn from a non-chivalric narrative and, when faced with a situation imported from a different paradigm, remained frozen until animated by a figure from an appropriate mode. This interplay of chivalric and non-chivalric is clearly involved in the treatment of the logistical problems of the quest where a romantic figure is seen to encroach upon a more materially based genre and needs to accept its norms before he can proceed. Semiotically the interplay may be analysed as the intervention of the specific ideological sub-codes of Robarts' audience, first to effect a final 'closure' of the romance as chivalric text and second to reopen it as the particularised reproduction of their own needs and interests.

After refusing payment Edward finally takes a reward: 'The Marchants which had received the benefit of his valour, and freed from those men of mischiefe which had despoyled them of all if hee had beene absent generally besought him to take in worth those they had presented.' In the world of this romance even chivalry has a commercial value, a value which might even seem degrading in the medieval scheme. In Robarts chivalry is not degraded; it is transformed into a new type of romance narrative, structured by different codes and premised on a different ideology. The realistic elements that in Middle English romances had had the sole function of providing occasional relief or new strategy for the plot now become foregrounded as the most privileged elements in the text. This process seems to me more overt in Robarts than in any other of the many early popular authors who wrote what are recognisably chivalric romances.

In *Honour's Conquest* Robarts may be seen to draw on the traditions of the Middle English romances while at the same time preparing the ground for his last work, *Haigh for Devonshire*, a piece of artisan realism in the manner of Deloney, but not plagiarised from him as some commentators would have us believe.[27] There is not the space to discuss this work here, nor would such a discussion be appropriate in the context of this attempt to map a particular line of influence in literary history in the terms of an item of semiotic theory. It is sufficient to say that, in this work, the processes of transformation described above are fully carried through and chivalric ideology is wholly displaced by mercantile concerns within the conventional structures of romance narrative. With the closure of the medieval text there is an opening onto another world. Robarts incites his reader to virtue and it is plain that in seventeenth-century London the citizen might be inspired by being shown recognisably modern figures articulated on the one hand by the structures of medieval romance and on the other by the ideological sub-codes of contemporary patriotism and mercantilism. It is this fusion of two types of organisation, a fusion of historically separate elements, which creates the space for a distinctive and integrated Model Reader who will be able to make coherent the heterogeneous components of the text.

Early popular literature is a rich and still relatively undiscovered area. This essay has attempted to provide some information and ideas for further study, but I hope that it has also gone some way towards establishing the validity of work on popular texts as an aspect of literary criticism rather than of social history. It will be seen that the model of literary history which underpins this essay is essentially dialectical and this is to be expected if we accept that literature is a product of the process of history and that its history will be determined by that process. But, at the level of a case study, I think that it may be valuable to 'translate' the grand dialectical process into the terms of semiotics, for, if history itself may be read as a textualisation, why should not the history of textualisaton, which is the study of literature, appropriate the analyses of history?

NOTES

1. R. H. Hilton, *The English Peasantry in the Later Middle Ages* (Oxford: Oxford University Press, 1975) pp. 3–19.
2. R. S. Neale, *Class in English History* (Oxford: Basil Blackwell, 1981). See also B. Hindess and P. Q. Hirst, *Pre-capitalist Modes of Production* (London: Routledge and Kegan Paul, 1975) pp. 299–301.
3. P. Laslett, *The World We Have Lost* (London: Methuen, 1971). A

detailed critique of Laslett's theory can be found in Neale, *Class in English History*, pp. 68–99.

4. R. Williams, *Culture* (London: Fontana, 1981) p. 155.
5. Recent work on Renaissance literature has done something to redress this balance. See for example J. Dollimore, *Radical Tragedy* (Brighton: Harvester, 1984); A. Sinfield, *Literature in Protestant England* (London: Croom Helm, 1983); D. Aers *et al.*, *Literature, Language and Society in England, 1580–1680* (Dublin: Gill and Macmillan, 1981); J. Drakakis (ed.), *Alternative Shakespeares* (London: Methuen, 1985). The best account of the development of an ideology of English Studies may be found in C. Baldick, *The Social Mission of English Criticism* (Oxford: Oxford University Press, 1983).
6. Two recent works on Elizabethan and Jacobean fiction are P. Salzmann, *English Prose Fiction, 1558–1700* (Oxford: Oxford University Press, 1985; and D. Margolies, *Novel and Society in Elizabethan England* (London: Croom Helm, 1985).
7. Thomas Nashe, *Anatomie of Absurditie*, in *Works*, ed. R. B. McKerrow, 5 vols (Oxford: Clarendon Press, 1904–10) I, p. 111.
8. Sir Philip Sidney, *An Apology for Poetry*, ed. G. Shepherd (Manchester: Manchester University Press, 1973) p. 127.
9. For this approach see J. Simons, 'Medieval Chivalric Romance and Elizabethan Popular Literature' (unpublished PhD thesis, Exeter, 1982).
10. Eco's position is to be found most conveniently in his *The Role of the Reader* (London: Methuen, 1981), esp. pp. 3–43, 47–66 and 175–199. Readers will note that many of the texts mentioned were first published in the reign of Elizabeth; however, the popularity of some of the romances meant that they were republished throughout the reign of James.
11. Eco, *The Role of the Reader*, p. 3.
12. Ibid., p. 9.
13. Ibid., p. 8.
14. Ibid., p. 22.
15. The fullest general account of the Middle English romances is that of D. Mehl, *The Middle English Romances of the Thirteenth and Fourteenth Centuries* (London: Routledge and Kegan Paul, 1968).
16. H. R. Jauss, *Toward an Aesthetic of Reception* (Brighton: Harvester, 1982) p. 87. Jauss's article 'The Alterity and Modernity of Medieval Literature', in *New Literary History*, x (1979) 181–229, comes to a model of literary development similar to my own but from the viewpoint of reception aesthetics and hermeneutics rather than semiotics.
17. J. Kristeva, *Semeiotike: recherches pour une sémanalyse* (Paris: Editions du Seuil, 1969) p. 55.
18. E. Gosse (ed.) in *The Complete Works of Samuel Rowlands*, 4 vols (Glasgow: Hunterian Club, 1880). The significance of a work such as *Guy* may be seen by analysing the proposition that one way of discovering the Model Reader in the text is to consider the type of hero whose adventures are to be recounted. From the point of view

of reception aesthetics H. R. Jauss's 'Levels of Identification of Hero and Audience', *New Literary History*, v (1974) 283–317, should be consulted here.

19. On Robarts see Simons, 'Medieval Chivalric Romance', pp. 237–69; L. B. Wright, 'Henry Robarts: Patriotic Propagandist and Novelist', *Studies in Philology*, xxix (1932) 176–99; and W. R. Davies, *Idea and Act in Elizabethan Fiction* (Princeton: Princeton University Press, 1969) pp. 261–5.

20. On this 'imperialism' see P. Hulme's interesting essay 'Hurricane in the Caribbees: the Constitution of the Discourse of English Colonialism', in F. Barker *et al.* (eds), *1642: Literature and Power in the Seventeenth Century* (Colchester: University of Essex, 1981) pp. 55–83.

21. E. M. Blackie (ed.), *Friendly Farewell, Given by a Welwiller to the Right Worshipful Sir Frauncis Drake Knight* (Cambridge, Mass.: Harvard University Press, 1924).

22. See Davies, *Idea and Act*, p. 266.

23. On the development of the term 'literature' see R. Williams, *Keywords* (London: Fontana, 1976) pp. 150–4.

24. Ed. J. P. Collier in *Illustrations of Old English Literature*, 3 vols (London, 1866).

25. Ed. Sir W. Foster in *The Voyages of Sir James Lancaster to Brasil and the East Indies*, Hakluyt Society, 2nd ser., Lxxxv (London, 1940) pp. 52–74.

26. Davies, *Idea and Act*, p. 263.

27. See for example A. Chevalley, *Thomas Deloney: le roman des métiers au temps de Shakespeare* (Paris, 1926) p. 137; E. A. Baker, *The History of the English Novel*, 4 vols (London, 1929) ii, 198. Wright, *Idea and Act*, p. 197, defends Robarts against the unfair charge.

3

Nashe, Rhetoric and Satire

NEIL RHODES

There are certain obvious respects in which Nashe is a marginal figure in English Renaissance literature. His contribution to the central literary forms of the period, drama and poetry, was negligible; he boasted rather unconvincingly that he could have been a university lecturer if he had wanted to; all his early writing was designed to secure a patron. He claimed that he had written 'in all sorts of humours privately', and his published work is certainly variegated. *Pierce Penilesse* (1592) begins as a complaint about the plight of poor arts graduates and drifts into a series of portraits of unsavoury London types. *Christs Teares over Jerusalem* (1593) develops some of this material into a hysterical pseudo-sermon on the iniquities of the city (in which Nashe adopts the persona of Christ), while *The Terrors of the Night* (1594) is a treatise on nightmares. He wrote two lengthy diatribes against the Cambridge don Gabriel Harvey, *Strange Newes* (1592) and *Have With You to Saffron-Walden* (1596); an account of the various mishaps that befall a page boy on a trip to the continent, *The Unfortunate Traveller* (1594); and finally an elaborate encomium for the Great Yarmouth fishing industry, *Lenten Stuffee* (1599). (He had lain low in Yarmouth after the banning in 1597 of his lost play, *The Isle of Dogs*.) There are some other odds and ends.

What are we to make of this jumble sale? The first thing to say is that it is futile to look in Nashe for consistent points of view or characteristic themes; in fact, we can discard the notion of content altogether. His single, overwhelming interest was in language itself – in language as a living source of energy, something inexhaustibly potent and infinitely malleable. All his writing is a self-conscious and self-congratulatory exhibition of his own power to exploit the resources of the medium, other objectives (besides money) being incidental. His texts constantly disrupt and parody the procedures of formal rhetoric with puns, authorial

25

interpolations, facetious changes of stylistic register, and cascades of grotesque imagery.[1] In many ways Nashe's work displays, or seems to display, the qualities which contemporary literary theory has celebrated in modernist and post-modernist texts, and has sought in earlier literature. One classic statement of the principles of this linguistic *jouissance* is that of Roland Barthes on de Sade. Barthes tells us that 'the pleasure of reading him clearly proceeds from certain breaks (or certain collisions): antipathetic codes (the nobles and the trivial, for example) come into contact; pompous and ridiculous neologisms are created. . . . As textual theory has it: the language is redistributed.'[2] Barthes goes on to explain that the pleasure of reading derives from the point or 'site' at which two edges meet in a text, one being 'an obedient, conformist, plagiarising edge', the other being 'violent' and 'subversive'. In the case of Nashe we may describe this site as that of the collision between rhetoric and satire.

But before going further I want to consider the concept of the 'subversive', since the term has strong ideological implications. Verbal exuberance and irresponsibility is characteristic of a good deal of Elizabethan and Jacobean literature: Shakespeare is a notable example. Indeed, any discussion of Nashe's language is of relevance to Shakespeare, and *vice versa*, since the two writers, who were exact contemporaries, share a similar fascination with its ludic possibilities. Both seem to enjoy, as much as T. S. Eliot was dismayed by, the sheer slipperiness of language, and both are reckless in exploiting that condition. Terry Eagleton takes this as his starting point in his recent book on Shakespeare, and remarks that his celebration of verbal excess would seem to be at odds with the conservative ethic of the plays:

> settled meanings, shared definitions and regularities of grammar both reflect and help to constitute, a well-ordered political state. Yet it is all this which Shakespeare's flamboyant punning, troping and riddling threaten to put into question. His belief in social stability is jeopardized by the very language in which it is articulated.[3]

Most of us would be less sure about what Shakespeare believed, but let that pass. The essential point is that Eagleton assumes that there is a correlation between the prevailing styles of linguistic practice in a society and the politics of the state. The same point is often made by critics of eighteenth-century French literature, where the extreme formality of poetic diction is said to reflect (and to have helped constitute?) the absolutism of the *ancient régime*. Such a simple equation is quite untenable in the context of the English Renaissance, for the simple reason that the high-water mark of rhetorical excess in sixteenth-century literature, the age of Lyly, Sidney, Marlowe, Nashe and Shakespeare, coincides with the zenith of Tudor absolutism. Conversely, the period of political upheaval and civil war in the first half to the seventeenth century is marked in literature by a shift towards much tighter, plainer, more concise forms of expression. The most verbally extravagant work of English prose in the seventeenth century, and quite untypical of its period, is Sir Thomas Urquhart's wildly enthusiastic version of Rabelais (1653). Urquhart was a staunch Royalist.

It is therefore very difficult to see how a connection can be made between a 'subversive' literary style (i.e. rhetorical excess, rhetoric as play) and radical political and social ideas. In this period the reverse would seem to be the case. For example, we can compare the way in which Nashe handles the subject of violent rebellion with passages by Sir Philip Sidney and Thomas Dekker on similar themes. Nashe's account of the Anabaptist revolt in Münster in *The Unfortunate Traveller* is a rhetorical extravaganza of base amplification:

> That day come, flourishing entred *John Leiden* the Botcher into the field, with a scarffe made of lysts like a bow-case, a crosse on hys brest like a thred bottome, a round twilted Taylors cushion buckled like a Tankard-bearers device to his shoulders for a target. . . . Perchance here and there you might see a felow that had a canker-eater scull on his head, which served him and his ancestors for a chamber pot two hundred yeeres, and another that had bent a couple of yron dripping pans armour-wise, to fence his backe and his belly.[4]

This is very like the description of Petruchio arriving at his wedding in *The Taming of the Shrew*, or some of the caricatures in *Pierce Penilesse*, such as Dame Niggardize. Each is an elaborate exercise in the low style, a farrago of absurd detail which in the above case serves to puncture Leiden's 'flourishing' pretensions by presenting his martial ostentation in terms of worn-out household utensils and the like. The rebels are proles pretending to be soldiers, figures of fun. Having established this, Nashe swiftly changes into cassock and surplice ('Peace, peace there in the belfrie, service begins') to preach a diatribe against religious sects, using the example of the Anabaptists of 1534 to attack the Puritans of the 1590s ('Anabaptists . . . Puritans . . . villaines').

The account of the massacre of Leiden's men then shows Nashe shifting his rhetorical ground yet again, as he moves into an elevated style more appropriate to a description of the exemplary behaviour of the imperial troops:

> The Emperialls themselves that were their Executioners (like a father that weepes when he beates his childe, yet still weepes and stil beates) not without much ruth and sorrow prosecuted that lamentable massacre; yet drums and trumpets sounding nothing but stearne revenge in their eares, made them so eager that their handes had no leasure to aske counsell of their effeminate eyes.   (ii, 240–1)

The rhetorical patterning lends a spurious dignity to a spectacle which by the end of the paragraph has become one of 'mangled flesh hung with goare'. The pompous mixture of *sententia* – this hurts me more than it hurts you – and periphrasis is repellent in the context, and the effect is aggravated by the fact that Nashe uses an elevated conceit about hands and eyes to try to convince us that the troops are weeping ruefully as they carry out the slaughter.

The account of the Münster rebellion is only one of a series of bravura rhetorical performances which make up *The Unfortunate Traveller*. Another is the tournament scene in which Nashe parodies the chivalric elegance of Sidney's *Arcadia*, and it is certainly true that Sidney's work operates on a more consistent rhetorical level than Nashe's. The *Arcadia* brims with tropes and figures; its style is so mannered and ornamental that Sidney's devotee Abraham Fraunce was moved to publish a compendium of its eloquence entitled *The Arcadian Rhetorike* (1588). But for all that, Sidney's treatment of war is less complacent than Nashe's. Surveying the battlefield after the combat between Kings Amphialus and Basilius in book iii, Sidney writes,

> for at the first, though it were terrible, yet Terror was deckt so bravelie with rich furniture, quilte swords, shining armours,

pleasant pensils, that the eye with delight had scarce leasure to be afraide: But now all universally defiled with dust, bloud, broken arrows, mangled bodies, tooke away the maske and sette foorth Horror in his owne horrible manner.[5]

Sidney's is a variation on the hands–leisure–eyes periphrasis used by Nashe, and the variation is significant. In Nashe's description the figure is used to *disguise* the horror of the spectacle; it is an elaborate way of saying that the soldiers were too frenzied to see what they were doing. Sidney, however, is aware that the flamboyant trappings of battle are deceptive, and the bald phrase 'tooke away the maske' seems also to call into question his own stylistic procedures – 'Sweet smoke of rhetoric!' as Armado says in *Love's Labour Lost*. One reason why Sidney is prompted into his sober observations is that the mangled bodies belong to noblemen. When dealing with a subject more closely approximate to Nashe's – a rebellion by churls – the stylistic playfulness becomes chillingly insensitive. One of the headings to chapter 25 of book ii refers to Dorus and Zelmane's 'five memorable strokes', each of which turns slaughter into a rhetorical conceit. A tailor has his nose struck off by Basilius, and he

(being a suiter to a seimsters daughter, and therefore not a little grieved for such a disgrace) stouped downe, because he had hard, that if it were fresh put to, it would cleave on againe. But as his hand was on the grounde to bring his nose to his head, *Zelmane* with a blow, sent his head to his nose.

And a miller is wittily disposed of by Dorus,

who setting his foote on his neck (though he offered two milche kine, and foure fatte hogs for his life) thrust his sword quite through, from one eare to the other; which toke it very unkindlie, to feele such newes before they heard of them, in stead of hearing, to be put to such feeling.

Aristocratic *hauteur* turns execution into antimetabole, a joke which is justified by the parenthetical jibes at the social status of the victims; and the victims themselves are reified as assemblages of parts, detachable and reattachable, in a way that resembles the system of rhetoric itself.

Both Sidney and Nashe, then, in rather different ways, use rhetoric as a smokescreen, in which amplification, its tropes and figures, is anything but subversive.[6] *Arcadia* is a product of the 1580s, a period before rhetoric encounters satire; its elegant verbal façade is not subjected to the parodic shifts of stylistic level which typify Nashe's work of the 1590s. But paradoxically it is the relative stylistic consistency of Sidney's work which allows him occasionally to stand back and see through 'the maske', while Nashe's more acrobatic exercises in the rhetorical gymnasium leave him too fully engaged to reflect critically upon his subject matter. And there is another difference between them worth noticing here, which is that Sidney is an aristocrat with Puritan sympathies, while Nashe is a man of the middle classes with, as we have seen, violent anti-Puritan prejudices. The crucial point is that it is the Puritans who speak with an increasingly radical voice during this transitional period between Elizabethan and Jacobean, and it is the Puritans who abandon rhetoric in favour of the truthfulness of the plain style. As far as the Elizabethan establishment was concerned, it was the plain style which was subversive, not the exuberant troping of a Nashe, a Sidney or a Shakespeare.

Thomas Dekker's *Work for Armourers* (1609) provides an illustration. Though not himself a Puritan, Dekker shares with a Puritan writer such as Philip Stubbes a senstitivity towards cruelty which is rare in this violent age. On the subject of bear-baiting Stubbes comments, 'What christen heart can take pleasure to see one poore beast to rent, teare, and kill another, and all for his foolish pleasure?'[7] Unfortunately he rather spoils the impression of compassion by following this with a gloating account of the collapse of a bear-baiting stadium which crushed two or three hundred men, women and children. Dekker, on the other hand, writing in a Puritan manner but without the religious zeal, turns from the suffering of animals to the suffering of humanity:

methought this whipping of the blinde *Beare*, moved as much pittie in my breast towards him, as the leading of poore starved wretches to the whipping posts in *London* (when they had more neede to be releeved with foode) ought to move the hearts of Cittizens, though it be the fashion now to laugh at the punishment.[8]

Dekker's compassion is reflected in the careful sobriety of his style; the observation is all the more forceful for the absence of rhetoric, and for its sense of quiet control. He then continues with a penetrating allegory of the relationship between Poverty and Money. Asking why these two nations should not be in bitter conflict, he explains their mutual dependence: Poverty needs Money, and Money needs large supplies of cannon fodder. But Money then breaks the league by instructing her subjects to have nothing to do with the poor, barring them from her rich cities and setting up 'whipping-postes and other terrible engines' in every street. Violent rebellion is now imminent, and the army of Poverty lays siege to Money, bringing with it Dearth, Famine and the Plague. As a result Money is so debilitated that a truce is called and the status quo resumed: 'The rich men feast one another (as they were wont) and the poore were kept poore still in pollicy, because they should doe no more hurt'. Dekker's pamphlet illustrates the increasing social awareness of the Jacobean period, but it also illustrates how a plain style can be effective in making radical points. A few years earlier Dekker had been imitating Nashe; the move away from Nashe is a move towards effective social criticism.

It is clearly a mistake to consider verbal excess and rhetorical flamboyance as indicators of radical intention in the writing of this period. This aspect of Nashe, Shakespeare and their contemporaries is a product of the intensely verbal nature of the Tudor grammar-school education, with its stress on rhetoric as a performing art and its insistence on *copia* as the source of true eloquence. The concept of *copia*, in fact, which was built into the sixteenth-century educational system, lies behind the extraordinary linguistic exuberance of the literature of the latter end of the period. The word means 'abundance' or 'plenty'; it implies amplification, elaboration and facility of discourse, what Abraham Fraunce called 'Braverie of Speach'.[9] School text-books such as Erasmus's *De Copia Verborum* were vast repositories of eloquence, thesauruses of rhetorical amplification, and Erasmus begins his book with the claim that 'The speech of man is a magnificent and impressive thing when it surges along like a golden river, with thoughts and words pouring out in rich abundance.'[10] *Copia* is verbal opulence, deriving as it does from Ops, the goddess of plenty, riches and power. But it would be wrong, at least in a sixteenth-century context, to regard that goddess as a jewelled whore, as though figurative excess might represent the subversively feminine aspect of rhetoric.[11] 'Bravery' could mean a flamboyant display of finery (as in Sidney's description of the troops), or of words (as in Fraunce's phrase), but the term retained the meaning of courage. As W. J. Ong puts it, 'Rhetoric at its most impressive peak was heroic and masculinising through its association with puberty rites', and he goes on to illustrate how mastery of expression was acquired by boys in an all-male environment under constant threat of physical punishment.[12] And rhetoric also acquires these characteristics through its essentially combative nature. Debate was a central part of sixteenth-century rhetorical education in which the emphasis on speech as *performance* turned feats of eloquence into demonstrations of power and disputation into gladiatorial combat. Words are instruments of persuasion, weapons of praise or blame, and their effective use can destroy an adversary. Henry Peacham writes in *The Garden of Eloquence* that the

> figures and formes of speech conteined in this book . . . are as martial instruments both of defence and invasion, and being so, what may be either more necessary, or more profitable for us, then to hold those weapons alwaies readie in our hands, wherewith we may defend our selves, invade our enemies, revenge our wrongs.[13]

It is through this tissue of concepts – *copia*, 'bravery', rhetoric as performance and language as power – that we should approach the writing of Nashe.

I suggested earlier that Barthes's two 'edges' (the 'obedient, conformist, plagiarizing edge' and the 'violent' or 'subversive' edge) might be identified in the context of Nashe's writing with rhetoric and satire. For there is another aspect of *copia* which points to the dispiriting side of rhetoric: books such as Erasmus's, or Fraunce's or Peacham's, may have been copious storehouses of eloquence, but they also encouraged *copying*, and the endless repetition of prefabricated linguistic units. Nashe undoubtedly revered the humanist writers and educators who were responsible for some of this, but he despised the servile use of collections of commonplaces: '*Licosthenes* reading (which shows plodding and no wit)', he sneers in *Have With You to Saffron-Walden* (III, 123 – Lycosthenes being the author of one such collection). Everywhere he stresses the importance of originality: 'the vaine which I have (be it a *median* vaine, or a madde man) is of my owne begetting, and cals no man father in England but my selfe' (I, 319); of spontaneity: 'give me the man whose extemporall veine in any humour will excell our greatest Art-maisters deliberate thoughts; whose inventions, quicker than his eye, will challenge the prowdest Rhetoritian' (III, 312); and of imaginative energy: 'He tels how he tost his imagination like a dogge in a blanket', he says of Pierce in *Pierce Penilesse* (I, 306).

The exuberant satire of this last work established Nashe's reputation and also formed part of the basis for his notorious combat of eloquence with Gabriel Harvey. Harvey had been elected Professor of Rhetoric at Cambridge in 1574, though he had left this post by the time he came to blows with Nashe, and his name was a byword for vanity, affectation and pomposity – 'the prowdest Rhetoritian' of his day, in fact. While there were personal motives for the quarrel, the opening exchange in Harvey's *Foure Letters* (1592) and Nashe's *Strange Newes* focuses the debate on rhetoric and satire. Harvey's chief grumble is that the vein which Nashe says is of his own begetting is 'the Invective vaine, a sturring and tickeling vaine: the Satyricall humour, a puffinge and swellinge humour', and that Nashe has abandoned the 'heavenly Eloquence' of a Sidney or a Spenser for an 'Aretinish mountain of huge exaggerations'.[14] Nashe did indeed admire the Italian satirist Aretino, but for the very qualities which in his own writing challenged the blandness and ponderousness of formal rhetoric: originality, spontaneity, imaginative energy – the violent edge of eloquence.[15]

For it is not just that Nashe's writing is morally indifferent to violence; it is in itself a language of violence. It travesties, yet at the same time revitalises, the humanist values of *copia*, 'bravery' and rhetoric as power, as he transfers them to satire and invective. Harvey is to be physically crushed by the power of his words:

Ile baite thee worse than a bull, so that thou shalt desire some body on thy knees to help thee with letters of commendation to *Bull*, the hangman, that he may dispatch thee out of the way before more affliction come upon thee . . . thou shalt bee

double girt with girds, and scoft at till those that stand by do
nothing but cough with laughing.   (I, 319–20)

And he then continues in the manner of Peacham by describing
rhetoric as a martiall art: 'With the wast of thy words I lay wast all
the feeble fortifications of thy wit. . . . Ile present thee with my
whole artillerie store of eloquence' (I, 321). But, despite the
violence of these threats in *Strange Newes*, Nashe claimed in the
second of his attacks on Harvey, *Have With You to Saffron-Walden*,
that he was motivated not by hatred but by a determination to
prove his 'sufficiencie' (III, 19). And this is entirely credible, for
the violence of Nashe's language is in part the product of his
precarious status as 'writer' at a time when such a term had little
meaning as a description of status. Everywhere his obsession
with his own stylistic virtuosity testifies to the fact that his self-
sufficiency is guaranteed only by the power of his pen, and it is
this fact which leads to his adulation of Aretino. In Aretino Nashe
saw an image of the professional writer as superman: 'His pen
was sharp pointed lyke a poinyard; no leafe he wrote on but was
lyke a burning glasse to set on fire all his readers. . . . Princes hee
spard not, that in the least point transgrest' (II, 264–5). In
belabouring Harvey Nashe aimed to be, if not the scourge of
princes, then at least the scourge of superannuated dons.
     This he achieved in *Have With You to Saffron-Walden*. The book
begins as a debate between four characters, one of whom, Piers
Penilesse, represents Nashe himself. After a fairly staid beginning
one of them turns to Piers with the words 'O peace, peace,
exercise thy writing tongue, and let us have no more of this plaine
English' (III, 33). And it is a remarkably apt phrase, for the
'writing tongue' which is responsible for the onslaught on Harvey
delivers a conspiciously oral performance. (By contrast, Harvey's
own oratorical style seems deliberately *written*.) In order to ridicule
his adversary Nashe falls into the conversational patter of the
stand-up comedian and raconteur, indulging in a riot of absurd
images of the 'incomprehensible corpulencie' of the product of
Harvey's literary labours. The vast turgidity of his prose style is
hiliariously captured by Nashe as he turns Harvey's book into a
grossly physical object:

Carrier, didst thou bring it by wayne, or on horse backe. By
wayne, sir, & it hath crackt me three axeltrees, wherefore, I

hope you will consider me the more. . . . I tooke and weighed [it] in an Ironmongers scales and it counterpoyseth a Cade of Herring and three Holland Cheeses. You may beleeve me if you will, I was faine to lift my chamber door off the hindges, onely to let it in, it was so fulsome a fat *Bonarobe* and terrible Rouncevall. Once I thought to have cald in a Cooper that went by and cald for worke, and bid him hoope it about like the tree at *Grays-Inne* gate, for feare it should burst, it was so beastly. . . . Credibly it was once rumord about the Court, that the Guard meant to trie masteries with it before the Queene, and, in stead of throwing the sledge or the hammer, to hurle it foorth at the armes ende for a wager. (III, 33–6)

It has to be said that, while this is a wonderful piece of comic invention, its success does not depend upon the rhetorical extravagance and verbal violence which is more generally typical of Nashe's prose style; it is rhetorical in character largely in its sense of language as performance. But *Have With You*, like all Nashe's writing, is stylistically very versatile, and elsewhere in the book he lambasts Harvey in a quite different vein. Here, for instance, he selects one of Harvey's more pedantic terms and spatters it with a volley of grotesque epithets:

lets have halfe a dozen spare-ribs of his rethorique . . . . with a continuat *Tropologicall* speach I will astonish you, all to bee-spiced & dredged with sentences and allegories . . . . *Tropologicall*! O embotched and truculent! No French gowtie-leg, with a gamash upon it is so gotchie and boystrous. (III, 41)[16]

This is rhetoric *as* satire, a kind of counter-rhetoric in which the monstrous display of verbiage becomes a barrage of calculated rhetorical violence. The words are truly weapons.

In between writing *Strange Newes* and *Have With You* Nashe attempted something very different, an invective sermon entitled *Christs Teares over Jerusalem*. In some ways it is his most bizarre work. He begins by bidding 'A hundred unfortunate farewels to fantasticall Satirisme' and asks Christ to 'Newe mynt my mind to the likenes of thy lowlines: file away the superfluous affectation of my prophane puft up phrase, that I may by thy pure simple Orator' (II, 12, 15–16). The image of the newly minted coin is apt enough; it is one that Donne uses frequently in his religious verse and prose. But purity and simplicity are stylistic virtues of which Nashe was incapable, and his adopted role as preacher merely provides him with another opportunity for a display of shattering rhetorical violence. Having assumed the persona of Christ weeping for the sins of Jerusalem and its impending destruction, he suddenly recasts the Saviour in the role of Tamburlaine, flaunting his red and black flags and threatening that the blood of the righteous shall 'staine the Skye with cloddered exhalations, interrupt the Sunne in his course, and make it sticke fast in the congealed mudde of gorie Clowdes' (II, 21). Nashe has a curious way with tears, as we saw earlier, and, despite his farewell to 'Satirisme', he slips back into the language of satire in his portrayal of the weeping Christ: 'I have sounded the utmost depth of dolour, and wasted myne eye-bals well-neere to pinnes-heads with weeping (as a Barbar wasteth his Ball in the water) . . .' (II, 36). In fact, Christ's tears are not tears at all. In a passage where Christ prays that his tears will soften the stony hearts of the Jews Nashe uses the word 'stone' as a *Leitmotiv* until the tears actually become stones, missiles which will rain down on the unfortunate inhabitants of the city (II, 23f.). It sounds rather like Shelley's poem about the Peterloo massacre, 'The Mask of Anarchy';

> Next came Fraud, and he had on,
> Like Eldon, an ermined gown;
> His big tears, for he wept well
> Turned to mill-stones as they fell.
>
> And the little children, who
> Round his feet played to and fro,
> Thinking every tear a gem
> Had their brains knocked out by them.

And, as Jerusalem suffers from fire and the sword, plague and famine, Nashe entertains us with a story about a mother who eats her child.

In the second half of the book Nashe turns his attention to what he considered to be the analogous plight of contemporary London. The exotic villainies paraded before the reader are a prelude to what is perhaps the real point of *Christs Teares*, namely the prospect of damnation. It is a prospect which releases his imagination in a way which renders his earlier pieties about stylistic simplicity quite obsolete:

> Your morne-like christall countenaunces shall be netted over and (Masker-like) cawle-visarded with crawling venomous wormes. Your orient teeth Toades shall steale into theyr heads for pearle; Of the jelly of your decayed eyes shall they engender them young. In theyr hollowe Caves, (theyr transplendent juice so pollutionately employd,) shelly Snayles shall keepe house. (II, 138–9)

This is a passage which perhaps only Nashe could have written. The mixture of verbal extravagance ('transplendent . . . pollutionately') and horribly obsessive physicality is curiously linked to the homely image of the 'shelly snails', while the disgusting spectacle of the caul of worms is counterbalanced by the *Tempest*-like sea-change of teeth becoming pearls. The reader is being pulled in a number of different directions at the same time. The passage has considerable imaginative density, but Nashe's imagination is not under control, just as throughout *Christs Teares* we may feel that his rhetorical strategy is not under control. This was noticed by contemporary readers, for in the Preface to the second edition (1594) Nashe records that some carpers 'exclaim that it is a puft-up stile, and full of prophane eloquence: others object unto me the multitude of my boystrous compound wordes', to which he replies, 'no winde that blowes strong but is boystrous, no speech or wordes of any power or force to perswade but must bee swelling and boystrous' (II, 183–4). 'Boystrous' is one of Nashe's favourite words, and, although he applies it adversely to Harvey's style, it is perhaps the single most appropriate epithet to describe Nashe's own blend of rhetoric and satire, or rhetoric *as* satire. His boisterousness is something that he cannot rein in, which is why the puffed-up profanity that he intended to avoid in *Christs Teares* is precisely what he achieved.

His next work, *The Unfortunate Traveller*, is his most famous, partly because it has been misleadingly thought of as a proto-novel. A recent critic has observed that

> In a remarkable proleptic experiment . . . Nashe began to define and develop the essential principles governing modern prose

narrative. . . . Nashe marks a vital stage in the transformation of narrative into a subversive medium. . . .[17]

This is a version of the commonplace that Nashe in some sense anticipates Sterne and Joyce, and the appearance of the buzz-word 'subversive' would imply that like them he is deliberately disrupting an earlier more mimetic or realistic form of narrative. But what? A fifteenth-century George Eliot, perhaps. If narrative became a subversive medium in the late sixteenth century, then what are we to make of the subsequent development of the novel? In fact, in so far as it is a narrative at all, *The Unfortunate Traveller* is a picaresque tale like the Spanish *Lazarillo de Tormes*, which had recently been translated into English (1586); that is to say, it is an episodic account of the antics of a young rogue (*picaró*) in the course of his travels. But what it resembles more closely is the Roman *satura* (e.g. Petronius's *Satyricon*), in that it is a satirical medley or farrago, extemporal and digressive, which deliberately mixes up different genres. *The Unfortunate Traveller* veers from jest-book farce to sermon, from burlesque epic to encomium to tragedy, and the reader is constantly being buttonholed and invited to admire Nashe's dexterous shifts of genre. It is 'subversive' only in the sense that it is a comic celebration of rhetorical disorder.

And it is indeed an obsessively rhetorical work: not so much a narrative as a cornucopia of set speeches, in which every kind of declamatory style is performed and parodied. In the first episode, Jack Wilton, the roguish page who acts as master of ceremonies, tells of a fairly ferocious practical joke that he plays on an army cider-seller, and as with the other episodes in the work it is chiefly an occasion for a bravura display of rhetorical extravagance. Here Jack persuades the cider-seller of his soft-hearted and merciful nature:

[I] have wept all my urine upwarde. The wheele under my citie bridge carries not so much water over the citie, as my braine hath welled forth gushing streames of sorrow: I have wepte so immoderately and lavishly that I thought verily my palat had bin turned to pissing Conduit in *London*. My eyes have bin dronke, outragiously dronke, wyth giving but ordinarie entercourse through their sea-circled Ilands to my distilling dreriment. (II, 213)

Those tears again! It seems probable that in view of the reception of *Christs Teares* Nashe has taken the first opportunity to parody his own 'puft-up style', turning the lachrymose violence of the sermon into a ludicrous flood of hyperbole. And again and again in *The Unfortunate Traveller* an episode is merely a frame for a fantastical piece of oratory. Indeed, when Jack and his master, the Earl of Surrey, pay a visit to the University of Wittenberg little happens but academic speechifying of the most grotesque kind. They are welcomed by a 'bursten-belly inkhorne orator called *Vanderhulke'* – probably another dig at Gabriel Harvey, who is given this nickname in *Have With You*:

> welcome, sayd I? O orificiall rethorike, wipe thy everlasting mouth, and affoord me a more Indian metaphor than that, for the brave princely bloud of a Saxon. Oratorie, uncask the bard hutch of thy complements, and with the triumphantest troupe in thy treasurie doe trewage unto him. . . . Why should I goe gadding and fisgigging after firking flantado amfibologies?
>
> (ii. 248)

And so we continue through Nashe's own panegyric on Aretino, Surrey's rhapsodies to his mistress, Geraldine, the tragical lament of a 'noble and chast matrone called *Heraclide'* who has been raped, to the final speech from the scaffold by the murderer Cutwolfe. In the last, Cutwolfe tells how he killed the bandit Esdras of Granado, who is in fact the perpetrator of the rape. He explains that he proposed to Esdras that he would spare him, provided that he first poured execrations on God and Christianity. Esdras complies with hair-raising vehemence, and Cutwolfe comments, 'These fearefull ceremonies brought to an end, I bad him ope his mouth and gape wide . . . therewith made I no more ado, but shot him ful into the throat with my pistoll: no more spake he after' (ii, 326). Esdras is literally shot through the mouth for shooting his mouth off. O orificiall rhetoric!

With Cutwolfe's execution the 'narrative' comes to an abrupt halt. Nothing has been concluded; no plot has been unfolded. There is merely a sense of rhetorical exhaustion. As Nashe observes earlier when telling of Heraclide, 'conjecture the rest, my words sticke fast in the myre and are cleane tyred; would I have never undertooke this tragicall tale' (ii, 292). For all his claims to verbal mastery, one frequently feels that he is mastered by, even possessed by, his rhetorical *furor*, and it is not always easy to agree with C. S. Lewis's verdict that 'he rides the nightmare'.[18] The impression of power mingles with an impression of impotence: behind the self-assertiveness of the showman lies the precariousness of the compulsive talker, and, as a writer who has to keep on writing (not *about* anything, but in order to survive), his situation is extremely unstable.

His last work, *Lenten Stuffe*, is an extended illustration of that condition. Great Yarmouth had provided him with a safe haven when he was in danger of arrest, and, while Nashe says of himself that 'My state is so tost and weather-beaten that it hath nowe no anchor-holde left to cleave unto', the town is 'firmely piled and rampierd against the fumish waves battry' (III, 156). At the end of the book he claims to have been the first person to write in praise of the sea, and it does seem that he has found the ideal subject for his 'boystrous' style. The turbulence of the diction is perfectly adapted to the turbulence of the sea itself, and a constant sympathy is evoked between words and weather. His own comment on the temper of the book is apparently contradictory, for while it is 'a light friskin of my witte', it is also 'my true vaine to be *tragicus Orator*' (III, 151–2), yet metaphorically contained within that contradiction is both the froth and surge of the 'fumish waves'. The sea releases his imagination in the same way that hell does in *Christs Teares*: ships after a storme 'were driven in swarmes, and lay close pestred together as thicke as they could packe; the next day following, if it were faire, they would cloud the whole skie with canvas, by spreading their drabled sailes in the full clue abroad a drying' (III, 158); the sea washes people's heads 'with his bubbly spume or Barbers balderdash' (III, 160); Cerdicus 'on those embenched shelves stampt his footing, where cods and dogfish swomme' (III, 161); fishermen 'furrowe up the rugged brine and sweepe through his tumultuous oous' (III, 186); swimming the Hellespont, Leander 'sprawled through the brackish suddes to scale [Hero's] tower', and, after he drowns in the 'the churlish frampold waves', Hero 'thought to have kist his dead corse alive againe, but as on his blew jellied sturgeon lips she was about to clappe one of those warme plaisters, boystrous woolpacks of ridged tides came rowling in, and raught him from her' (III, 196–8). Despite the leanness of its title, *Lenten Stuffe* is as fulsome and copious as anything Nashe wrote; it is his ultimate piece of bravery, and there is a deliberate discrepancy between the plenitude of the language and the triviality of the subject, which is the red herring. The book, and with it Nashe's writing career, ends in a frantic crescendo of comic hyperbole:

> The puissant red herring, the golden *Hesperides* red herring, the *Meonian* red herring, the red herring of red Herrings Hal, every pregnant peculiar of whose resplendent laude and honour to delineate and adumbrate to the ample life were a woorke that would drinke drie foure-score and eighteene Castalian fountaines of eloquence, consume another *Athens* of facunditie, and abate the haughtiest poeticall fury twixt this and the burning zone and tropike of Cancer. My conceit is cast into a sweating sickenesse, with ascending these few steps of his renowne; into what a hote broyling saint Laurence fever would it relapse then, should I spend the whole bagge of my winde in climbing up to the lofty mountaine creast of his trophees?   (III, 226)

Is Nashe a mere wind-bag, then (or, to use a term of his own, a 'wind-fucker')? This absurd swansong seems ironically to acknowledge his enthralment in language, while the self-parody enables him to reassert his rhetorical mastery. It is a balancing act between rhetoric and satire. There is no doubt that he subscribed to the values of *copia*, and that he admired some of the things that he parodied, such as humanist models of eloquence and the work of Sidney. At the same time, satire, whether in the form of invective, caricature, burlesque or *satura*, provides the cutting edge to his writing and constantly disrupts the rigidity of formal rhetoric. From the froth and surge of Nashe's prose, at its most 'boystrous' in *Lenten Stuffe*, comes a vivid sense of the materiality of language, and it is the satirical edge which also produces the plastic, quasi-physical quality of his writing and saves it from mere wind-baggery. The collision between rhetoric and satire is at the heart of Nashe's peculiar, if limited, literary achievement, but, although he must remain a marginal writer, as I suggested at the beginning, there is an important sense in which he is entirely representative of the 1590s. His ambiguous attitude towards rhetoric and his experiments with satire reflect the growing disillusionment of the last decade of Elizabeth's reign.[19] In the following decade Sir Francis Bacon was to issue his famous attack in the *The Advancement of Learning* (1605) on the humanists' obsession with the power of words (as opposed to 'matter') and on the fulsome and figurative values of *copia*. It is precisely those values which Nashe's work both celebrates and questions.

NOTES

1. See N. Rhodes, *Elizabethan Grotesque* (London: Routledge and Kegan Paul, 1980). I should perhaps note that, just as this book uses the term 'Elizabethan' to cover early Jacobean literature, so the present volume uses 'Jacobean' to cover late Elizabethan literature.
2. *Barthes: Selected Writing*, ed. S. Sontag (London: Fontana, 1983) p. 405 (from *The Pleasure of the Text*).
3. T. Eagleton, *William Shakespeare* (Oxford: Basil Blackwell, 1986) p. 1.
4. *The Works of Thomas Nashe*, ed. R. B. McKerrow, rev. edn (Oxford: Basil Blackwell, 1958) II, 232–3. All references to Nashe's works are to this edition.
5. Sir Philip Sidney, *The Countesse of Pembroke's Arcadia*, ed. A. Feuillerat (Cambridge: Cambridge University Press, 1912) p. 392.
6. I have myself used the term rather uncritically elsewhere (see Rhodes, *Elizabethan Grotesque*, p. 156). This seems a good opportunity to look at it more critically.
7. Philip Stubbes, *The Anatomie of Abuses*, ed. F. J. Furnivall (London, 1877–9) p. 178.
8. *The Non-Dramatic Works of Thomas Dekker*, ed. A. B. Grosart (London, 1885) IV, 99.
9. Abraham Fraunce, *The Arcadian Rhetorike* (London, 1588).
10. Desiderius Erasmus, *Literary and Educational Writings*, vol. 2, ed. C. R. Thompson (Toronto: University of Toronto Press, 1978) p. 295.
11. As does C. Norris, 'Post-structuralist Shakespeare: Text and Ideology', in *Alternative Shakespeares*, ed. J. Drakakis (London: Methuen, 1985) pp. 51–3. It is Dr Johnson, not Norris, who is responsible for the derogatory aspect of the metaphor.
12. W. J. Ong, *Rhetoric, Romance and Technology* (Ithaca, NY: Cornell University Press, 1971) p. 14 and ch. 5 ('Latin Language Study as a Renaissance Puberty Rite').
13. Henry Peacham, *The Garden of Eloquence*, 2nd edn (London, 1593).
14. Gabriel Harvey, *Foure Letters and Certeine Sonnets*, ed. G. B. Harrison (London: Bodley Head, 1922) pp. 30–67.
15. See Rhodes, *Elizabethan Grotesque*, ch. 2.
16. 'Gamash': a kind of leggings, 'Gotchie', i.e. bloated, swollen, is a coinage of Nashe's (see *Works*, IV, 322).
17. K. Ryan, 'The Extemporal Vein: Thomas Nashe and the Invention of Modern Narrative' in *Narrative: From Malory to Motion Pictures*, ed. J. Hawthorne (London: Edward Arnold, 1985) p. 53. A forceful criticism of this kind of argument has been made by J. Dollimore, himself a far from untheoretical critic: 'there is a naive error, common in literary

studies, of describing the inception of a particular movement in terms of its subsequent historical development; that is, of telescoping the development back into its inception and reading it off as already contained ("encoded") there' – *Radical Tragedy* (Brighton: Harvester, 1984) p. 7.

18. C. S. Lewis, *English Literature in the Sixteenth Century* (London: Oxford University Press, 1954) p. 416. The point about Nashe's entrapment in rhetoric is well made by J. V. Crewe in his excellent theoretical study *Unredeemed Rhetoric: Thomas Nashe and the Scandal of Authorship* (Baltimore: Johns Hopkins University Press, 1982).

19. See S. S. Hilliard, *The Singularity of Thomas Nashe* (Lincoln, Nebr.: University of Nebraska Press, 1986).

4

The Luck of the English

VALERIE PITT

When the Church of England set itself to revise its forms of worship Auden's was the sharpest comment. 'Why', he asked, 'Spit on your luck?' The word is apt: the Book of Common Prayer you might say, happened more by luck than judgement. For, as it emerged, in 1662, as a Schedule to the Act of Uniformity, it was clearly not the product of a single intention, or a single mind, not even Cranmer's, or indeed of a single generation. It was evolved over and out of a century and a half of political conflict and bloodstained theological controversies for whose shibboleths it was written and rewritten, in turn legally enforced and legally proscribed. Its authors and sponsors, and in the seventeenth century its revisers, lived often on the edge of martyrdom – at best, exiled or deprived of their preferments; at worst, beheaded or burnt – and they were not, in that situation, consciously concerned with the literary merit of their new Prayer Book. With the headsman closing in on him, a man's preoccupation is not usually with the quality of his style. Indeed, the image of the Prayer Book as a baroque masterpiece, a proper setting for the eloquence of Jacobean and Caroline divines, is grossly misleading. Its worship is altogether plainer, simpler and more serviceable, more for common use, than the splendours of Jeremy Taylor, say, or John Donne. The virtues of its prose, fitness or function and almost hereditary feel for the lie of the language are certainly 'literary' virtues in the sense that they belong to good writing in any genre, but the Book of Common Prayer is not, in fact, literature: it is, precisely, prayer.

It is, I mean, an Office book, a working manual which contains the prescribed forms through which the Church, sometimes in the congregation, but more often through the routine diurnal devotions of the minister, fulfils its office, or duty, of prayer for and on behalf of mankind. The book also includes instructions, and, on occasion, arguments, for the use of those forms, and most of it is immemorial. The theology of the period was much occupied about the specific wording and the arrangement of prayers: who did what, and how and when, but the essential structures of public prayer had been in place for generations and were 'given' to the writers of the Prayer Book in much the same way as the structures of Greek tragedy were 'given' to the Athenian dramatists. In the mists of antiquity the Christian Church had established the method of its Office as a recitation, daily, of the Jewish Psalter. 'Seven times a day', the Scriptures said, 'will I praise thee', and so the Church did. In the same Scriptures Jesus said, 'Do this in remembrance of me', and Paul said, 'As often as ye break this bread and drink this cup ye do show forth the Lord's death until he come' – and so the Church did that too. The Reformers and the revisers of the liturgy endeavoured to redirect and simplify the services, contracting seven of them, for instance, to two, but these were – they had to be – the boundaries of their endeavours. Public worship must include confession and praise and must be based on the recitation of psalms. There must also be prayers of petition, readings from Scripture and instruction both for the minister and the people. True, the more radical of the Protestant reformers wished to abandon set forms and ceremonies and rely on the 'liberty of the Spirit' – that is, on a trust that they would be moved to pray extempore – but the divines of the English Church had no truck with that. They required (in part for extra-theological reasons) a uniformity of practice and therefore a *common* prayer book, therefore a conformity, however unwilling and modified, with traditional practice.

The Restoration divines who were responsible for the Prayer Book of 1662 were 'given' rather more than the inheritance of antiquity and the Middle Ages. What they had was the *Prayer Book*, basically that of the Elizabethan Settlement proscribed under the Protectorate, and two earlier versions, of 1549 and 1552, discarded as too Papist and too Protestant respectively; a Scottish Prayer Book much loved by Laudian Englishmen but repudiated by the Scots; and various private attempts, notably in the Durham Book, usually by august literary figures, to revise or rewrite various offices or prayers. They had also to reckon with the Authorised Version of the Bible, which had not yet been incorporated into the services, with the *Exceptions* against the

Prayer Book which the Presbyterians, led by Richard Baxter, had presented at the Savoy Conference, and with Baxter's own radical alternative book *The Reformation of the Liturgy*. Moreover, the context in which they undertook their revision was not, religiously speaking, propitious. The 1662 Prayer Book was to a much greater degree even than the Prayer Book of 1559 a political act. It completed the Restoration, undoing Cromwell and the reign of the saints not merely at the centre of government at St James's but in every parish in England. It might, it would, have been better for everyone if the King and his advisers had recognised that attendance at public worship was not a suitable measure of citizenship, especially after a civil war. Again, especially after a civil war in which your own religious practices have been proscribed and insulted, resistance to the shibboleths of your erstwhile masters is a political demonstration. Hence the sharpness of the Establishment's replies to, for example, the Presbyterian 'Exceptions' to the ceremonies at Confirmation when the Bishop lays hands on the heads of the confirmands, which was said to be contrary to the Thirty-Nine Articles: 'It is the apostolic ordinance and you misinterpret the Article'.

The bishops, in fact, and after them Convocation and Parliament, were having little or no truck with the Puritan *Exceptions*. Indeed, they could not respond to them, for what the Presbyterian divines wanted was freedom and space, though, if necessary, within prescribed structures, for the minister to pray and exhort extempore, and that, after all, is scarcely compatible with the concept of *common* prayer. It is difficult not at least to sympathise with the episcopal irritation. Though for different reasons, it is just as tedious to a modern mind as it was to the bishops to follow arguments in which high issues of conscience turn on 'tokens of spousage', kneeling in Church, or the use of the *Apocrypha* in public worship. Yet these apparent trivialities were, of course, no more than foam streaks on a deep sea of cultural as well as political division in which the Puritan mind was still at the radical edge of change. The bishops, on the other hand, constantly supported their position by reference to what was 'given' in theology or liturgical practice: 'apostolic ordinance', 'usage', 'Catholic tradition'. So the Book of Common Prayer more or less kept the common English Christian in continuity with the Christian past.

The historian of liturgy is apt, on this account, to argue that the

1662 Book is *essentially* the Prayer Book that Parliament suppressed in 1645, by which he usually means that the revisers avoided any radical changes in the Order for Holy Communion. That argument, however, ignores the shift and settle in the make-up and language of the Prayer Book as the revisers in each generation worked through and authorised the different versions of 1549, 1552, 1559, 1604 and 1662. For, when it finally appeared in the Annex to the Act of Uniformity, the Book of Common Prayer was almost geologically layered. Its base rock was Cranmer's work and that of his collaborators in 1549, but fathoms under that lay the ancient uses of the medieval Church. The congregation heard, or so the King's men told the Cornish rebels who objected to the innovation, 'the self same words in English which were in Latin, saving a few things taken out'.

That is a statement which needed qualification after 1552: the revision of that year was a theological subsidence radiating fissures across the foundations, and after that there was an endless shift and deposit of new prayers and rubrics as each new generation added to, deleted from or altered something in the text. The editing in 1662 was especially thorough: the assembled divines reformed 'disorderly' collects, reordered certain minor services, such as the Burial Service and the Order for the Consecration of Bishops, and added new prayers, of which the most significant, because they have grown the most familiar to congregations and are, besides, triumphs of the liturgist's art, were the Prayer for All Conditions of Men and the General Thanksgiving. The most radical linguistic change, however, stems from the bishops' agreement at the Savoy Conference to use the Authorised Version of the Bible rather than the Tyndale–Coverdale translation for the readings and psalms. It is true that someone – the printers perhaps – forgot about the Psalms, so that congregations not dulled down by the modern Alternative Services Book still praise God in Coverdale's splendidly direct English:

Hold not thy tongue, O God, keep not still silence: refrain not thyself, O God.

Save me, O God: for the waters are come in, even unto my soul.
   I stick fast in the deep mire, where no ground is: I am come into deep waters, so that the floods run over me.

I am weary of my crying: my throat is dry: my sight faileth me for waiting so long upon my God.

That directness is characteristic of the Tudor Prayer Books and has not disappeared from the 1662 version:

Hear us, calling out of the depth of misery, and out of the jaws of this death, which is ready now to swallow us up: Save, Lord, or else we perish. The living, the living, shall praise thee. O send thy word of command to rebuke the raging winds and the roaring sea; that we, being delivered from this distress, may live to serve thee.

This, though it is a prayer for rescue from the present danger of storm at sea, is perhaps unusually immediate. Ordinarily the effect of the 1662 editing was to smooth and subtilise the original as in Cosin's rewriting of the Collect for the 11th Sunday after Trinity. Cranmer's version runs,

God, which declarest thy almighty power, most chiefly in shewyng mercy and pitie; Geve unto us abundauntly thy grace, that we, running to thy promises, may be made partakers of thy heavenly treasure.

Cosin has changed this to

O God, who declarest thy almighty power most chiefly in shewing mercy and pity: Mercifully grant unto us such a measure of thy grace, that we, running the way of thy commandments, may obtain thy gracious promises, and be made partakers of thy heavenly treasure.

It has to be said that Cosin's version is an improvement on Cranmer's. There are hundreds of these amendments not only in the text of the services but also, as the Authorised Version was substituted for earlier translations, in the readings: for instance,

There was a certain rich man, which was clothed in purple and fine linen, and fared sumptuously every day. And there was a certain beggar named Lazarus, which was laid at his gate full of sores, and desiring to be fed with the crumbs which fell from the rich man's table: more over the dogs came and licked his sores. And it came to pass that the beggar died, and was carried by the angels into Abraham's bosom

is substituted for

There was a certaine riche man, which was clothed in purple and fyne white, and fared deliciously every day. And there was a certaine begger named Lazarus which lay at his gate full of sores, desyring to be refreshed with the crummes which fell from the riche man's borde, and no man gave unto him. The dogges came also and licked his sores. And it fortuned, that the begger dyed, and was caried by the Angels into Abrahams bosome.

Nearly every change is in itself minor, but as the changes accumulate they alter the character of the 1662 Book. It may be built on a strong Tudor base but it is a seventeenth-century book, not *essentially* the same book as that suppressed in 1645 but continuous with it.

It had a different kind of distinction, for the revisers were writers of considerable power and skill – though, oddly, as literary figures they don't exist. The 'canon' might just admit Cosin, but it knows nothing of, say, Reynolds, or of Robert Sanderson, to whom Convocation entrusted the revision of the Burial Service and the Ordinal. This indifference is not really surprising: the art of composing liturgy, though at the root of literature (what else were the Homeric Hymns or the Psalms?) is out of the ken of literary critics. It is not merely that its matter is not words on the page but words in the mouth: that is also true of poetry and drama. It is that it is a radically impersonal art: it is *rite*, written for public use, for the common, not the individual, voice. That imposes certain conditions on the writing which the 'best authors' do not or cannot always meet. It is a notable fact that the great preachers of the century were not very successful when they tried their hand at public prayer. They over-elaborate:

We sinners . . . expecting with fear and trembling thy formidable and glorious return to judge the quick and the dead when thou shalt render to every man according to his works, do humbly present to thee, O Lord, this present sacrifice of remembrance and thanksgiving, humbly and passionately praying thee not to deal with us according to our sins, nor recompense us after our transgressions; but according to thy abundant mercy, and infinite goodness, to blot out and take away the handwriting that is against us in the book of remembrance which thou hast written: and that thou wilt give us spiritual, celestial and eternal gifts . . . .

And so on. Having once got going Jeremy Taylor lets pious emotion carry him into 'passionately praying' with 'fear and trembling', which is not commonly the state of the Anglican worshipper early on a Sunday morning. What is more important, however, is that the prayer is for its purpose badly articulated. The quotation is only part of it – part that is, of a single sentence, and so phrased that to say it properly the celebrant would need the breath control of a trained opera singer. Yet good liturgical prayer *must be written to be spoken* and that by men and women with little or no ability to manage their own voices:

Almighty God / Father of all mercies; / We thine unworthy servants do give thee most humble and hearty thanks / For all thy goodness and loving-kindness / To us and to all men; / We bless thee for our creation, / preservation, / and all the blessings of this life; / But above all for thine inestimable love / In the redemption of the world by our Lord Jesus Christ; / For the means of grace, And the hope of glory.

This prayer is meant to be said together by the Minister and the people and it is printed very carefully with capital letters to indicate the phrasing. It is no accident that it is so beautifully balanced. Whoever wrote it (said to be Reynolds or possibly Sanderson) was clearly thinking not about the fear and trembling of his soul or its potential enjoyment of celestial gifts and pleasures but about the function of his language: about how and where the prayer was to be used.

He had, they all had, other and now long-lost advantages: in 1662 they were still the inhabitants, just, of a non-literate culture – that is, one in which the ordinary forms of social communication were oral, so that the skilled writer, especially if he were a preacher, wrote for speech, his work was to be spoken and heard, not silently read from the printed page. Moreover, addressed to a church congregation, it was inevitably addressed to an amorphous audience: in that culture sharp social and educational divisions did not differentiate sinner from sinner; the moral and legal obligations to public worship required everyone to be in church with their betters and, or, their subordinates. Besides, for the most part English was not yet distinguished into a common and a literary language. I say 'for the most part' because, of course, the seventeenth century is the age of a developed baroque prose: the more or less conscious endeavour of a good many writers to distance themselves from the vulgarities of the vulgar tongue. That option was not open to the liturgical writers, partly because they were revising an existing plain Tudor text but mostly because the techniques of ornate prose will not work in common prayer – as the passage from Jeremy Taylor shows. He cannot leave well alone but elaborates and ornaments both his themes and his syntax beyond the concentration of the listener. To hold that concentration the writer requires, flatly, a vocabulary so plain as to be almost banal and a strong sense of balance and rhythm:

We commend to thy fatherly goodness all those who are anyways afflicted, or distressed, in mind, body or estate.

O Eternal Lord God, who alone spreadest out the heavens and rulest the raging of the sea; who hast compassed the waters with bounds until day and night come to an end: be pleased to receive into thy almighty and most gracious protection the persons of us thy servants and the ship in which we sail.

It is perhaps worth noting how much of the Prayer Book's vocabulary is monosyllabic or disyllabic and how little of it is, in spite of the prevailing literary fashions, latinate or neologistic; or, again, how much of it, setting aside the theological words, is still part of the common stock. The syntax is a different matter, but then that difference is partly dictated by the rhetorical requirements of prayer. Vocative sentences which address and define the properties of God invite, for instance, a periodic structure:

O God, whose never-failing providence ordereth all things both in heaven and earth: We humbly beseech thee to put away from us all hurtful things . . . .

> O Lord, who never failest to help and govern them whom thou dost bring up in thy stedfast fear and love: Keep us we beseech thee, under the protection of thy good providence . . . .

Otherwise the ordinary sentence structures of the exhortations and the readings from the Authorised Version are startlingly uncomplicated:

> There was a man of the Pharisees, named Nicodemus, a ruler of the Jews. The same came to Jesus by night, and said unto him, Rabbi, we know that thou art a teacher come from God; for no man can do these signs that thou doest, except God be with him.

The passage is typical; almost any gospel reading is couched in the very simplest of English sentence patterns.

> I am the good shepherd and know my sheep and am known of them . . . .

> Pilate therefore took Jesus, and scourged him. And the soldiers plaited a crown of thorns, and put it on his head . . . .

It seems extraordinary, very extraordinary, that works of this fundamental plainness are thought to be difficult or over-elaborate. What has happened, of course, is that the reputation of the Authorised Version and the Prayer Book is coloured by that of the ornate prose of the period, the elaborate tropes and syntactical flourishes represented by *Urn Burial* and *Holy Living* and *Holy Dying*, the 'amplifications, digressions, and swellings of style' which Bishop Sprat attacked in his *History of the Royal Society*.

In fact the Royal Society's committee 'for improving the English language' was set up in 1664, nearly contemporaneously with the reintroduction of the Book of Common Prayer, and it is very revealing to consider the editing of that Book in the context of the contemporary debates about plain language. The 1662 revisers were by no means uninfluenced by the baroque movement in prose when they were not writing liturgically. Sanderson's Preface to 1662 shows that:

> By what undue means, and for what mischievous purposes the
> use of the Liturgy (though enjoined by the laws of the land,
> and those laws never yet repealed) came, during the late
> unhappy confusions, to be discontinued, is too well known to
> the world, and we are not willing here to remember.

That is not really surprising: it was the familiar mode of much of
their devotional formation. The baroque preachers were of their
own political and religious party. And it would not be true to
suggest that, in spite of the necessary plainness the liturgy
required and the editors practised, their party idiom *never* crept
into the services, at least in the matter of amplification – as in the
prayer for use in ships at sea. Generally speaking, however, the
revisers, if they had had any literary ambition to succeed as
baroque writers, were working against two forces. The first was
their inherited pastoral insistence that, following St Paul, they
'would have such language spoken to the people in the Church,
as they might understand, and have profit by hearing the same'.
Latinate sentences are not, in practice, easy to follow in church so
that one can 'have profit by hearing the same'. The other was the
character and energy of their base text. When Sprat talks of that
'close, naked, natural way of speaking' which prefers the language
of workmen and merchants before the language of wits or
scholars, he might well have been describing the language of
Cranmer or Miles Coverdale, and certainly that language resisted
and resists any attempts to amplify it with 'swellings of style'.
There was an inherent tension in the revision between the style, a
modified and modest baroque, with which the revisors were most
comfortable and the nervous energy of their originals. Seventeenth-
century preachers will write like seventeenth-century preachers,
especially when they are praying, with a certain, if chastened,
elaborateness:

> Merciful Lord, we beseech thee to cast thy bright beams of light
> up on thy Church, that it being enlightened by the doctrine of
> thy blessed Apostle and Evangelist *Saint John* may *so walk in the
> light of thy truth, that it may at length attain to the light of everlasting
> light*.

This collect (for St John the Evangelist) appeared in 1549 without
the italicised phrases, which were added in 1662 and may fairly be

described as 'swellings of style'. The effect of such 'swellings' here and elsewhere is a certain loss of pace which, I suppose, might be thought a disadvantage. Certainly the 1662 Book is a degree less spontaneous, less fresh and racy, than that of 1549 or 1559. The Bishops' Committee had many merits and some of them were literary, but not the vividness of vision which, for instance, saw Dives in 'purple and fyne white' or the Cranmerian economy to leave the two lines of a prayer as two lines if they say what is wanted. Yet the baroque manner has its own excellencies which have their proper place, though perhaps not in the collects. When Laud prayed for the High Court of Parliament (the prayer appears in 1662 but we think Laud wrote it when he was Bishop of St David's) he weights his phrases, desiring

> that all things may be so settled by their endeavours, Upon the best and surest foundations, that peace and happiness, truth and justice, religion and piety, May be established among us for all generations.

As we have seen, this careful weighing may lead from poise to ponderousness, but not, surely, here. The effect of the deliberate rhetorical balance is to slow the speaking voice and that is a liturgical merit, especially in the set-piece prayers which are the special contribution and characteristic of the 1662 Prayer Book. It is a book which has its own virtue.

The general effect of the revision, the editing of a text written in a lively English just discovering its own qualities as a literary language, by divines educated in a more formal tradition, is to impart, as we read it, a certain stateliness to the services, parallel perhaps with the Laudian imposition of physical dignity and ceremony on church proceedings. After the informalities of the Civil war, the liberty of the spirit desired and practised by the radicals – and so mocked by Swift in *A Tale of A Tub* – the Prayer Book had its appeal. Yet it is deeply conservative: conservative in its very nature, certainly, as ritual always is, but the more so since the ritual actions are reinforced by language used ceremonially, ritually used, as it were, not to convey meaning so much as to clothe it, to present prayer and praise not too gorgeously but decently habited. Sprat's metaphor is interesting here: he and his friends wanted a *'close, naked,* and natural way of speaking', which is not quite the same thing as asking for simple speech or

plain words. What they wanted was not just language
'understanded of the people' but a language which was language
not drapery. The language of 1662 is, as I have said, plain
enough, but at moments, not all the time, it can envelop its own
meanings like an oversize surplice. And like a surplice it comes to
be treated as a specially religious garment not for everyday use.
Though 'understanded of the people', 'it belongs to a special,
ceremonial world in a way that, say, the language of Coverdale's
Psalms does not.

There is another way in which the 1662 Prayer Book is
conservative. In the 1930s R. W. Chambers, in a discussion of
Roper's *Life of More*, argued for what he called 'the continuity of
English prose', tracing the vigour of the native rhetoric to the
devotional traditions of the Middle Ages, the necessary instruction
of a Christian people, in sermons, saints' lives, and works of
spiritual instruction such as the *Ancrene Riwle*. Since these had to
be written in a language 'understanded of the people' they
preserved as it were in an underground stream a native language
under threat from that of the conquering Norman. In a sense
Tyndale and Coverdale and Cranmer simply reassert that the
language of English religion is and ought to be English – and
draw on the vigour of their predecessors. We may, I think, argue
that the 1662 Prayer Book is the last public document in that
tradition. An obvious example will illustrate the point. In the
Middle Ages the marriage vows (the 'espousals') were for obvious
reasons spoken in the vernacular. The bride took the groom

> to my wedded husband to have and to hold from this day
> forward for better for worse, for richer for poorer, in sickness
> and in health, to be bonere and buxum in bed and at the board
> till death us departe, if holy Church it will ordain; and thereto I
> plight thee my troth.

Cranmer tidied that, and the 1662 revisers, for once agreeing with
the Puritans, modified one phrase, 'death us departe' as obsolete –
otherwise the text is continuous (or was until the Alternative
Services Measure) from the thirteenth or fourteenth century to the
present day. In the 1662 revision the bride takes the groom

> to my wedded husband, to have and to hold from this day
> forward, for better for worse, for richer for poorer, in sickness

and in health, to love, cherish and to obey, till death us do part, according to God's holy ordinance and thereto I give thee my troth.

What is significant here is less the repetition, through centuries, of the same phrases as the consistency with which the Prayer Book makers follow the lie of the vernacular. The necessary rhythm, which for the spouses is mnemonic, is created by breaking the sentences into smaller spoken units, by doublets and by exploiting the rules not so much of English prose as of alliterative verse: for instance, in the Middle Ages the bride was required to 'be bonere and buxum in bed and at the board'. And that remained the pattern in 1662. The bishops were careful to retain the alliteration and balance in revising the marriage vow, writing not 'till death parts us' but 'until death us do part'. Indeed, their mild baroque is itself instinctively alliterative. God is addressed as he who 'rulest the raging of the sea', is asked to ensure that the Church is 'so guided and governed by thy good spirit', and is given 'humble and hearty thanks' for 'the means of grace and for the hope of glory'. The rhythms of past states of the language have so got into the revisers' blood and breath that even when they are writing from a different rhetorical culture they cannot help repeating them. So 1662 not only conserves its predecessor, like a basilica built round the shrine of a saint; it also perpetuates some at least of it inherited modes. And, since for two and a half centuries, until the invention of sound radio, the 1662 Prayer Book supplied the core of the only spoken public English commonly heard (Sunday by Sunday or intermittently) by a fair proportion of Englishmen, it may fairly be argued that the Prayer Book kept some of those modes live in the language, preserved indeed what Chambers called the continuity of English prose. It might also be argued that that was disastrous: that in fact there was no such coherence between the language of a sixteenth-century divine and the man or woman in the twentieth-century omnibus, that our common speech has so changed over the centuries that the people in the streets have no ear for the language spoken in church nor the Church for the language spoken in the streets. But that is another theme.

5

The Borders and their Ballads

STEPHEN KNIGHT

Everybody of Scottish origin and anybody with knowledge of the British poetic tradition will know Border ballads. They appear regularly in poetic anthologies; they have been favourites in schools past and in some cases present; they have their own Penguin anthology edited by William Beattie.

There is in the public domain a fairly clear idea of the essence of the Border ballad. Down from the late sixteenth and early seventeenth centuries, it seems, comes the image of an austere world, one of violence and vengeance, of brave men, broad swords, bold horses and bleak moors. The life of the archetypal Border ballad is riding and raiding across the cold hills and steep dales of the Border territories, and the poetry seems to have a burly vigour, a true Scots tang, to it.

That notion contains some validity, in a number of qualified ways, but there is a good deal more to be said on the subject. This essay will study the surprising variety of ballads that can be associated with the Borders and the ways in which they have changed, or have been changed. It will be argued that this often too simply conceived body of poetry is in fact a highly mobile and volatile set of cultural productions, embedded in which is both a whole series of historical contexts and also a fascinating set of examples of the ways in which culture is produced and of the reasons why it is produced in certain forms. The real relations between the Borders and their ballads are much more complex and much more informative than the simple and romantic notion commonly held of the Border ballads as the brisk poetry of a braw people.

What do people think of when Border ballads come to mind? Of Kinmont Willie, perhaps, faithlessly captured by the distasteful

Lord Scroop of England, but valiantly rescued by his kin and
friends, as they surge in good-humoured violence across the
Border to Carlisle – the whole recounted in spanking stanzas of
stirring verse. Or 'The Death of Parcy Reed', a tragic heroic ballad
from the English Middle March, where betrayals, vengeance and
harsh action bear down on the hard-handed and strong-minded
hero – a more rugged and less quaint northern poem, than
'Kinmont Willie'. Or perhaps the intricate joking and fighting of
'Dick o' the cow', the tale of a half-foolish man who yet manages
to outwit the most formidable of all the Border clans, the
Armstrongs of Liddesdale, in all their strength. Or, yet again, a
sterner Armstrong ballad, that of 'Johnie Armstrong', who was
summoned to see his king and there betrayed and hanged – a
song both poignant and powerful.

These are typical 'riding' ballads and there are others like them,
related to them, extending and reworking their themes and
introducing other motifs of courage, endurance, malice and
treason. But they are surprisingly few. Beattie only prints nine
true 'riding' ballads: 'The Song of the Outlaw Murray', 'Johnie
Armstrong', 'The Lochmaben Harper', 'Jamie Telfer of the Fair
Dodhead', 'Kinmont Willie', 'Dick o' the Cow', 'Jock o' the Side',
'Hobie Noble' and 'Archie of Ca' Field'.

'Hughie the Graeme' is not clearly a riding ballad, though it has
contacts with the form; 'Graeme and Bewick' is definitely not one.
Appearing early in his edition, Beattie's nine have a privileged
weight, but still look light in a book of fitty-two ballads. Beattie
might have printed others – 'Rookhope Ride', 'The Raid of the
Reidswire', 'The Lads o' Wamphrey', 'The Fray o' Suport' and of
course 'The Death of Parcy Reed', which he presumably omits
because it takes place entirely in England. But, even if the genre
were fully represented (and Child omits some of those examples),
the 'riding' ballad is still much less common than its reputation
might suggest.

Another odd thing comes to mind. George Macdonald Fraser is
well known as the author of the Flashman series (not so well
known, unfortunately, for his golfing stories, as in *McAuslan in the
Rough*), but he is also the author of a solid and scholarly history of
the Borders in their true raiding and riding period, the sixteenth
century. *The Steel Bonnets*, as the book is finely called, is a classic
on the subject. But, strange to say, under 'ballads' the index is
almost silent: a passing reference is made to their vigour and

fame, but this genuinely historical analysis finds little role for the ballad texts. Fraser's book is very different from James Reed's *The Border Ballads*, which merely comments on the texts as if they were historical, with no sense of the context of their own production.

The heart of the matter is that very few indeed of what we know as Border ballads, which seem to relate to the conditions of mid- to late-sixteenth-century southern Scotland and northern England, do actually date from that period or even within a century or so. The well-known battle poems 'Chevy Chase' and 'The Battle of Otterburn' are definitely late-sixteenth-century in origin, and they relate to the ballad genre in some way. They are epic ballads, it seems, and among their versions they do have the variability of details and of overall impact that are normally found within ballads and their variants. But they are long, quite learned and essentially literary, not true, orally generated, ballads.

One powerful Scots ballad does exist in manuscript from the late sixteenth century, a rarity and a benchmark. This is 'Captain Car', which has later variants called 'Edom o' Gordon' – both about the same dark event, but identifying differently the commander on the day. An Aberdeenshire ballad, about an occurrence in the Gorden–Forbes conflict in the late sixteenth century, its language, technique and attitudes recall many of the Border ballads, and David Buchan, a fine scholar of the ballad, has argued that the lowlands of the north-east, Aberdeenshire in short, should be seen as continuous with the Borders, because they were economically and demographically similar, had very similar cultures and did in fact produce similar ballads.

But it might be asserted that Aberdeenshire was not a borderland. Actually it did have a border, with the Highlands, but that is not the point. The point is, and this is most important, that the Borders do not matter originally as *borders*; the earliest riding ballads from the Borders have no consciousness of national rivalry as a problem. The bold Scots and the vengeful English do not appear in the early ballads, or not in the early versions of ballads that were continually remade. That consoling nationalism is basically a product of the late-eighteenth-century period of ballad remaking and ballad editing: the period, that is, of Sir Walter Scott and the remarkable group of scholarly and patriotic men who worked with and around him and did so much to shape a national consciousness.

Now this statement may seem surprising, even shocking, but it is so, and can be supported in some detail. It is of course generally true that earlier cultures were not aware of the nation as an identification point, relying rather on the more organic patterns of family, village, area. Two examples of early ballads will clarify and elucidate the point that has just been made about nationalism as a later growth in the ballad, not originally a border matter at all.

'Johnie Armstrong' is certainly early and Jacobean; the broadside versions indicate it was about in the seventeenth century. For this evidence, as for so much else in ballad study, Child's great edition is the most convenient source (including the additions, notes and corrections scattered through his volumes, traceable through the title index in the last volume).

One of the early versions of 'Johnie Armstrong' tells this story:

1 Is there never a man in all Scotland,
     From the highest state to the lowest degree,
  That can shew himself now before the king?
     Scotland is so full of their traitery.

2 Yes, there is a man in Westmerland,
     And John Armstrong some do him call;
  He has no lands nor rents coming in,
     Yet he keeps eightscore men within his hall.

3 He has horse and harness for them all,
     And goodly steeds that be milk-white,
  With their goodly belts about their necks,
     With hats and feathers all alike.

4 The king he writ a lovely letter,
     With his own hand so tenderly,
  And has sent it unto John Armstrong,
     To come and speak with him speedily.

5 When John he looked the letter upon,
     Then, Lord! he was as blithe as a bird in a tree:
  I was never before no king in my life,
     My father, my grandfather, nor none of us three.

6 'But seeing we must [go] before the king,
      Lord! we will go most valiantly;
   You shall every one have a velvet coat,
      Laid down with golden laces three.

7 'And you shall every one have a scarlet cloak,
      Laid down with silver laces five,
   With your golden belts about your necks,
      With hats [and] brave feathers all alike.'

8 But when John he went from Guiltknock Hall!
      The wind it blew hard, and full sore it did rain:
   'Now fare you well, brave Guiltknock Hall!
      I fear I shall never see thee again.'

9 Now John he is to Edenborough gone,
      And his eightscore men so gallantly,
   And every one of them on a milk-white steed,
      With their bucklers and swords hanging down to
         the knee.

10 But when John he came the king before,
      With his eightscore men so gallant to see,
    The king he moved his bonnet to him;
      He thought he had been a king as well as he.

11 'O pardon, pardon, my soveraign leige,
      Pardon for my eightscore men and me!
    For my name it is John Armstrong,
      And a subject of yours, my leige', said he.

12 'Away with thee, thou false traitor!
      No pardon I will grant to thee,
    But, to-morrow before eight of the clock,
      I will hang thy eightscore men and thee.'

13 O how John looked over his left shoulder!
      And to his merry men thus said he:
    I have asked grace of a graceless face,
      No pardon here is for you nor me.

14   Then John pulled out a nut-brown sword,
        And it was made of mettle so free;
     Had not the king moved his foot as he did,
        John had taken his head from his body.

15   'Come, follow me, my merry men all,
        We will scorn one foot away to fly;
     It never shall be said we were hung like doggs;
        No, wee'l fight it out most manfully.'

16   Then they fought on like champions bold –
        For their hearts was sturdy, stout, and free –
     Till they had killed all the kings good guard;
        There was none left alive but onely three.

17   But then rise up all Edenborough,
        They rise up by thousands three;
     Then a cowardly Scot came John behind,
        And run him thorow the fair body.

18   Said John, Fight on, my merry men all,
        I am a little hurt, but I am not slain;
     I will lay me down for to bleed a while,
        Then I'le rise and fight with you again.

19   Then they fought on like mad men all,
        Till many a man lay dead on the plain;
     For they were resolved, before they would yield,
        That every man would there be slain.

20   So there they fought couragiously,
        'Till most of them lay dead there and slain,
     But little Musgrave, that was his foot-page,
        With his bonny grissell got away untain.

21   But when he came up to Guiltknock Hall,
        The lady spyed him presently:
     'What news, what news, thou little foot-page?
        What news from thy master and his company?'

22   'My news is bad, lady,' he said,

'Which I do bring, as you may see;
My master, John Armstrong, he is slain,
And all his gallant company.

23 'Yet thou are welcome home, my bonny grisell!
Full oft thou hast fed at the corn and hay,
But now thou shalt be fed with bread and wine,
And thy sides shall be spurred no more, I say.'

24 O then bespoke his little son,
As he was set on his nurses knee:
'If ever I live for to be a man,
My fathers blood revenged shall be.'

Johnie lives on his own stern resources, is *de facto* an independent baron. The king of Scotland objects to this, calls him up, arrests and executes him, but not before Johnie speaks with noble disdain for this treachery. The dynamic of this austere ballad is the liberty of the baron against the king, that great medieval theme that is inscribed in the very pattern of the Round Table, where the king was only first among equals, and a theme embedded in the awkward realities of the feudal system. This is a late feudal ballad, for all its setting in the lawless Border region.

Johnie is said to be a man of Westmorland, but that is a passing mention of origin, not the basis of a national consciousness. In any case, he now lives at Gilnockie, Liddesdale, and recognises as monarch the King of Scotland. Armstrong came from the 'debatable land', an area not recognised as Scottish until 1552 and after that, in reality, a land set apart from English and Scottish law. Generally speaking, Fraser shows how meaningless the whole Border was in many ways: the Graham family in particular revelled in having homes in both countries. Much of the action of the ballads does not work along chauvinistic lines. Parcy Reed dies when his English rivals join their Scots friends against the English Reed family; that is a late ballad in terms of its collecting date, but the same pattern of minimal nationalism is seen in an early one, the seventeenth-century 'Jock o' the Side', in which John Armstrong (a different one) is taken prisoner and held in the 'New Castle' on the Tyne. The ballad tells how his half-brother Hobie Noble leads a rescue, but this early version never notices that a Scotsman is being released from English captivity. There is no simple nationalist self-construction in process here; it is later simplifications which develop reductive ideas such as English traitors and brave true Scots. The Borderers may well have been scoundrels, but at least they were not patriots.

Another famous ballad has an originally 'unpatriotic' structure later turned into chauvinism, more sharply than in 'Johnie Armstrong'. 'Sir Patrick Spens' must be the best known of all the ballads, but it has a fairly early version quite different from the familiar account. In that, Sir Patrick has a 'braid letter' from the king ordering him to sea; he goes to Norway, where he and his men are insulted; they leave at once in spite of bad omens about the weather, and are drowned – tragic, proud, fated, but true Scots to the watery last. There is, though, a crucially different version:

1   The king sits in Dumferling toune,
      Drinking the blude-reid wine:
   'O whar will I get guid sailor,
      To sail this schip of mine?'

2   Up and spak an eldern knicht,
      Sat at the kings richt kne:
   'Sir Patrick Spence is the best sailor
      That sails upon the se.'

3   The king has written a braid letter,
      And signd it wi his hand,
   And sent it to Sir Patrick Spence,
      Was walking on the sand.

4   The first line that Sir Patrick red,
      A loud lauch lauched he;
   The next line that Sir Patrick red,
      The teir blinded his ee.

5   'O wha is this has don this deid,
      This ill deid don to me,
   To send me out this time o' the yeir,
      To sail upon the se!

6   'Mak hast, mak haste, my mirry men all,

Our guid schip sails the morne':
'O say na sae, my master deir,
For I feir a deadlie storme.

7 'Late late yestreen I saw the new moone,
Wi the auld moone in hir arme,
And I feir, I feir, my deir master,
That we will cum to harme.'

8 O our Scots nobles wer richt laith
To weet their cork-heild schoone;
Bot lang owre a' the play wer playd,
Thair hats they swam aboone.

9 O lang, lang may their ladies sit,
Wi thair fans into their hand,
Or eir they se Sir Patrick Spence
Cum sailing to the land.

10 O lang, lang may the ladies stand,
Wi thair gold kems in their hair,
Waiting for thair ain deir lords,
For they'll se thame na mair.

11 Haf owre, haf owre to Aberdour,
It's fiftie fadom deip,
And thair lies guid Sir Patrick Spence,
Wi the Scots lords at his feit.

Here the action is much simpler. Sir Patrick both laughs and weeps at the braid letter – he knows the season is dangerous. But, faithful to royal orders, he sets sail in spite of the omens, and, now on the outward journey, all are drowned. It is a quite different story with a quite different meaning. Here it is the power of the king to command and destroy that is central – just as it was in 'Johnie Armstrong', and just as it in reality was in the disputed martial politics of sixteenth-century Scotland. This is no Border ballad, but one that shows how generalised were the central issues of the genuine Jacobean ballads associated with Scotland, whether on its borders or not.

The short version is the earlier; Percy has it among his papers, and others record it from oral delivery. The long version is found in *Minstrelsy of the Scottish Border*, and Scott says he combined two variant versions with some stanzas sung by Mr Robert Hamilton. Most ballad scholars would take that to mean that Sir Walter did the revising work himself; the other editions that print this version are by Motherwell and Buchan, 1827 and 1828, and their ballads appear to be sung variants of Scott's literary text. Scott's version, it is clear, constructs a notion of Scottish honour in the face of international scorn and sets aside the notion of any dissension within this nation itself.

Scott's status as the originator of the historical novel, in some ways a major force in the development of the novel itself, has been well charted, especially by critics outside England – Germans have long admired Scott's power and the Hungarian Marxist critic Georg Lukács made him an initiating figure for the topic of his book *The Historical Novel*. But it has not been properly recognised that Scott has a similar status in the ballad itself. His practices varied from text to text and deserve closer study. Andrew Lang opened up the topic and C. E. Zug has recently gone further. It is clear that, like most editors until this century – and some in it – Scott felt it proper to emend, correct, rewrite his sources, and in doing so was a major creator of a new consciousness both in terms of Scottish self-consciousness and in terms of literary taste.

It was Scott, for example, who imposed the term 'Border ballads', simply through his title *Minstrelsy of the Scottish Border*. It is basically a fanciful title. The poems are not minstrel poems in the strict sense of being produced by professional singers; as has been argued here, they are not consciously Border-oriented, nor in any nationalistic way Scottish. Rather, as Buchan showed, they belong to a type of social and economic world that produced this kind of culture, which included the Scottish north-eastern lowlands and some English counties as well.

Taking the hypothesis that the early 'riding' ballads are non-nationalistic and the later ones nationalistic, it is possible to re-examine the texts and see how they fall into these categories. Some which are not recorded early seem like the early ballads and none that pass directly through Scott's hands are without some chauvinist reshaping. 'Archie of Ca' Field', for example, is recorded from oral tradition by Percy in the eighteenth century, and so is not very early, but it has no sense of Anglo-Scottish rivalry. Archie is apparently an Armstrong and he is imprisoned in Dumfries, that great Maxwell stronghold. 'The Song of the Outlaw Murray', which Child prints last of all because he doubts its oral character, is in fact very like 'Johnie Armstrong' in its feudal concerns (though its language is basically very late eighteenth-century, even nineteenth-century), speaking of Murray's hold on the Ettrick Forest and the king's partial failure to control him. This is not history: but it does seem to be the sort of projected anxiety about freedoms that is basic to this sort of ballad in the fading of feudalism. Child reports that a note on a now lost manuscript attributed a version to the seventeenth century, for what that is worth. It would be nothing unusual for such a song to survive for 300 years with only lexical changes and no major reshaping.

But there are clear cases of radical restructuring, even of ballads newly composed. 'Kinmont Willie', Scott says in his note, bears a striking resemblance to a historical narrative from 1596. I think nobody now doubts that the reason for this resemblance is that good Sir Walter himself composed 'Kinmont Willie'. It is a quite brilliant pastiche of the language, the idioms and the attitudes of the riding ballads, but added to it are some of the central values of Sir Walter's world: the nationalism of course, and the braw humour of the now self-conscious Scots, but also the literary consciousness of the Edinburgh lawyer turned novelist; the poem is full of finely polished ruggedness and detailed historical comments, and it is richly studded with the names that so fascinated Scott and his contemporaries, the names of their own country. These excerpts make clear the thematic and formal patterns of Scott's creation of a tradition:

1   O have ye na heard o the fause Sakelde?
       O have ye na heard o the keen Lord Scroop?
    How they hae taen bauld Kinmont Willie,
       On Hairibee to hang him up?

2   Had Willie had bur twenty men,
       But twenty men as stout as he,
    Fause Sakelde had never the Kinmont taen,
       Wi eight score in his companie.

3   They band his legs beneath the steed,
       They tied his hands behind his back;

They guarded him, fivesome on each side,
  And they brought him ower the Liddel-rack.

4 They led him thro the Liddel-rack,
     And also thro the Carlisle sands;
   They brought him to Carlisle castell,
     To be at my Lord Scroope's commands.

5 'My hands are tied, but my tongue is free,
     And whae will dare this deed avow?
   Or answer by the border law?
     Or answer to the bauld Buccleuch?'

6 'Now haud thy tongue, thou rank reiver!
     There's never a Scot shall set ye free;
   Before ye cross my castle-yate,
     I trow ye shall take farewell o me.'

7 'Fear na ye that, my lord', quo Willie;
     'By the faith o my bodie, Lord Scroop', he said,
   'I never yet lodged in a hostelrie
     But I paid my lawing before I gaed.'

8 Now word is gane to the bauld Keeper,
     In Branksome Ha where that he lay,
   That Lord Scroope has taen the Kinmont Willie,
     Between the hours of night and day.

9 He has taen the table wi his hand,
     He garrd the red wine spring on hie;
   'Now Christ's curse on my head,' he said,
     'But avenged of Lord Scroop I'll be!

10 'O is my basnet a widow's curch?
      Or my lance a wand of the willow-tree?
    Or my arm a ladye's lilye hand?
      That an English lord should lightly me. . . .

35 And when we cam to the lower prison,
      Where Willie o Kinmont he did lie,
    'O sleep ye, wake ye, Kinmont Willie,

Upon the morn that thou 's to die?'

36 'O I sleep saft, and I wake aft,
      It's lang since sleeping was fleyd frae me;
    Gie my service back to my wyfe and bairns,
      And a' gude fellows that speer for me.'

37 Then Red Rowan has hente him up,
      The starkest men in Teviotdale:
    'Abide, abide now, Red Rowan,
      Till of my Lord Scroope I take farewell.

38 'Farewell, farewell, y gude Lord Scroope!
      My gude Lord Scroope, farewell!' he cried;
    'I'll pay you for my lodging-maill
      When first we meet on the border-side.'

39 Then shoulder high, with shout and cry,
      We bore him down the ladder lang;
    At every stride Red Rowan made,
      I wot the Kinmont's airns playd clang.

40 'O mony a time,' quo Kinmont Willie,
      'I have ridden horse baith wild and wood;
    But a rougher beast than Red Rowan
      I ween my legs have neer bestrode.

41 'And mony a time,' quo Kinmont Willie,
      'I've pricked a horse out oure the furs;
    But since the day I backed a steed
      I nevir wore sic cumbrous spurs.'

42 We scarce had won the Stanesbaw-bank,
      When a' the Carlisle bells were rung,
    And a thousand men, in horse and foot,
      Cam wi the keen Lord Scroope along.

43 Buccleuch has turned to Eden Water,
      Even where it flowd frae bank to brim,
    And he has plunged in wi a' his band,
      And safely swam them thro the stream.

44   He turned him on the other side,
         And at Lord Scroope his glove flung he:
     'If ye like na my visit in merry England,
         In fair Scotland come visit me!'

45   All sore astonished stood Lord Scroope,
         He stood as still as rock of stane;
     He scarcely dared to trew his eyes
         When thro the water they had gane.

46   'He is either himsell a devil frae hell,
         Or else his mother a witch maun be;
     I wad na have ridden that wan water
         For a' the gowd in Christentie.'

Scott's baronial home was originally a ramshackle farmhouse called Clarty Hole, muddy pond. Out of the murky waters of Border reality he distilled lucid and spiritually refreshing draughts of culture. Looking to the past, he served the present. At Abbotsford he built a living museum of Scottishness, but it also had modern life. Hung about with arms and memorabilia, it was one of the first houses thereabouts to have gas lighting and was stuffed with those mechanical metal knick-knacks the nineteenth century loved so much.

A much more specific but equally telling piece of ideological creativity is found in Scott's treatment of 'Jamie Telfer of the Fair Dodhead'. This is referred to regularly as a classic of 'raising the water': that is, rounding up the neighbours and the relatives who live along the same stream to help you gain justice and your livestock back – 'hot trod' if the pursuit was within six days, 'cold trod' after that. The historical accuracy of the depiction of the process in 'Jamie Telfer' is itself rather suspect: actual cultural material surviving from within an operating society rarely contains structural analysis or comprehension of that society. Epics date from well after the real existence of the heroic world.

The major hero of 'Jamie Telfer', the laird who throws his weight nobly behind wee Jamie, is the bold Buccleuch. His baptismal name was but Sir Walter Scott, and Scott the novelist claimed, with some reason, descent from him. But this is not a complete creation as in 'Kinmont Willie'; Scott himself draws attention to another version of 'Jamie Telfer' and Child found it in time for volume v of his collection. Here, instead of Gilbert Elliot being the craven who refuses to ride for Jamie and Buccleuch being the bold leader, the roles are exactly reversed. Scott inscribed his family's heroism with a few strokes of the pen. And he tidied up the poem elsewhere: in the original version the English captain was wounded in the 'left ba' stone', but Scott made this more decent, in a slightly obscure way, by changing the wound to 'the right leg bone'.

It is perhaps not hard to guess the name of the man from whom Scott received Jamie Telfer. It was indeed one James Telfer, a ballad scholar and very likely the author of this whole text, as he certainly wrote the opening stanzas of his version of 'Parcy Reed'. It is important to note that, while Scott was unusual in the range of his learning and the literary power of his re-creations, he was one of a sizable kind, one of a group of urban intelligentsia who were not so much rediscovering as constructing rural and popular bases for their own perilously baseless personalities in the rapid development of a new social formation in Edinburgh.

The 'Border ballads', so called and so often remembered, owe more to those men, their own needs and their own skills, than they do the Borderers themselves. But that is not to slight the Borderers as cultural producers. The Borders are actually very important in the ballad world for something more than giving rise to a few riding and raiding ballads and a whole self-consciousness for a later generation. If only eight, at most nine, of Beattie's ballads are about raiding and riding, what are the other forty-three about? They are in fact classics of the great British ballad stock.

The Border areas are a major source for what are called the 'big' ballads, the powerful narrative songs which present both the problems and the imaginations of an earlier and non-literate communal culture. Only Aberdeenshire can surpass the Borders as a source – and that is probably owing to the fact that these areas remained basically medieval right up to the abrupt modernisation of Scottish society. A literate class interested in the past had access there to quite antique material, as they did only in a few parts of the English-speaking world – Somerset for example, or the Appalachian mountains in America, which maintained a basically late-medieval tradition unbroken until the twentieth century.

From the Borders stem classics such as 'Clerk Saunders',

'Broomfield Hill', 'The Twa Sisters', 'The Daemon Lover' and 'Johnie Cock'. These are not riding and raiding ballads, though they are often bloodstained and full of pain and honour, treason and truth. A recurring motif, as in so much popular culture, is the relationship between man and woman and the many strains and delights it can bring. Most of the big ballads deal with the family in some way or other, especially with the problem-causing marriage of a daughter – 'Clerk Saunders' is the archetype. These ballads ran richly through the Border culture, and sometimes they lie behind what have been taken as riding ballads. There is a short and poignant lament for 'Rare Willie Drowned in Yarrow':

1   Willy's rare, and Willy's fair,
        And Willy's wondrous bony,
     And Willy hegth to marry me,
        Gin eer he marryd ony.

2   'Yestreen I made my bed fu brade,
        The night I'll make it narrow,
     For a' the live-long winter's night
        I lie twin'd of my marrow.

3   'O came you by yon water-side?
        Pu'd you the rose or lilly?
     Or came you by yon meadow green?
        Or saw you my sweet Willy?'

4   She sought him east, she sought him west,
        She sought him brade and narrow;
     Sine, in the clifting of a craig,
        She found him drowned in Yarrow.

How did Willie come to that end? In terms of the dominant, Scott-moulded idea of Border ballads, perhaps he encountered a playful group of Armstrongs or Johnstones, or perhaps the wilful theft of a cow had brought him to grief. Not so. There are other and fuller versions of the song in existence, also from the Borders and from elsewhere, and they tell an even starker story. It was all because of love; rather than see him married to the girl who speaks those stanzas, his mother had him pursued and murdered. The full story is told in some of the versions of 'The Dowie Dens of

Yarrow'; Scott has a diluted variant in 'Annan Water'. Another relative, 'The Water o' Gamrie', shifts the death scene to the Moray Firth, and a westerly version is 'The Mother's Malison', also known as 'Clyde Water'. So here the Borders preserve a fine type of a widely known story. That is the sort of thing, no doubt, that Jock Armstrong or James Johnstone would hum as they went about, watching for the probably equally musical Martin Elliot or Robert Maxwell.

Culture does not reflect reality; it presents a processed version of the problems that are recognised by a society. A central reason for the bleak conditions on the Borders in the mid to late sixteenth century was in fact nationalistic: the English lowering of the price of beef was making the traditional pastoral economy of those rather unprofitable pastures almost hopeless, and so raiding became increasingly an economic activity. But there is no recognition of that reality in the culture. The rich poetry of the Borders is that of an active, communal, orally productive people. They sang, as we know to our benefit, of love and jealousy, of pride and blood. And when they thought about politics they thought of the power of the king and his agents, and how true Borderers, on both sides, would rather do without such restrictions. If there is any ballad that speaks for the Borders and the Borderers as they felt, thought and sang in the sixteenth century, it must be that superb ballad 'Johny Cock', which the great scholar F. J. Child, who knew and loved the tradition so much, called 'this precious specimen of the unspoiled traditional ballad'. Without any early version, it is still widespread, non-nationalistic, non-literary and wonderfully potent:

1 Johny he has risen up i the morn,
   Calls for water to wash his hands;
   But little knew he that his bloody hounds
   Were bound in iron bands.

2 Johny's mother has gotten word o that,
   And care-bed she has taen:
   'O Johny, for my benison,
   I beg you'l stay at hame;
   For the wine so red, and the well baken bread,
   My Johny shall want nane.

3   'There are seven forsters at Pickeram Side,
        At Pickeram where they dwell,
    And for a drop of thy heart's bluid
        They wad ride the fords of hell.'

4   Johny he's gotten word of that,
        and he's turnd wondrous keen;
    He's put off the red scarlett,
        And he's put on the Lincolm green.

5   With a sheaf of arrows by his side,
        And a bent bow in his hand,
    He's mounted on a prancing steed,
        And he has ridden fast oer the strand.

6   He's up i Braidhouplee, and down i Bradyslee,
        And under a buss o broom,
    And there he found a good dun deer,
        Feeding in a buss of ling.

7   Johny shot, and the dun deer lap,
        And she lap wondrous wide,
    Until they came to the wan water,
        And he stemd her of her pride.

8   He 'as taen out the little pen-knife,
        'T was full three quarters long,
    And he has taen out of that dun deer
        The liver bot and the tongue.

9   They eat of the flesh, and they drank of the blood,
        And the blood it was so sweet,
    Which caused Johny and his bloody hounds
        To fall in a deep sleep.

10 By then came an old palmer,
        And an ill death may he die!
    For he's away to Pickram Side,
        As fast as he can drie.

11 'What news, what news?' says the Seven Forsters,
　　'What news have ye brought to me?'
　'I have noe news,' the palmer said,
　　'But what I saw with my eye.

12 'High up i Bradyslee, low down i Bradisslee,
　　And under a buss of scroggs,
　O there I spied a well-wight man,
　　Sleeping among his dogs.

13 'His coat it was of light Lincolm
　　And his breeches of the same,
　His shoes of the American leather,
　　And gold buckles tying them.'

14 Up bespake the Seven Forsters,
　　Up bespake they ane and a':
　O that is Johny o Cockleys Well,
　　And near him we will draw.

15 O the first y stroke that they gae him,
　　They struck him off by the knee;
　Then up bespake his sister's son:
　　'O the next 'll gar him die!'

16 'O some they count ye well-wight men,
　　But I do count ye nane;
　For you might well ha wakend me,
　　And askd gin I wad be taen.

17 'The wildest wolf in aw this wood
　　Wad not ha done so by me;
　She 'd ha wet her foot ith wan water,
　　And sprinkled it oer my brae,
　And if that wad not ha wakened me,
　　She wad ha gone and let me be.

18 'O bows of yew, if ye be true,
　　In London, where ye were bought,
　Fingers five, get up belive,
　　Manhuid shall fail me nought.'

19   He has killd the Seven Forsters,
        He has killd them all but ane,
     And that wan scarce to Pickeram Side,
        To carry the bode-words hame.

20   'Is there never a boy in a' this wood
        That will tell what I can say;
     That will go to Cockleys Well,
        Tell my mither to fetch me away?'

21   There was a boy into that wood,
        That carried the tidings away,
     And many ae was the well-wight man
        At the fetching o Johny away.

'Johny Cock' bears a vigorous voice: it speaks of the naturalness of hunting for sport and food; the love of life in the open; being at one with the created world; riding and raiding in an unchauvinist fashion; facing one's fate and future like a man; turning a bold face to the Crown and its mealy-mouthed officers. The ballad shapes unforgettably the persona of Johny Cock and itself creates his survival, perhaps in the body, but certainly in the spirit. Great vigour and a richly operative popular culture are embodied in that ballad, and those are the central features of the Borders and their ballads. The riding ballads are indeed a part of that potent culture, but not the only part, however much they were selected out by later editors and commentators. The whole complex of ballad culture from that part of the world deserves to be studied, in a much more detailed and discriminating way than has been usual in previous treatments.

REFERENCES

W. J. Beattie (ed.), *Border Ballads* (Harmondsworth: Penguin, 1952).
D. Buchan, *The Ballad and the Folk* (London: Routledge and Kegan Paul, 1972).
F. J. Child (ed.), *The English and Scottish Popular Ballads*, 5 vols, repr. edn (New York: Dover, 1965). All ballads quoted from this source.
G. M. Fraser, *The Steel Bonnets* (London: Plan, 1974).
A. Lang, *Sir Walter Scott and the Border Minstrelsy* (London: Longman, 1910).

G. Lukács, *The Historical Novel* (London: Merlin, 1962).

J. Reed, *The Border Ballads* (London: Athlone, 1965).

Sir Walter Scott, *Minstrelsy of the Scottish Border*, 3 vols (Kelso and Edinburgh: Constable, 1802–3).

C. E. Zug, 'Sir Walter Scott and the Ballad Forgery', *Studies in Scottish Literature*, viii (1970) 52–64.

6

The Poetry of John Donne: Literature, History and Ideology

WILLIAM ZUNDER

Donne was part of the second generation of Elizabethan writers: the generation that included Shakespeare and Jonson, and which reached maturity in the 1590s and the first decade of the seventeenth century. Typically of this generation, he was born into the urban middle class. He was born in 1572, the son of a London ironmonger. Less typically, he was born into a family that was also Catholic. Donne's early career was a characteristic example of sixteenth-century social rising. From a prosperous bourgeois household he went, first, to university, probably to both Oxford and Cambridge; then, between 1591 and 1594, perhaps longer, to the Inns of Court in London, to study law. In 1596 and 1597 he took service with one of the great aristocrats of the time, the Earl of Essex, on the Cádiz and Islands expeditions against the Spanish. And in 1597 or 1598 he became secretary to Sir Thomas Egerton, the Lord Keeper, a post at the heart of the Elizabethan government. In December 1601, however, he secretly married Egerton's niece, Ann More, without her father's consent, and in the following year he was dismissed by Egerton because of it. Donne's later career is, consequently, quite different in character, yet still typical of his class and time, the early years of the reign of James I. It was a period of economic dependence on those above him; of a series of attempts, between 1607 and 1614, to regain government office through patronage, all of them unsuccessful; and of a decision, in January 1615, when he was ordained, and when he virtually ceased writing poetry, to pursue a career in the Church of England.[1]

The society that Donne was born into was one that was

undergoing basic change. There was, to begin with, the rise of capitalism. At the beginning of the sixteenth century England was no longer feudal. The Middle Ages were over. By the last decades of the century – the 1580s and 1590s – England was capitalist.[2] The effects of this transformation were enormous. There was the rise of humanism, and the secularisation of education. There was the rise of Protestanism, and the dislocation from continental Europe, in particular the confrontation with Catholic Spain. There was the rise of nationalism, and the growth of a strong, centralised state, focused on the monarchy and the court. There was the rise of Parliament; the beginning of English imperialism; and the rise of science.

Nevertheless, though English society was changing, the dominant ideology of the time continued to stress the fundamental principles of the preceding age. The informing ideas of Aquinas in the thirteenth century are those of Hooker at the end of the sixteenth. All reality, including social reality, is hierarchical. There is a chain of being, connected by mutual dependence, stretching from the lowliest inanimate object up to God himself. This notion was intensified in the early years of the seventeenth century in the direction of royal absolutism: the claim that, despite traditional ideas of limited monarchy, the sovereign was, in fact, answerable only to God. A key figure in this intensification was James I, whose *Basilikon Doron* ('The Gift of the King'), a defence of absolute monarchy, appeared in 1599.

The outstanding work of Donne's early career is Satire III, long recognised as a major poem. Donne probably wrote it in 1594 or 1595, at the juncture between leaving the Inns of Court and seeking the patronage of Essex. It belongs to a moment of transition in his life. The other Satires are responses to the economic and social changes of the sixteenth century, in a way that is characteristic of the tradition of satire in the century, from Wyatt onwards. Satires I and II are responses to the rise of capitalism; Satires VI and V, to the increased power of the court and the central government, in particular to the Court of Star Chamber. And these changes are viewed, again characteristically, in traditional terms. Satire III, on the other hand, is a response to the religious changes of the century: to the rise of Protestanism.

As usual, Donne is highly contemporary. And the early part of the poem reviews current English activity in the mid 1590s: the war in the Netherlands against the Spanish; exploration and privateering – the beginning of English imperial expansion – seen as a commercial activity, undertaken 'for gain' (l. 26); diving and mining, part of the developing capitalist enterprise at the end of the century; and a vogue for amatory bullying (ll. 17–28).[3] Against this activity, chosen to represent English society at its most typical and dynamic, are placed the four traditional points of reference: of the devil, the world and the flesh, and the soul (ll. 33–42). The difficulties of religious belief that the sixteenth century gave rise to were considerable. Donne's own experience is a case in point. But it is clear from the assurance with which he turns to these four traditional points that he has not lost confidence in the fundamental certainties of the dominant view. The difficulty for Donne comes with the question of particular ecclesiastical allegiance: which church to belong to. And, though his upbringing as a Catholic in a Protestant nation posed the question to him with especial urgency – and Elizabeth's government in the 1590s was paranoid about Catholic subversion – he is, all the same, expressing a typical quandary of the time.

The next section of the poem (ll. 43–69) reviews the possible choices: 'Seek true religion. O where?' (l. 43). And Donne draws on his humanist education to sketch satirical portraits of the current options in the manner of Juvenal. Donne characterises the contemporary churches as women sought by male lovers: part of a tendency in Donne throughout his career to see questions in terms of sexual relations. Mirreus chooses Catholicism because of its ancestry and splendour. Crants chooses Calvinism because of its plainness and novelty. Graius opts for the Church of England, because it is local; while Phrygius, knowing that some churches are imperfect, rejects them all, and Gracchus, thinking them all much the same, accepts all of them. But Donne affirms the dominant assumption that there is only one, universal Church:

> but unmoved thou
> Of force must one, and forced but one allow;
> And the right; . . . .
>
> (ll. 69–71)

And it is a Church that is susceptible of rational, in fact historical, inquiry:

> ask thy father which is she,
> Let him ask his; though truth and falsehood be
> Near twins, yet truth a little elder is;
> Be busy to seek her, believe me this,
> He's not of none, nor worst, that seeks the best.
>
> (ll. 71–5)

What distinguishes the choices made by Mirreus and the others is that none of them is made as the result of a dispassionate search for the truth. As the poem moves into its central section (ll. 76–88), Donne acknowledges that both the Catholic and Protestant positions may all be wrong: 'To adore, or scorn an image, or protest, / May all be bad' (ll. 76–7). What matters is the search itself:

> doubt wisely, in strange way
> To stand inquiring right, is not to stray;
> To sleep, or run wrong is.
>
> (ll. 77–9)

What the lines amount to is an insight into the positive nature of inquiry. The position adopted is one of reserved judgement. And what is advocated as a solution to the contemporary difficulties of belief is a positive scepticism: 'doubt wisely'. In the last years of the sixteenth century this is a radical advocacy to make.

The lines are followed by a classic expression of the difficulty of reaching the truth. It is a passage that Donne took great care over, as the many revisions in the manuscripts suggest. And it is one that F. R. Leavis, in a piece of criticism which is itself classic, singled out as an exemplary instance of enactment, of the verse movement acting out the sense, in this case a sense of effort:[4]

> On a huge hill,
> Cragged, and steep, Truth stands, and he that will
> Reach her, about must, and about must go;
> And what the hill's suddenness resists, win so.
>
> (ll. 79–82)

Though difficult to reach, truth is, nevertheless, attainable. There is no ultimate scepticism in the poem. And, after a characteristic moment of syntactical compression (ll. 86–7) – the sense of difficulty, again – there is, surprisingly, a moment of democratic openness. This is expressed in an image of the sun, one of a series of sun images that recur throughout Donne's work:

> Hard deeds, the body's pains; hard knowledge too
> The mind's endeavours reach, and mysteries
> Are like the sun, dazzling, yet plain to all eyes.
>
> (ll. 86–8)

The whole section belongs to that phase in Donne's life at the Inns of Court described by Izaak Walton in his biography of Donne, first printed in 1640. It was a phase when he surveyed 'the body of divinity, as it was then controverted betwixt the reformed and the Roman church', and when he 'had betrothed himself to no religion that might give him any other denomination than a christian'.[5]

There is a sense of exhilaration in the last section of the poem (ll. 89–110), and a sense of defiance, as Donne proceeds to set limitations to royal power in matters of belief. 'Keep the truth which thou hast found', he says (l. 89), because

> men do not stand
> In so ill case here, that God hath with his hand
> Signed kings blank-charters to kill whom they hate,
> Nor are they vicars, but hangmen to Fate
>
> (ll. 89–92)

– the traditional notion of limited monarchy, but also a deliberate diminution of royal status in the word 'hangmen'. The truth is one thing; the law, another. And the law can justify complete opposites, both Catholic and Protestant. At the Last Judgement – once more, a basic certainty – the authority of Philip II of Spain, or Pope Gregory XIV, or Henry VIII, or Martin Luther, all representative leaders or enforcers of sixteenth-century opinion, will not be sufficient:

> will it then boot thee
> To say a Philip, or a Gregory,
> A Harry, or a Martin taught thee this?
> Is not this excuse for mere contraries,

Equally strong; cannot both sides say so?
(ll. 95–9)

And Donne exemplifies the argument in a powerful river image,
which narrows the idea of limited monarchy to exclude from it
jurisdiction in matters of faith. Legitimate rule becomes tyranny, a
traditional term, when it seeks to dictate opinion. At a time when
the dominant view took it for granted that rulers decided their
subjects' religion – *cuius regio, eius religio*, 'The region has the
ruler's religion' – this is a revolutionary stand to take:

> That thou mayest rightly obey power, her bounds know;
> Those past, her nature, and name is changed; to be
> Then humble to her is idolatry.
> As streams are, power is; those blessed flowers that dwell
> At the rough stream's clam head, thrive and prove well,
> But having left their roots, and themselves given
> To the stream's tyrannous rage, alas are driven
> Through mills, and rocks, and woods, and at last, almost
> Consumed in going, in the sea are lost.
> (ll. 100–8)

And the poem concludes with a warning which is also an assertion
that freedom of conscience is divinely sanctioned:

> So perish souls, which more choose men's unjust
> Power from God claimed, than God himself to trust.
> (ll. 109–10)

There are similarities between Donne's position in the central
and last sections of the poem and contemporary developments in
France as a result of the wars of religion: the idea of religious
toleration in the *politique* thinkers, among them Jean Bodin, whose
Six livres de la république ('Six Books on the Republic') appeared in
1576, four years after the notorious massacre of French Protestants,
the Huguenots, on St Bartholomew's Day, 1572; and the idea of
the right to resist unlawful authority, elaborated in the *Vindiciae
contra Tyrannos*, first published in 1579, and translated and
reprinted many times (a version in English, *A Defence of Liberty
against Tyrants*, appeared in 1648 at the height of the English
revolution). The idea of the right of resistance was a development

within Calvinism initiated by John Knox in Geneva in the 1550s. And Donne's poem stands as a landmark in the growth of religious toleration and liberty of conscience in England. It stands near the beginning of a tradition that was to include such classic, if diverse, defences of freedom of thought and expression as Browne's *Religio Medici* ('The Religion of a Doctor'), written in the mid 1630s and first printed in 1642, the year the Civil War broke out, and Milton's *Areopagitica*, published two years later. It is a tradition that was to culminate in the seventeenth century in the philosophy of Locke and in the Toleration Act of 1689.

And yet Donne's position here is profoundly incompatible with his affirmation earlier in the poem of the indivisibility and universality of the Church. If there is one true Church, how is it possible to stand back asking which one it is? And how is it possible for each individual to make his or her own choice, when there is only one choice to be made? It is an incompatibility similar to the contradiction in Hooker, the first five books of whose *Of the Laws of Ecclesiastical Polity* appeared in 1593–7, where the Church of England is claimed to be both national and universal. In each case the contradiction is something specific to England in the 1590s.

The radicalism of Satire III is intensified in the poems that Donne wrote immediately after his marriage: poems such as 'The Anniversary'; 'The Good Morrow'; the two 'Valedictions', 'forbidding Mourning' and 'of Weeping'; and 'The Sun Rising'. It can be seen most clearly in the use Donne made, again, of the image of the sun.

The sun occupied a central position in the idea of the chain of being, and, among other things, was a symbol of the monarch. Shakespeare's use of it in *Richard II*, which he wrote about the same time as Donne wrote Satire III, probably in 1595, is typical of its use at the end of the sixteenth century. There is, for example, Bolinbroke's description of Richard as he appears on the walls of Flint Castle: 'See, see, King Richard doth himself appear, / As doth the blushing discontented sun' (III.iii.62–3).[6] Shakespeare's position in the play is basically the same as Hooker's in the *Laws*. And it was the dominant position in England at the time. Rebellion was wrong. But the monarch had no divine right to absolute rule. The monarch must rule with consent. But there was little or no right to resist. Shakespeare's position is unaltered in *Troilus and Cressida*, which was most likely written late in 1602, in the last months of Elizabeth's reign before her death in March 1603, and which contains a classic exposition of the idea of the chain of being. This comes in Ulysses' famous speech on 'degree' and hierarchy (I.iii.75–137). The pre-eminence of the sun in the chain, and of monarchy, is carefully preserved:

> The heavens themselves, the planets, and this centre,
> Observe degree, priority, and place,
> Insisture, course, proportion, season, form,
> Office, and custom, in all line of order;
> And therefore is the glorious planet Sol
> In noble eminence enthron'd and spher'd
> Amidst the other, whose med'cinable eye
> Corrects the ill aspects of planets evil,
> And posts, like the commandment of a king,
> Sans check, to good and bad.
>
> (I.iii.85–94)

Shakespeare almost certainly had a passage from Hooker in mind when he wrote the speech: the passage on the law of nature at the end of book I, chapter 3.2, of the *Laws of Ecclesiastical Polity*, first printed in 1593 ('Now if nature should intermit her course . . .').

In 'The Sun Rising', which Donne probably wrote in 1603, a few months after the accession of James I, the sun is deliberately downgraded:

> Busy old fool, unruly sun,
> Why dost thou thus,
> Through windows, and through curtains call on us? . . .
> Saucy pedantic wretch, go chide
> Late school-boys, and sour prentices. . . .
> Call country ants to harvest offices. . . .
>
> (ll. 1–3, 5–6, 8)

The monarchy is downgraded with it: 'Go tell court-huntsmen, that the King will ride' (l. 7). The king referred to is James himself, whose passion for hunting was well known, and whom Donne probably met on 10 August 1603, when, on the first royal

progress of his reign, James visited Pyrford, the country house in
Surrey belonging to Ann Donne's cousin, Sir Francis Wolley,
where Donne had been living since his marriage, and where
James spent the night. The visit to Pyrford was almost certainly
the occasion of the poem.

Against the sun, and against monarchy, is placed sexual love
between a man and a woman, which is seen as transcending
history:

> Must to thy motions lovers' seasons run? . . .
> Love, all alike, no reason knows, nor clime,
> Nor hours, days, months, which are the rags of time.
>
> (ll. 4, 9–10)

And both are overturned in the interest of the individual love-
relationship. In a strict sense, the poem is revolutionary:

> Thy beams, so reverend, and strong
> Why shouldst thou think?
> I could eclipse and cloud them with a wink,
> But that I would not lose her sight so long:
> If her eyes have not blinded thine,
> Look, and tomorrow late, tell me,
> Whether both th' Indias of spice and mine
> Be where thou left'st them, or lie here with me.
> Ask for those kings whom thou saw'st yesterday,
> And thou shalt hear, All here in one bed lay.
>
> (ll. 11–20)

There is, however, an immediate contradiction in the poem.
Although the principle of social hierarchy is overturned, Donne
continues to think of the individual relationship in terms of the
dominant, hierarchical ideology. As the homily 'Concerning Good
Order and Obedience' puts it, 'Some are in high degree, some in
low; some kings and princes, some inferiors and subjects; priests
and laymen, masters and servants, fathers and children, husbands
and wives, rich and poor; and every one have need of other.'[7]
The homily was among those first published in 1547, as one of the
earliest acts of the reformed Church in England, and was deeply
familiar to the rest of the sixteenth century as a result of being
read out regularly in church. Like the passage on the law of

nature in Hooker, it too most probably lies behind Ulysses' speech on 'degree' in *Troilus and Cressida*. And, while the Catholic recusancy of his family may have made it less familiar to him than to others, Donne thinks of the man in the relationship as superior to the woman, though they are mutually bound to each other. He sees the relationship in terms of the dominant patriarchy of the age. And there is a further contradiction, because he sees the relationship in terms which affirm the social hierarchy which has just been denied. The man rules the woman as the king rules his people:

> She 'is all states, and all princes, I,
> Nothing else is.
>
> (ll. 21–2)

The priority of the relationship, and its self-sufficiency, is, nevertheless, asserted. Line 22 has a definite finality about it.

> Princes do but play us; compared to this,
> All honour's mimic; all wealth alchemy.
> Thou sun art half as happy as we,
> In that the world's contracted thus;
> Thine age asks ease, and since thy duties be
> To warm the world, that's done in warming us.
> Shine here to us, and thou art everywhere;
> This bed thy centre is, these walls, thy sphere.
>
> (ll. 23–30)

The poem is a monument in the development of individualism in England. It is an individualism that was to be formulated in the middle years of the seventeenth century by Hobbes, whose *Leviathan* first appeared in 1651, two years after the execution of Charles I by Parliament, and three years after the publication of the *Defence of Liberty against Tyrants*. It is an individualism that was, once more, to reach a culmination at the end of the century in the ideas of Locke. Yet there is another, and basic, contradiction in the poem. Donne rejects the feudal principle of hierarchy, though he does so incompletely and contradictorily. But he also rejects the new capitalist society that had been forming itself around him in the preceding quarter of a century. The woman is more important than 'both th' Indias of spice and mine', both the

East Indies, the current source of spices, and the West Indies –
America – the source of precious metals; in each case, a source of
fabulous wealth. And not only is 'honour' – social distinction – a
charade, 'mimic', in comparison with the individual love-
relationship: all wealth is a sham, 'alchemy', the pseudo-science
of the day (l. 24). Donne attempts to occupy a space between
feudalism and capitalism that, in the specific historical conditions
of England in the first decade of the seventeenth century, did not
exist. He attempts to do this by transcending history altogether.
And the attempt is made by means of a total commitment to
romantic love: 'Love, all alike, no season knows, nor clime'. It is
something which it is impossible to do.

By 1606, when Donne left Pyrford to set up home nearer London
at Mitcham, or 1607, when he started to apply once more for
government office (for a vacancy in the household of Anne of
Denmark, James I's queen), it is apparent that his commitment to
the individual love-relationship was waning. This can be seen in
such a poem as 'Love's Alchemy', which he probably wrote about
this time. The poem expresses profound feelings of disillusion
and disappointment with love; even, in the poem's last two lines,
feelings of bitterness.

> Some that have deeper digged love's mine than I,
> Say, where his centric happiness doth lie:
> I have loved, and got, and told,
> But should I love, get, tell, till I were old,
> I should not find that hidden mystery;
> Oh, 'tis imposture all:
> And as no chemic yet the elixir got,
> But glorifies his pregnant pot,
> If by the way to him befall
> Some odoriferous thing, or medicinal,
> So, lovers dream a rich and long delight,
> But get a winter-seeming summer's night.
>
> Our ease, our thrift, our honour, and our day,
> Shall we, for this vain bubble's shadow pay?
> Ends love in this, that my man,
> Can be as happy as I can; if he can

Endure the short scorn of a bridegroom's play?
    That loving wretch that swears,
'Tis not the bodies marry, but the minds,
    Which he in her angelic finds,
    Would swear as justly, that he hears,
In that day's rude hoarse minstrelsy, the spheres.
    Hope not for mind in women; at their best
    Sweetness and wit, they are but mummy, possessed.

The poem does not endorse these feelings. The reference to marriage in lines 15–17 and 21–2, and the reference to the Neoplatonic conception of spiritual union in lines 18–20, bring into the poem a norm that 'places' the sentiments expressed. The poem, in other words, is fundamentally ironical. And the norm is, essentially, the dominant notion of marriage as a lifelong commitment, universally available and, for any sexual relationship, universally obligatory. And it is this norm that the poem ultimately, by implication, affirms. Yet, the feelings are expressed all the same. And there are other poems written in the years between Donne's leaving Pyrford and his ordination which express similar feelings of disenchantment, or of doubt about the sufficiency of the relationship: poems such as 'Farewell to Love', or 'A Fever' and, most searchingly, 'A Nocturnal upon S. Lucy's Day'.

What happens is that the commitment is transferred from the individual human relationship to an individual religious relationship: from Ann Donne to God. It is a transference in a virtually Freudian sense. And it is registered in the *Holy Sonnets* Donne wrote between 1609 and 1611; in particular, in 'What if this present were the world's last night?', most likely written in 1609. In a way that is characteristic of these poems, drawing, as they do, on contemporary techniques of religious meditation, Donne imagines himself at the end of the world, on the world's 'last night', about to meet God at the Last Judgement, and with the prospect of either heaven or hell immediately before him. He generates a sense of crisis. And the transference is made initially through the Petrarchan conceit of the woman's image in the lover's heart (ll. 2–8). Donne uses the conceit elsewhere – in 'The Damp', for instance, which he probably wrote in the 1590s. Here, the picture of Christ, implicitly, replaces that of the woman in the man's heart. God replaces Ann. And in the poem's last six lines, the sestet of the sonnet, which forcefully answers the octave, human love is rejected. It is seen as 'idolatry', false worship. And it is superseded by divine love. Even so, the new love takes the form of the old:

> What if this present were the world's last night?
> Mark in my heart, O soul, where thou dost dwell,
> The picture of Christ crucified, and tell
> Whether that countenance can thee affright,
> Tears in his eyes quench the amazing light,
> Blood fills his frowns, which from his pierced head fell,
> And can that tongue adjudge thee unto hell,
> Which prayed forgiveness for his foes' fierce spite?
> No, no; but as in my idolatry
> I said to all my profane mistresses,
> Beauty, of pity, foulness only is
> A sign of rigour: so I say to thee,
> To wicked spirits are horrid shapes assigned,
> This beauteous form assures a piteous mind.[8]

It is a transference, too, that Donne describes in retrospect some ten years later, in 1619, in the sonnet he wrote about Ann's death two years previously: 'Here the admiring her my mind did whet / To seek thee God; so streams do show the head' (ll. 5–6). And the transference is confirmed:

> Since she whom I loved hath paid her last debt
> To nature, and to hers, and my good is dead,
> And her soul early into heaven ravished,
> Wholly in heavenly things my mind is set
>
> (ll. 1–4)

though the new love is not settled. It is like a troubled marriage or affair. Donne wants more love, greater assurance. 'But though I have found thee', he says to God, 'and thou my thirst hast fed, / A holy thirsty dropsy melt me yet' (ll. 7–8). But the irrationality of this is acknowledged, since God himself is an anxious lover, chasing Donne's soul rather than Ann's, offering him all his own soul, and jealous not only, tacitly, of Ann and other beautiful rivals – saints and angels – but also of ugly competitors for Donne's love, the world, the flesh, and the devil:

But why should I beg more love, when as thou
Dost woo my soul for hers; offering all thine:
And dost not only fear lest I allow
My love to saints and angels, things divine,
But in thy tender jealousy dost doubt
Lest the world, flesh, yea Devil put thee out.

(ll. 9–14)

And in 'A Hymn to Christ', probably written a short while later in the same year, the rejection of human love is complete. Donne addresses God directly, referring to England: 'I sacrifice this Island unto thee, / And all whom I loved there, and who loved me' (ll. 9–10).

In this development of an inner individualism Donne stands at the head of a tradition that extends into the last decades of the seventeenth century. It is an Anglican tradition and, at the time of the Civil War, Royalist. There is the piety of Herbert, whose mother was a patroness of Donne from his early days at Mitcham, who became one of Donne's close friends by the time of Donne's ordination, and whose poems were published in *The Temple* in 1633, the year in which he died. Between 1633 and 1679 *The Temple* was printed thirteen times. There is the mysticism of Vaughan, whose *Silex Scintillans* ('The Sparking Flint') first appeared in 1650, the year before *Leviathan*. And there is the near-solipsism of Traherne's prose *Centuries*, written in the early years of the Restoration, probably between 1669 and 1674, the year of his death.

With Donne, the public face of this inner individualism takes two forms. On the one hand, there is complaint at the passing of the feudal order, which, by the end of the first decade of the seventeenth century, was irreversible. The most celebrated example of this occurs in *The First Anniversary: An Anatomy of the World*, which Donne wrote in 1611 for another patron, Sir Robert Drury, on the death of his daughter, Elizabeth, a year previously. It is one of the few poems of Donne to have been printed in his lifetime, by 21 November 1611. Donne draws on Shakespeare, on Gloucester's speech in *King Lear* (I.ii.100–19), written about 1604–5. The whole traditional order, from its ideological superstructure (ll. 205–11) to its social base (ll. 211–19), is acknowledged to have disintegrated:

And new philosophy calls all in doubt,
The element of fire is quite put out;
The sun is lost, and th' earth, and no man's wit
Can well direct him where to look for it.
And freely men confess that this world's spent,
When in the planets, and the firmament
They seek so many new; they see that this
Is crumbled out against to his atomies.
'Tis all in pieces, all coherence gone;
All just supply, and all relation:
Prince, subject, father, son, are things forgot,
For every man alone thinks he hath got
To be a phoenix, and that then can be
None of that kind, of which he is, but he.
This is the world's condition now. . . .

(ll. 205–19)

And, on the other hand, there is espousal of the absolutist pretensions of the Stuart court. The radicalism of Satire iii, and of such poems as 'The Sun Rising', gives way to the absolutism of James I.

This is evident, partly, in the abject self-degradation of the verse letters Donne wrote to his patronesses in the half-dozen years before he was ordained, mostly to the Countess of Bedford between 1608 and 1612. The Countess of Bedford was a leading figure at the Jacobean court, and a favourite of Anne of Denmark. From 1603 to about 1620 she was one of the most influential women in England. And in 'This twilight of two years', which Donne probably sent to her as a new year's gift in 1610, not long after he had written 'What if this present were the world's last night?', he describes himself as 'One corn of one low anthill's dust, and less', as 'not an inch', whereas the Countess herself is 'infinity' (ll. 28, 30). But it is clearest in the Epithalamion he wrote for the wedding of the Earl of Somerset to the Countess of Essex on 26 December 1613. The marriage was a contemporary scandal, coming, as it did, on the heels of the Countess's dubious divorce. And in 1616 the couple were to be disgraced and imprisoned for the murder, just before the marriage, of Sir Thomas Overbury, who had opposed it. It was a continuing scandal that did enormous damage to the standing of the court. But, since 1607, Somerset had been James's favourite. And, though he was to be replaced in 1614 by the future Duke of Buckingham, he was the most powerful patron Donne had found. Donne casts the Epithalamion in the form of an eclogue, a pastoral dialogue, largely as a means of apologising to Somerset for not attending the wedding. And in it there is direct endorsement of Jacobean absolutism. Once more, Donne uses sun imagery: a characteristic of the apologists of absolutism, on the continent as well as in England. Just as, in contemporary chemistry, base metals underground need the sun's rays to be turned into gold (ll. 61–4), so the people need the practice of kingship in order to be truly civilised. The people are passive, waiting for wisdom and honour in the way that, according to Protestant theology, they wait for the gift of faith from God (ll. 65–8). There is no sense of any limitation on monarchy, or of any other centres of authority or power: custom, for instance, or the law. The lines are a classic utterance of absolutist sentiment. And they have the recondite reference and involuted syntax typical of the public poems Donne wrote in the years preceding his entry into holy orders

> The earth doth in her inward bowels hold
>   Stuff well disposed, and which would fain be gold,
> But never shall, except it chance to lie,
>   So upward, that heaven gild it with his eye;
> As, for divine things, faith comes from above,
>   So, for best civil use, all tinctures move
> From higher powers; from God religion springs,
>   Wisdom, and honour from the use of kings.
>
> (ll. 61–8)

Donne's final position is one of dissociation between the inner commitment and the outer life. It is ironical that this should be the concluding observation, since the starting-point for the discussion of Donne in the twentieth century, Eliot's famous review of Grierson's similarly famous anthology of the metaphysical poets, praised Donne for the absence of dissociation.[9] Yet Donne ends his career in a state of self-alienation. You can see this in the Holy Sonnet he wrote on the Church. It was written a year or so after the sonnet on Ann Donne, in the period 1620–2. Both poems exist in the same, single manuscript, and were probably copied from Donne's own papers. Neither was printed or, unusually, circulated while Donne was alive. By 1620 Donne was not only an ordained priest of the Church of England, but also a royal chaplain, rector of Keyston in Huntingdonshire and of Sevenoaks in Kent, and Reader in Divinity at Lincoln's Inn. In 1619 he was chaplain to the embassy James I sent to Germany under Viscount Doncaster, in an attempt to mediate between the Catholic and Protestant forces at the start of the Thirty Years War. His departure was the occasion of the 'Hymn to Christ'. In 1621 he was to be appointed Dean of St Paul's Cathedral. And by 1630, the year before his death, he was being considered for a bishopric. And yet the sonnet reveals no allegiance to any particular church. It has basically the same structure as Satire III. Each alternative is viewed in turn: the Catholic Church, and the Protestant churches on the continent and at home (ll. 1–10). But the outcome, if anything, is even less sure than it had been nearly thirty years before. Instead of the positive scepticism of the earlier poem, and its defiance of unlawful authority, there is an otherworldly longing of a kind later developed by Vaughan and here expressed in the paradoxical, sexual terms of Donne's inner individualism:

> Show me dear Christ, thy spouse, so bright and clear.
> What, is it she, which on the other shore
> Goes richly painted? or which robbed and tore
> Laments and mourns in Germany and here?
> Sleeps she a thousand, then peeps up one year?
> Is she self truth and errs? now new, now outwore?
> Doth she, and did she, and shall she evermore
> On one, on seven, or on no hill appear?
> Dwells she with us, or like adventuring knights
> First travail we to seek and then make love?
> Betray kind husband thy spouse to our sights,
> And let mine amorous soul court thy mild dove,
> Who is most true, and pleasing to thee, then
> When she' is embraced and open to most men.
>
> (ll. 11–24)

What is absent from the poem is any connection between the inner self and the institutional form.

NOTES

1. See R. C. Bald, *John Donne: A Life* (London: Oxford University Press, 1970).
2. M. Dobb, *Studies in the Development of Capitalism*, rev. edn (London, 1963) p. 18.
3. All quotations from Donne's poetry are taken from *John Donne: The Complete English Poems*, ed. A. J. Smith (Harmondsworth: Penguin, 1971).
4. F. R. Leavis, 'Imagery and Movement' (1945), in Leavis (ed.), *A Selection from 'Scrutiny'*, vol. I (Cambridge: Cambridge University Press, 1968) pp. 236–7.
5. Izaak Walton, *The Lives of John Donne, Sir Henry Wotton, Richard Hooker, George Herbert and Robert Sanderson* (1640–78; repr. Oxford: Clarendon Press, 1927) p. 25.
6. Quotations from Shakespeare are taken from *William Shakespeare: The Complete Works*, ed. P. A. Alexander (London: Collins, 1951).
7. *The Two Books of Homilies* (Oxford, 1859) p. 105.
8. Terry Eagleton discusses the phenomenon of transference in Freudian psychotherapy in *Literary Theory* (Oxford: Basil Blackwell, 1983) pp. 159–60.
9. T. S. Eliot, 'The Metaphysical Poets' (1921), in *Selected Essays*, 3rd edn (London: Faber and Faber, 1951) pp. 281–91.

7

Donne's Masculine Persuasive Force

HELEN CARR

As in the pleasure gardens, she saw herself in the black pupil of his squint. 'My face in thy eye, thine in mine appears. And true plaine hearts doe in the faces rest.' John Donne, 1572–1632, alias Jack Donne, alias the Dean of St Paul's. In the school poetry book, between extracts from Shakespeare and 'The Rape of the Lock' by Alexander Pope. How all the young girls loved John Donne.[1]

This evocation of John Donne as romantic ideal in Angela Carter's *The Magic Toyshop* struck an immediate chord when I read it. It was just how he was regarded in my grammar school, though perhaps our Leavisite teacher saw to it that we didn't formulate it in quite that way. 'How all the young girls loved John Donne', Melanie thinks. It's not entirely clear whether she means the young girls in Donne's poems or in her school. Carter's prose suggests the ambiguity is in Melanie's mind, mirroring the (other) school-girls' passionate identification with those girls addressed within the poems. Melanie's is just the kind of naïve, onastic reading that our teachers and lecturers warned us against. Besides, she's a fictional character who constantly transforms all the books she reads into imaginative sustenance from her erotic self-discovery. Yet all the same, her response to John Donne and his aliases is worth thinking about. Angela Carter has astutely captured something quite significant about the persona – or rather personae – that Donne created in his love poetry. Their range of attitudes and feelings – impatience, desire, mastery, energy, tenderness – together suggest something very recognisable still as ideally 'masculine'.

Words such as 'masculine' or 'manly' have often been applied to Donne, particularly since the nineteenth century, when 'manliness' becomes so vital a characteristic, especially perhaps in the context of poetry, that etiolater of Victorian masculinity. Warburton was talking of Donne's 'manly wit' in 1751. In 1815 Coleridge was advising those who found Donne's metres harsh, 'Read . . . Donne's satires as he meant them to be read, and as the sense and passion demand, and you will find in the lines a manly harmony.' Coleridge also talked of Donne's 'masculine intellect', and Emerson, besides including Donne among the books 'in which the English language has its teeth and bones and muscles largest and strongest', admired Donne's 'masculine' oratory. G. H. Lewes even more emphatically wrote, 'Honest John Donne – rough – hearty – pointed and sincere . . . was in every sense a man.' While those comments reveal much about the speakers themselves, it is important to look at what in Donne's writings gave rise to them.[2]

In Elegy XVI, Donne himself speaks of his 'words' masculine persuasive force'. The *OED* gives 1629 as the first use of 'masculine' to mean 'having the appropriate excellencies of the male sex; virile; vigorous, powerful'. But in this Elegy the word clearly already has this meaning. Up till then the word only conveyed a biological maleness. Here it is already taking on the implications of gender as well as sex.

During the last twenty years the historical and psychological construction of 'femininity' has been extensively analysed – mainly, though not exclusively, by feminist women. Less attention has been given to the concept of masculinity, though there are signs that that is changing. Books have appeared with such titles as *The Sexuality of Men*, *Masculinity* and *Male Fantasies*.[3] As I write, *Marxism Today* is organising a one-day conference on men and their media representations, and the publishers' autumn catalogues reveal a whole clutch of new academic studies of masculinity. It would not be entirely true to say that masculinity has only become visible since the advent of feminism, for 'manhood' has had its own vigorous ideological power. But in a sense it was largely undistinguished from human nature, the norm from which femininity declined. As masculine and feminine have emerged as binaries explicable only in terms of their difference, masculinity has been thrown into relief.

Foucault's history of sexuality dates the beginning of the modern sense of sexuality to the second half of the eighteenth century. In a recent article, 'Reason, Desire and Male Sexuality', Victor Seidler has suggested that in beginning its history at that date Foucault ignores the seismic changes that had shaken ideas about sexuality during the seventeenth century. Seidler is particularly concerned with Cartesianism and the view of man it implies, arguing that Foucault should have taken the same historical starting-point as for his earlier work *Madness and Civilization*. In the seventeenth century the idea of Reason becomes identified with masculinity, and women, as Foucault argued of the mad, become silent embodiments of irrationality. Although I do not think that all of Seidler's article is equally cogent, his general point is an important one. Feminist historians have shown that the seventeenth century with its burgeoning bourgeois capitalism was a time of significant change in the economic and ideological constraints placed on women, and certainly not merely in terms of the 'repressive hypothesis' which Foucault attacks. With the growth of the gentry and the middle classes, women became economically less productive, their leisure a tribute to their husband's or father's success, their participation in society as a whole increasingly restricted. Marriage, which in the medieval period had provided for the establishment of genealogies for the aristocracy and of economic units for the rest, became for the middle classes enmeshed in monetary transactions while also, paradoxically, carrying a new emphasis on what Lawrence Stone calls 'affective' relationships. Although the Western tradition remained saturated by ideas about the nature of women and men that had existed from the time of the Greeks, and although some of the sexual stereotypes around in the Middle Ages are here today, between the sixteenth and the eighteenth centuries a shift took place. Women continued to be seen in dualistic terms, either evil temptress or beatific virgin. But, as Pat Caplan puts it, while in the medieval period the most dominant of those images for women was Eve, by the eighteenth century it was the Virgin Mary. At the same time the image of women's sexuality changed from that of dangerous sensuality to one of sexual anaesthesia. What was the corresponding change for men?[4]

That there were changes is clear. Critics and historians have in recent years become very aware of the surprising fluidity in the early seventeenth century of ideas of gender and sexual roles. Linda Woodbridge for example writes,

> Literature for the English High Renaissance abounds in dialogue, epithet, incident, and costume which suggest changing sex roles – the constant juxtaposition of fop and virago, each of whom partakes of the other's sexual 'nature'; the high incidence of transvestism in the drama; to imputing of effeminacy to civilian men; the literary attention being paid to assertive city women; the charge of lewdness which can so often be read obliquely as a protest against liberty.[5]

Quite what this fluidity implies is debatable. For men, one element is clearly the move from a martial ideal to the civilian norm. Juliet Dusinberre argues that this shifting of gender boundaries shows that the playwrights were admirers and defenders of women in opposition to James I's misogynist court: the Puritans had made possible a new kind of feminism, based on their commitment to scriptural notions of equality of all believers and to the new status of Christian marriage as no longer inferior to celibacy.[6] Dusinberre has, however, been strongly criticised: in other ways the Puritans were adamant believers in male superiority, and she can cite only a small handful of putatively feminist texts to set against the proliferation of misogynist writing. Yet the very fact that the texts are so contradictory is in itself evidence of the shifting and uncertain sense of what gender might imply. Linda Woodbridge follows the passage I quoted above with a simple, common-sense response:

> What we know about the real-life female transvestite movement, about the traumas of transition to a peace-time society, about the new way of life women were encountering and creating in a London which was suddenly a large city, suggests that literature was here reflecting life – that sex roles were changing and the distinction between the sexes diminishing, just as literature shows.[7]

The trouble with that explanation is that the distinction between the sex roles, certainly by the end of the century, had not diminished, merely reformed itself in different terms, which most feminists would argue were more rigid than before. Already families were increasingly patriarchal. The change from a feudal to a capitalist economy brought a new set of distinctions and differences to gender, and new patterns of marriage and sexual relations. It certainly did not dissolve differences. The anxiety over gender identity was part of a wider disruption of certainty. With metaphysical and social coherence in question, any sure identities dissipate or crack, as Jonathan Dollimore has argued, quoting Donne himself.[8]

> And new philosophy calls all in doubt . . .
> 'Tis all in pieces, all coherence gone,
> All just supply, and all relation;
> Prince, subject, father, son are things forgot.
>
> (p. 276)

In the early seventeenth century traditional misogynism coexists with new pleas for women, libertinism with fear of damnation, martial ideals with new mercantile endeavours. And comments on gender cannot always be read literally. As Lisa Jardine has argued, the trope of the strong-willed woman is often a sign of feared social upheaval.[9] In the witch-hunts deviant women come literally to embody all the threats of a changing, soon to be revolutionary, society.

Since masculinity has so long been the norm of humanity, changes in male self-definition, or in the ideology of manliness, are not easily recognised. In Donne's case, such changes have been identified as literary or formalistic, summed up perhaps in the familiar argument that Donne continued to use Petrarchan forms, but employed them much more dramatically than earlier writers. Yet part at any rate of what these literary shifts encoded were new representations of masculinity, seen throughout seventeenth-century society, but appearing in sharp focus in Donne's poetry.[10]

If women were seen as either Eve or Mary, whore or chaste, there was no equally powerful binary for men. Men were not defined primarily in terms of their sexuality, as women were. Rank and occupation were predominant. But, all the same, male sexuality was represented by two very different discourses, which reflect fairly clearly the Eve–Mary dichotomy. One was the medieval association of lust with the animal, the fallen brutish nature of man, only too easily awoken by the temptress woman. The other was the literary representation of the lovesick lover. In general, Elizabethan literary lovesickness is associated with weakness, and behaviour that would now be – or, at any rate, was until recently – labelled 'feminine': weeping, depression, dreaminess, concern with clothes. It would be anachronistic to see Benedick and Claudio precisely as 'effeminate' in their switch from arms to love-matters. The two remain alternative occupations for the courtier, but this self-abasing love-making sits uneasily with a martial concept of masculinity, and much of the humour of *Much Ado about Nothing* depends on the ludicrous contrast between the two sides of Benedick's character. The two roles don't reinforce each other, except in so far as lovers are more acceptable because they are also brave soldiers. And the lover is youth in its green immaturity, not youth in its full-bloodedness.

This conception of the lover pining humbly for his idealised mistress, a conception which had grown out of the courtly-love tradition, was increasingly mocked and burlesqued in the late sixteenth and early seventeenth centuries: the imagery associated with it could only be used self-consciously, Shakespeare's sonnets for example, if they are not anti-Petrarchan ('My mistress' eyes are nothing like the sun'), at any rate knowingly exploit the artificiality of Petrarchan conventions ('Shall I compare thee to a summer's day?/Thou art more lovely and more temperate'). As J. W. Lever argued over thirty years ago, these conventions were never wholly successful in England. He ascribes this to the difference in English traditions (the ebullient medieval lyric; Anglo-Saxon misogyny), which must be partly true, through also to the chill Northern soul, which seems more dubious.[11]

What Lever does not discuss is that this is a form which grew originally out of a feudal society. Although Chaucer had known and drawn on this tradition, most obviously in his translation of *The Romance of the Rose* and in *The Knight's Tale*, in the England of the sixteenth century it was even further from its social context than in the city states of Italy. Yet it was almost the only form in which romantic passion could be described, or, in other words, in which sexuality, even in the most etiolated form, could be expressed, other than in terms of fleshly degradation. By the time Donne wrote, there had entered two other models, Ovid's stylish eroticism and Puritan marriage, which were to evolve perhaps into the later binary of rake and respectable paterfamilias. The lustful Adam/melancholy lover could begin to change.

Courtly-love poetry, with its religion of love and its cult of the lady, was from the start a subversive form. Why it arose when it did remains in some senses unanswered. The trope can be traced to Arab sources, but that does not account for its persistence and development into one of the central modern European tenets, romantic love. But from its beginnings in the twelfth century it provided a discourse through which the accepted norms of feudal society could be questioned. Although the nature and formulation of that questioning varied, what all forms of courtly love shared was a structure which overturned accepted social hierarchies, and gave a new value to human subjectivity and emotion, a secular equivalent of St Bernard, the medieval mystics and the cult of the Virgin. This humanism has two poles in the courtly-love tradition: first, the lady – that is, human love usurping the divine; secondly and more constantly (because in some forms the lady is spiritualised entirely into some universal good), the supreme importance given to the sensibility of the lover – the *cor gentil*, as the Italian school called it. It would be a mistake to read these poems as in any literal way proto-feminist. The focus is far more on the male lover who is capable of these intensities of love and pain.[12]

Yet these poems certainly show sexual passion overturning traditional power relations. The man presents himself as supplicant and servant to the woman. Lovers are what Sidney calls 'rebels to Nature'. They reverse the accepted hierarchies. They construct a microcosm – a traditional enough medieval/early Renaissance practice, but, instead of the microcosm echoing in miniature the macrocosm of God and the feudal order, it is a blasphemous parody of it. It is not surprising that there is evidence that some of the early practitioners of this poetry were involved with heretical sects, though it could also be a vehicle for a kind of *trahison de clercs*, the discontented, *déclassé* poet mocking the values which demean him. In the poems an individual asserts a new religious and social order of which he is creator, arbiter and centre. So, on one level, courtly love maps out one path towards Protestantism, capitalism, the end of feudalism. Yet at another level these early poems are curiously impotent. Not only do they present their central protagonist as passive, but there is no way in which they finally escape from the discourse of their age. They may invert and mock it but they have no means of negotiating new terms – in either sense. (One might argue that Dante did in his synthesis of courtly love with Christianity, but in doing so he changed them both.) On the whole courtly love remained an individualistic insertion into a world of fixed relationships. It is perhaps more fitting than we realise that a modernist such as Ezra Pound should have become so spell-bound by courtly love. On the one hand, the challenge to the feudal hierarchy in the name of the religion of love; on the other, the challenge to bourgeois custom in the name of the supremacy of art.

The Petrarchan tradition, the main form in which courtly love was known to English writers, is constantly present as imagery, allusion and butt in English writing in the late sixteenth century. Woodbridge suggests that the mockery of the convention of the lovelorn youth idolising his mistress reflects an uneasy awareness that the elevation of the woman was now a real possibility, that just because such conventions were less ludicrously contradictory of social practice they were perceived as more inflammatory. Again her view paints an unrealistically bright picture of women's lot, although I am sure she is right about the clash with a changed praxis. As affective sexual relationships became of more central importance it was increasingly nonsensical to operate with a model of sexual relationships so far from the usual social roles. And, as a critique of authority, it was an impossibly weak form for the breakdown in confidence that permeated the intelligentsia.

There remained too the uneasy awareness of the form's overt contradiction of Christian doctrine, in the fixing upon a mere woman of love which in theological terms should only be given to God. The Puritans were beginning to rehabilitate sex within marriage, though the Prayer Book had remained rather grudging about the matter. But the courtly-love tradition was essentially one of apostasy and antinomianism, qualities in ready supply elsewhere by 1600, but just because of that all the more bothersome here. In Philip Sidney's sonnet sequence *Astrophel and Stella*, published in 1591, tremendous tension remains within the form. For example, in a sonnet alluded to already Sidney writes,

> It is most true, that eyes are form'd to serve
> That inward light: and that the heavenly part
> Ought to be king, from whose rules who doth swerue,
> Rebels to Nature strive for their owne smart . . .
> True, that on earth we are but pilgrims made,
> And should in soule vp to our countrey moue:
> True, and yet true that I must Stella love.[13]

In this poem the Petrarchan or courtly appropriation of Christian imagery is reversed to represent the claims of that religious structure. But the poem bears a threatening trace throughout that contradicts its apparent orthodoxy. Its fatalistic ending, poised between defiance and despair, 'yet true that I must Stella love', asserts by its closure that the shadowed parody is more powerful than the overt assertion. But its protagonist remains static, powerless, humble in his hopeless love. The poem's struggle can have no outcome. Loved and lover are locked in insistent, unsatisfied need. Two absolutes face each other: the religious world, and the world of desire, equally imperative.

I do not want to suggest that Donne moves very far towards reconciling these contradictory pressures, only that he finds forms that engage more fully with them. On the cusp of the feudal/capitalist world, of aristocratic/bourgeois society, of Catholic/Protestant religion, of fidelistic/rational thought, his writing, with its complex imagery and desperate convolutions, encompasses a wide terrain of contemporary conflict and debate. The most striking change in Donne's use of Petrarchism is his attempt to bring together power and passion (which I would define not as precisely sexual or romantic, but perhaps as meaningful erotic passion) so that both become attributes of the 'masculine' or, in the terms of the poems, of the lover. In 'The Sun Rising', for example, Donne takes as the basic conceit the same fundamental mode of the Petrarchan tradition, and courtly love before it, the creation of the world of the lovers as a counter-cosmos. His counter-cosmos is presented very differently, as many critics have noted – witness his colloquial, irreverential tone, the dramatic vigorous language. But there are deeper and more structural changes. In the traditional Petrarchan poem the lady (not a word Donne often uses for the women in his poems) takes on the light-bearing qualities of the sun; she takes on royal authority over her servant lover. In 'The Sun Rising', the first time the comparison is drawn between the lovers and the sun itself this pattern seems to be continuing.

> Thy beams so reverend, and strong
> Why should thou think?
> I could eclipse and cloud them with a wink,
> But that I would not lose her sight so long:
> If her eyes have not blinded thine,
> Look . . . .
>
>   (p. 80)[14]

However, it should be noted that, even before the blinding light of the mistress's eyes are mentioned, the poet is already singly contesting the power of the sun. But, by the time the analogy with royal power enters the poem, the usual order, or rather disordering, has been disrupted, because the poet himself takes on the role of 'all princes', while the lady assumes the role of the possessed, that of 'all states'. At the end of the poem the counter, usurping sun is not the lady but them both: 'this bed thy centre is, these walls, thy sphere'.

This is a poem of post-coital celebration, of sexual success rather than failure and frustrated desire. But it is not simply a love poem. From its opening line, 'Busy old fool, unruly sun', it is also a poem about the usurpation of power, the young defying the old. There is a level at which such a poem must be seen in the context of Donne's other angry comments on the court, and of all those other defiant young Jacobeans – and this is a Jacobean poem – who are scornful of the inadequacy and corruption of their 'betters', ambitious young men who were impatient with the pedantry of custom. Yet – and this is a point to which I will have to return – on another level there is no more possible resolution for this poem than there was for Sidney's. If the model of authority is the sun, there is not much that can finally overturn it. The counter-world is ultimately bound within the discourse of the poem.[15]

Even when Donne is apparently most closely following the convention of the suppliant servant, he undermines the Petrarchan imagery. For example, in 'Lovers' Infiniteness', which depends entirely on the image of the besotted weeping lover, he transforms his entreaties into a commercial transaction, so that 'Sighs, tears, and oaths, and letters' are 'spent' in order to 'purchase' the beloved. His danger is that other men 'their stocks entire . . . can in tears, / In sighs, in oaths, in letters outbid' him. Humble subservience is transformed into competition for the ownership of an expensive object, bargained for in the market place. The lover is the merchant, the beloved the merchandise. But the poem questions this reassertion of the superiority of the masculine. The woman's love, it argues, cannot in any worthwhile sense be purchased, only given. The lovers 'will have a way more liberal', joining their hearts, so they 'shall / Be one, and one another's all' (p. 64).[16]

This tension between assertion of masculine strength and union of reciprocal giving is enacted again and again in Donne's poems of mutual love. His urgent imperatives dramatise the contradiction of the 'masculine persuasive force'. He orders or cajoles the women to acknowledge both his power and their equality. Claiming his right to possess, he presses her to give herself freely. This is the central dilemma of the newly emerging Puritan capitalist marriage, in which the man is indubitably superior but the partnership must be simultaneously intimate and equal. It is a paradox that reappears in Donne's divine poems, when they draw on sexual imagery for his relationship with God:

> Yet dearly I love you, and would be loved fain
> But am betrothed unto your enemy,
> Divorce me, untie, or break that knot again,
> Take me to you, imprison me, for I
> Except you enthral me, never shall be free,
> Nor ever chaste, except you ravish me.
>
> (p. 315)

Even in a poem such as Elegy x, 'To his Mistress Going to Bed' (p. 133), an openly erotic poem of masculine panâche which clearly owes far more to Ovid than to Petrarch, the imagery of conquest is entwined with that desire for mutuality. Donne proceeds by a series of commands. 'Come, Madam, come . . . Off with that girdle . . . Unpin that spangled breastplate . . . Off with that wiry coronet'. The central image is that of the conquistador:

> O my America, my new found land,
> My kingdom, safeliest, when by one man manned,
> My mine of precious stones, my empery,
> How blessed am I in thus discovering thee!

Yet he can only explore if his mistress grants him the licence. 'Licence my roving hands, and let them go/Before, behind, between, above, below'. She becomes both the English queen who permits the voyage and the American territory to be possessed. The pun here on discovering her is one made visually in contemporary depictions of European discovery, when America is allegorised as a naked Indian woman found by the clothed European man. There is an intimate connection between colonialist acquisition and the new emphasis on sexuality as a moment of virile possession. The imagistic linking of sexual and territorial appropriation occurs repeatedly ('search out the secret parts/Of the India'; 'Make her for love fit fuel/As gay as Flora, and as rich as Ind').[17]

Yet Donne is always questioning as well as creating this reification of the woman. His lyrics, quite literally, constantly pose her questions, even though they are always rhetorical ones. Like Pilate he does not wait for an answer;

> Stand still, and I will read to thee
> A lecture, love, in love's philosophy.
> (p. 62)

This is perhaps closer to what actually happens. But at least the speakers in Donne's poems believe women capable of understanding lectures in philosophy. Laying aside for the minute John Carey's probing of Donne's own ultimate uncertainty about the validity of reason, in this respect gender boundaries are less fixed than they were soon to be. As Victor Seidler argues, during the seventeenth century rationality becomes the province of men. So when Dryden censures Donne because he 'perplexes the minds of the Fair Sex with nice Speculations of Philosophy, when he shou'd ingage their hearts, and entertain them with the softnesses of Love', he is expressing a fairly new conviction that women can only be creatures of the emotions and unreason. A. J. Smith's surprise that the 'great age of wit and reason' should condemn Donne in this way does not allow for the fact that it was the age of sensibility, not the 'great age of wit and reason', for women.[18]

Donne's love poems, with their 'little room' which he wrestles to believe 'an every where', foreshadow in miniature the view of love and marriage as a private other world, a view that became pervasive by the latter part of the seventeenth century. As Catherine Belsey says, 'After 1660 the family progressively becomes a privileged, private place of retreat from a public world increasingly experienced as hostile and alien.' However, as she also notes, Donne's contemporary Webster was already contrasting the warm privacy of the domestic with the corrupt, malign public in *The Duchess of Malfi*.[19]

In poems such as 'The Ecstasy' and 'A Valediction Forbidding Mourning' the desire for mutual love intensifies to images of fusion. The urgent search for oneness in so many of the poems has complex origins. It cannot be separated from Donne's overwhelming experience of his 'nothingness', which in some senses emerges immediately out of the socially devastating consequences of his own love marriage. As he wrote to Sir Henry Goodyer of his exile from favour in Mitcham, 'to be no part of any body is to be nothing. . . . I stumbled . . . yet I would try again: for to this hour I am nothing, or so little, that I am scarce subject and argument good enough for one of my own letters.'[20] For Donne, as John Carey suggests, this longing for unity propogates in his vocabulary newly invented words to convey interconnectedness – 'intertouch', 'inter-assured' 'interanimate' – and lies behind the mingling, reflexive passion of his 'Sappho to Philaenis'; Donne's songs and sonnets constantly enact closeness where the Petrarchan convention enacted distance.[21] He dramatises scenes in which the lovers speak, look, touch:

> Our eyes were firmly cemented
>   With a fast balm, which thence did spring;
> Our eye-beams twisted, and did thread
>   Our eyes, upon one double string.
>
>   (p. 53)

'Husband and wife is one flesh', as Hamlet, following Genesis, puts it. This scriptural concept was central to the Puritan view of marriage. As early as 1542 Thomas Bacon wrote that marriage was

An hie, holye and blessed order of life, ordayned, not of man, but of God, yea and that not in this sinneful world, but in paradyse that most joyful garden of pleasure; which (Matrimonie) hath ever ben had in great honor and reverence among all nacions; wherein one man and one woman are coupled and knit together in one fleshe and body in the feare and love of God, by the free, lovinge, harty, and good consente of them both, to the extent that they two may dwel together, as one fleshe and body of one wyl and mynd in all honesty, vertue and godlines, and spend theyr lyves in equal partaking of all such thinges, as god shal send them in thenkes gevynge.[22]

In 1617 William Whateley expressed views even closer to the romanticised view of marriage which remains until the present day:

Love is the life and soule of marriage . . . where love is abundant it makes a supply of all other wants. . . . Love sweetens and seasons all estates . . . in whom it prevaileth, to them is marriage it selfe indeed, viz, a pleasing combination of two persons as into one home one purce, one heart, and one flesh.[23]

This view of equality within marriage was of course at total variance with the legal and economic subordinate position of women, and with the increasing power of fathers and husbands as heads of household.[24] The Puritans argued the superiority of the husband no less firmly than they extolled marriage partnership. William Guage told wives constantly to remind themselves that 'Mine husband is my superiour, my better', and used the analogy of the head and the heart to show that, though man and wife were one flesh, there must still be an hierarchical structure.[25] Many of Donne's love poems are of course not about, or not necessarily about, marriage. But I would argue that this contradiction at the heart of the ideology of bourgeois marriage is constantly at play in his writings. His male personae, varied, fragmentary though they be, insist that their words are charged with this masculine force, even when what they want to beget is a free response and mutual tenderness.

One set of poems in which Donne is forced to embrace a form very much closer to the traditional Petrarchan model are those written to his patronesses, where the genre – and social expediency – demanded that he conventionally praise them as the embodiment of all virtue, as 'Lauras', which name he applies to Elizabeth Drury. How poets cope with the problem of the self-effacement and studied compliment needed in writing poems to their patrons is a study in itself. David Aers and Gunther Kress have argued, convincingly, that Donne's verse letters must be interpreted as the work of a frustrated, alienated intellectual, compelled to hide or express obliquely any impatient scepticism or angry contempt.[26] And the sexual roles add to this conflict: for a poet who elsewhere refuses to accept this meek self-abasement before a woman, the humiliation is exacerbated, no matter how much he platonises her. Even in the Elizabeth Drury poems, writing about someone he had never known, and the daughter of a patron rather a patroness herself, Donne cannot pass over the difficulty of turning a woman into the 'idea of a woman', as he is reputed to have told Jonson he had done.

Most of these eulogistic poems have the distancing form of the verse letter, as well as imagery that places these women in other 'climes'. Compared with the seeming conceit-bound control of the songs and sonnets, their imagery often appears fractured and contradictory, the exception perhaps being the Elizabeth Drury poems, possibly just because there Donne takes incoherence and disorder as his theme. In *The First Anniversary: An Anatomy of the World*, the centre of the poem becomes not the woman, but the poet's own bitter disillusionment:

> This man, so geat, that all that is, is his
> O what a trifle, and poor thing he is!
> If man were anything, he's nothing now.
>   (p. 275)

In the 'sick world, yea dead, yea putrefied' of this poem Donne explores the corruption of sexuality, obsessed as he is, in so many of these poems, with the blight of Eve.

We are born ruinous . . . .
. . . mankind . . . laboured to frustrate
Even God's purpose; and made woman, sent
For man's relief, cause of his languishment . . .
For that first marriage was our funeral:
One woman at one blow, then killed us all,
And singly, one by one they kill us now.
We do delightfully ourselves allow
To that consumption; and profusely blind,
We kill ourselves, to propagate our kind.

(p. 273)

This fusion of traditional medieval misogyny and Jacobean despair is very different from Donne's Ovidian diatribes against women's inconstancy. It appears as almost the necessary complement to the effusive praise these poems demand: the one stereotype demands its counter-form. But, in addition, Donne had himself fallen from social grace through a woman. 'The sickness of which I died is that I began in your Lordship's house this love', he wrote to Sir Thomas Egerton after his marriage. To his wife's father he had already written, 'And though perchance you intend not utter destruction, yet the way through which I fall towards it is so headlong, that being thus pushed I shall soon be at the bottom.' His return in several of these poems to Eve, cause of the Fall of man, cannot be unconnected with his aggrieved sense of his unjust debarment from courtly fortune, and his enforced position as suppliant for grace. He awkwardly but persistently twists together the Petrarchan, Platonic ideal and the death-bearing biblical Eve. The terror of the consequences of trespass, which picks away at the masculine ebullience of the songs and sonnets, here poses itself as a challenge to the genre. Elizabeth Drury can only escape woman's corruption by taking on what Donne, following Paracelsus, identifies as the masculine qualities of alchemical fire.[27]

She took the weaker sex, she that could drive
The poisonous tincture and the stain of Eve,
Out of her thoughts, and deeds; and purify
All by a true religious alchemy.

(p. 275)

When Donne writes to the Countess of Bedford (whose flesh,

John Carey points out, he repeatedly petrifies, making it amber, crystal or whatever), he makes it clear that he can only deal with her as an exception to womankind

> The first good angel, since the world's frame stood,
>   That ever did in woman's shape appear.
>
> (p. 226)

> So in this pilgrimage I would behold
>   You as you'are virtue's temple, not as she.
>
> (p. 230)

In a poem to the Countess of Huntingdon he prefaces his praise of her in one poem by saying,

> In women so perchance mild innocence
>   A seldom comet is, but active good
> A miracle . . . .

> . . . we might fear that virtue, since she fell
>   So low as woman, should be near her end.
>
> (p. 236)

In his other poem to her, he rejects the convention of the Petrarchan lover at some length, before giving her the standard Petrarchan praise. He assures her that he will not

> vex your eyes to see
> A sighing ode, nor cross-armed elegy.
> I come not to call pity from your heart,
> Like some white-livered dotard that would part
> Else from his slippery soul with a faint groan,
> And faithfully, (without you smiled) were gone.
> I cannot feel the tempest of a frown,
> I may be raised by love, but not cast down.
>
> (p. 239)

As the Countess of Huntingdon was Sir Thomas Egerton's stepdaughter, living in the household at the time of Donne's marriage, she would have known perfectly well that love had, in

social terms, cast him down, and, if the date of 1603 is correct, did
so only a year earlier. The unexpectedly frank *double entendre*, 'I
may be raised by love', out of place in this genre, is an extra
flicker of Donne's defiance. Donne goes on to suggest an
evolution, a progress now completed to a more mature and manly
form of love. The days of mutual, humble confused love, he
suggests, are over:

> What pretty innocence in those days moved!
> Man ignorantly walked by her he loved;
> Both trembled and were sick, both knew not why.

Now man has learnt more: he has not only discovered 'the place'
he searches for (woman as territory again) but 'the nearest way',
which is not to plead but to assert himself.

> It is not love that sueth or doth contend;
> Love either conquers or but meets a friend . . .
> Let others sign and grieve; one cunning sleight
> Shall freeze my love to crystal in a night.
>
> (p. 240)

This masculine bravado is Donne's counter to his social
vulnerability, and the poem's imagery of distance paradoxically
gives him more space to insist on his own power within his 'side
of the earth'. The misogyny in these patronage poems should not
be read simply as an attack on womankind. Donne may or may
not have believed these misogynist statements literally: he at any
rate found them a useful available structuring of his experience,
and a displacement of his own guilts. In these public poems, as
opposed to his more intimate songs and sonnets, the misogyny
serves to preserve his fragile self-esteem and to express his anger
at his exclusion from fortune. This goes beyond Donne's individual
dilemma. Any analysis of the emergence of modern masculinity
will have to take into account how it has helped make possible the
necessary yet harshly restricted social mobility that capitalism
brought. When Donne writes his more personally framed love
poems, he can eschew the inimical stereotypes of Eve and Laura.
But the centrality – and fragility – of his dynamic, energised,
achieving masculinity remains.

There is no space here to explore the sexual imagery of Donne's
religious poetry (where God certainly is as often addressed in the
imperative mood as the women in the love poems). But I want to
end by looking briefly at one aspect of the irreconcilable yet
inextricably fused duality of love and religion in his writing.
Donne's love poetry is never solely about love. John Carey in his
brilliantly subtle study of Donne's life and work suggests that
Donne's obsession with woman's inconstancy springs from his
own anxieties about his betrayal of Catholicism. Carey's book in
fact constantly and persuasively looks at Donne's love poetry to
explain his preoccupations with the nature of the body, ambition,
his driving anxious sense of dividedness and displacement, and
above all his religious conflicts. Sometimes, however, Carey seems
to suggest that Donne only uses love poetry to write about more
important things. (The repeated, slightly old-fashioned jocularity
of Carey's references to the women in Donne's poetry as 'girls'
increases this sense that they are not to be taken entirely
seriously.[28]) I would argue quite the reverse. Donne again and
again attempts in these poems to make sexual relationships a
central organising frame. In a time which, as Christopher Hill
suggests, experienced itself much more as a crumbling, collapsing
world than a new beginning, Donne transmutes the religion of
love of his Petrarchan heritage into the exploration of images
which might briefly make his fragmenting world cohere.[29] Donne
draws into his love poetry a whole range of discourses from
mutually incompatible areas: Protestantism, Catholicism, Ovid's
paganism, stoicism, Neo-platonism, the counter-cosmos of the
courtly-love tradition. In the shifting, contradictory period of the
early seventeenth century, for a brief moment it was possible for
Donne's poetry to freight sexual relations with an ontological
weight that they were not again asked to carry for another 200
years. That use of sexual relations is certainly one reason for
Dryden's unease with Donne's love poetry. Lawrence Lerner has
argued that in the nineteenth century 'Dover Beach' marks a
moment of transition from a world of religious faith to one where
the only absolute signifier becomes the power of individual love.
When the Sea of Faith has withdrawn, the only answer is to say
as Arnold says, 'Ah, love, let us be true / To one another'.

But for Arnold there no longer remains a dominating alternative
metaphysic with absolute claims to comfort or threaten. Donne's
retreat to the little room of love always remains insecure. As I

suggested in my reading of 'The Sun Rising', in the end there is no possible negotiation between the world of that love poem and the world of social power and Christian doctrine without. Donne is reported to have suffered intense remorse later for his blasphemous love poetry. With his early and deep Catholicism, his imaginative horror at the corruptibility of flesh, he never attempts to work out the kind of reconciliation between sexuality and Christianity that Milton wrestles to achieve, even though he struggles in such poems as 'The Ecstasy' to fuse body and soul in love. The moralisation of premarital, male sexuality lies in the future.

Catherine Belsey has suggested we need a genealogy of romantic love. I have attempted here to outline one stage in its evolution. It is ironic, and possibly significant, that Donne's drawing-together of erotic passion and power, of tender intimacy and domination, as defining qualities of the masculine is played out against the loss of power he experienced through his own marriage. By contrast, earlier – or even contemporary and later – representations of sexual relations still put passion and power as mutually exclusive. Even in *Antony and Cleopatra*, Antony's political power is quite literally destroyed by his love of Cleopatra, for all that he is portrayed as so much greater that the cautious, bureaucratic Octavius. It is ironic, too, that a poet who choose to circulate his work in the aristocratic way around his friends, and felt that he lowered himself in publishing *The First Anniversary*, should return so often to images of the mercantile, trading world. Yet the capitalist world moralised and naturalised the libidinous possessive thrust of man in science, in colonialism, in business, in sexuality. The process begins at this period, as Bacon recognised when he talked of 'the masculine birth of science'. But, though Donne's writing is in so many ways shaped by this new pressure towards assertive masculinity, with its desire for possession and control, part of its greatness is that it also so powerfully problematises this new man, not least by his desperate search for a closer and fully equal love.[30]

NOTES

1. Angela Carter, *The Magic Toyshop* (London: Virago, 1981) p. 193.

2. Quotations from, in order of appearance: A. J. Smith (ed.), *John Donne: The Critical Heritage* (London: Routledge and Kegan Paul, 1975) p. 204; ibid., p. 271; Raoul Granqvist, *The Reputation of John Donne, 1779–1867*, in *Acta Universitatis Upsaliensis, Studia Anglistici Upsaliensia*, 24 (Uppsala, 1975) p. 161; Smith, *Donne: The Critical Heritage*, p. 304; Granqvist, *The Reputation of Donne*, p. 161.

3. Andy Metcalf and Martin Humphries, *The Sexuality of Men* (London: Pluto, 1985); Jeremy Weeks, *Masculinity* (Chichester: Ellis Harland, 1986); Klaus Theweleit, *Male Fantasies* (Oxford: Polity Press, 1987). There are also a number of papers on masculinity in *Sexual Difference*, a special issue of *Oxford Literary Review*, 8 (1986).

4. Michael Foucault, *The History of Sexuality*, vol. I (Harmondsworth: Penguin, 1979) and *Madness and Civilisation* (London: Tavistock, 1967); Victor Seidler, 'Reason, Desire and Masculine Sexuality' and Pat Caplan, Introduction, in Caplan (ed.), *The Cultural Construction of Gender* (London: Tavistock, 1987); Lawrence Stone, *The Family, Sex and Marriage, 1500–1800* (London: Weidenfeld and Nicolson, 1977). For a feminist historian's view, see Sheila Rowbotham, *Women, Resistance and Revolution* (Harmondsworth: Penguin, 1972) pp. 25–6. For further discussion of the association of women and nature in the eighteenth century see L. J. Jordanova, 'Natural Facts: a Historical Perspective on Science and Sexuality', in Carol P. MacCormack and Marilyn Strathern (eds), *Nature, Culture and Gender* (Cambridge: Cambridge University Press, 1980) and 'Naturalising the Family: Literature and the Bio-Medical Sciences in the Late Eighteenth Century', in L. J. Jordanova (ed.), *Languages of Nature* (London: Free Association Books, 1986).

5. Linda Woodbridge, *Women in the English Renaissance: Literature and the Nature of Womankind, 1540–1620* (Brighton: Harvester, 1984) p. 181.

6. Juliet Dusinberre, *Shakespeare and the Nature of Women* (London: Macmillan, 1975). Those who argue against her include Kathleen McLuskie, 'The Patriarchal Bard', in Jonathan Dollimore and Alan Sinfield (eds), *Political Shakespeare: New Essays in Cultural Materialism* (Manchester: Manchester University Press, 1985); Lisa Jardine, *Still Harping on Daughters: Women and Drama in the Elizabethan and Jacobean Period* (Brighton: Harvester, 1983); Jonathan Dollimore, *Radical Tragedy: Religion, Ideology and Power in the Drama of Shakespeare and his Contemporaries* (London: Methuen, 1984).

7. Woodbridge, *Women in the English Renaissance*, p. 181.

8. Dollimore, *Radical Tragedy*, p. 276.

9. Jardine, *Still Harping on Daughters*, p. 93.

10. For example, Donald Guss, 'Donne's Petrarchism' (1965), in John R. Roberts (ed.), *Essential Articles for the Study of John Donne* (Brighton: Harvester, 1975).

11. J. W. Lever, *The Elizabethan Love Lyric* (1956), University Paperback edn (London: Methuen, 1966).

12. For other views of the sexual politics of courtly love see Lilian S. Robinson, 'Women under Capitalism: the Renaissance Lady', in her book *Sex, Class and Culture* (London: Methuen, 1986), as well as Meg

Bogin, *The Women Troubadours: An Introduction to the Women Poets of Twelfth-Century Provence* (New York: Norton, 1980).

13. Philip Sidney, *Astrophel and Stella*, sonnet v.

14. All page references for the poems are to *John Donne: The Complete Poems*, ed. A. J. Smith (Harmondsworth: Penguin, 1973).

15. The line 'Go tell court-huntsmen, that the King will ride' dates this as a Jacobean poem: see for example Helen Gardner, in her edition of *The Elegies and Songs and Sonnets* (Oxford: Clarendon Press, 1965) p. 201, which says of this line, 'As Professor Praz was the first to point out, this is clearly a topical jest at King James's passion for hunting which, to his attendants' disgust, involved early rising.' The position of the alienated Jacobean intellectual is discussed in Mark H. Curtis, 'The Alienated Intellectuals of Early Stuart England', in Trevor Aston (ed.), *Crisis in Europe 1560–1660* (London: Routledge and Kegan Paul, 1965); David Aers and Gunter Kress, 'Darke Texts Need Notes: Versions of the Self in Donne's Verse Epistles', *Literature and History*, 8 (1978); and Dollimore, *Radical Tragedy*.

16. William Zunder has commented on the 'hierarchical, yet equal' relationships that Donne creates, in *The Poetry of John Donne: Literature and Culture in the Elizabethan and Jacobean Period* (Brighton: Harvester, 1982) p. 30. There is also a subtle discussion of the tension between mutuality and masculine egoism in 'The Good Morrow' in an article which I found only a few days before completing this essay: David Aers and Gunther Kress, 'Vexatious Contraries: a Reading of Donne's Poetry', in David Aers, Bob Hodge and Gunther Kress, *Literature, Language and Society in England, 1580–1680* (Dublin: Gill and Macmillan, 1981).

17. For a discussion of these allegorical depictions of America see Peter Hulme, 'Polytrophic Man: Tropes of Sexuality and Mobility in Early Colonial Discourse', and, of the sexual implications of the language of colonialism, my article 'Woman/Indian: "the American" and his other', both in Francis Barker *et al.* (eds), *Europe and its Others*, vol. II (Colchester, University of Essex, 1985).

18. Smith, in *Donne: The Complete Poems*, p. 13.

19. Catherine Belsey, *The Subject of Tragedy* (London: Methuen, 1985) p. 193.

20. See *John Donne: Selected Prose*, ed. Neil Rhodes (Harmondsworth: Penguin, 1987) p. 93.

21. John Carey, *John Donne: Life, Mind and Art* (London: Faber and Faber, 1981).

22. Preface to Miles Coverdale's translation of *The Christion State of Marriage* (1543), quoted in William Haller and Malleville Haller, 'The Puritan Art of Marriage', *Huntington Library Quarterly*, 5 (1942) 244–5.

23. Ibid., p. 268.

24. For discussion of the increasingly patriarchal family see Stone, *Family, Sex and Marriage,* and Rowbotham, *Women, Resistance and Revolution.*

25. Haller, in *Huntington Library Quarterly*, 5, p. 249.

26. Aers and Kress, in *Literature and History*, 8.

27. Carey, *Donne: Life, Mind and Art*. Donne's exploration of such

gendering (cf. his description of the true Church in Satire III) would need a study in itself. Aers and Kress in 'Vexatious Contraries' (in Aers *et al.*, *Literature, Language and Society*) also quote these letters, though to make rather different points. Again I would recommend this article as a fascinating study of the intermeshing of Donne's sexual and social anxieties.

28. I don't want to simplify Carey's complex response. He interestingly compares Donne to D. H. Lawrence in his treatment of the conscious body. Carey's is the most far-reaching and perceptive study of Donne so far. However, I would disagree with his wish to see Donne's writing as the expression of his unique imagination, rather than as a response – which is of course both imaginative and unique – to his historical context.

29. Christopher Hill, *The Intellectual Origins of the English Revolution* (Oxford: Clarendon Press, 1965).

30. See C. B. MacPherson, *The Political Theory of Possessive Individuality* (Oxford: Clarendon Press, 1962) p. 220: 'The basic assumptions of possessive individualism – that man is free and human by virtue of his sole proprietorship of his own person, and that human society is essentially a series of market relations – were deeply embedded in the seventeenth century foundations.' On science and masculinity see Brian Easlea, *Fathering the Unthinkable: Masculinity, Science and the Nuclear Arms Race* (London: Pluto, 1983).

8

'In Love with Curious Words': Signification and Sexuality in English Petrarchism

MALCOLM EVANS

Even a cursory survey of references to Petrarchism in critical writing on early-seventeenth-century English poetry reveals some interesting inconsistencies in terminology. There are critics and literary historians who write of the Petrarchism of Donne, Jonson and their followers, for example, while others have claimed that the poetry of Donne and Jonson, through its rejection of the ornate style, its use of more colloquial rhythms, and its tendency to resist or undermine certain conventional images, establishes a decisive break with this tradition.[1] But what may at first appear to be a critical disagreement, beyond which lie related debates about the centrality and value of Petrarchism in late-sixteenth-century poetry,[2] is an effect of these inconsistencies, which permit much of the work of seventeenth-century poets to be at once 'Petrarchan' in one sense and 'anti-' and 'un-Petrarchan' in another.

The problem of this ambiguity, trivial in itself, prompts other questions, which range from considerations of lyric form to the forces that govern what is and is not said about love at a particular historical moment – those factors determining the production and re-presentation of that curious intersection of public and private domains which Roland Barthes calls 'lover's discourse', the repertoire of gestures, images and scenarios that structure the experience of love and the subjectivity of the lover.[3] It is a problem that involves more than a pedantic disagreement over literary critical terminology. The question of what can and cannot be named 'Petrarchan' extends into broader areas of concern common to poets and literary theorists of the seventeenth century and contemporaries of Barthes: the relationship of language to what purports to exist outside or beyond it, and of semiotic codes and conventions to material social processes.

The first section of this essay outlines a relatively minor current in the history of Petrarch's influence, the highly codified and restrictive English Petrarchism of the late sixteenth century. The second deals with the 'Petrarchan' in a broader sense, as a discourse on love still highly influential throughout Europe in the seventeenth century, and the third examines its relationship to eroticism and the body. The fourth section attempts some tentative correlations of this broader phenomenon with other, analogous discourses, which operated in very different ideological arenas but were also addressed to the construction and regulation of 'love' and sexuality during this period of profound cultural change. The concluding section is modelled on the Petrarchan blazon and, more tentatively, on Walter Benjamin's proposal for a book made up entirely of quotations which surprise the wayfarer and relieve him (or her) of his convictions.

I

> O Petrarke, hed and prince of poets all,
> Whose lively gift of flowyng eloquence,
> Wel may we seke but finde not how or whence
> So rare a gift with thee did rise and fall.
> Peace to thy bones, and glory imortall
> Be to thy name.

These sentiments, from an anonymous sonnet in Tottel's *Miscellany* (1557), signal the increasing importance of Petrarchan models to English lyric poets in the second half of the sixteenth century. The next poem in this influential collection makes similar claims, and Puttenham's *Arte of English Poesie* (1589) again stresses eloquence, along with the importance of Wyatt and Surrey, who domesticated the sonnet and became 'chief lanternes of light' to later poets by 'imitating very naturally and studiously their maister Francis Petrarch'.[4] With the courtly vogue of the sonnet and the demands of printers for collections and sonnet sequences to satisfy a substantial market, there evolved, from the formal and emotional

range of Petrarch's love poetry, a more schematic code accessible
to any versifying talent. In this scheme the lady is a distant, often
cruel, goddess or saint-like figure. For the lover, who praises,
sighs, weeps and languishes, she is the only possible source of
comfort and grace. The form need only approximate that of the
Petrarchan sonnet – Thomas Watson's lyric below, for example,
has 18 lines arranged in three quartets, each followed by a
couplet. The language is elevated, the style fraught with the
antitheses and oxymora that constitute the lover's tumultous
passion. If the lady's eyes resemble the sun, her lips coral, her
skin alabaster and her voice music the product will be an example
of Elizabethan Petrarchism written by Watson, Barnabe Barnes,
Thomas Lodge, Giles Fletcher or one of a number of other writers.
Authorship, in most cases, is not a crucial issue. They are marked
by the essential anonymity Barthes ascribes to lover's discourse in
general.[5]

Watson's *Hecatompathia* (1581) gives some suitable examples of
the formula:

> Harke you that list to heare what sainte I serve:
> Her yellowe lockes exceede the beaten goulde;
> Her sparkeling eies in heav'n a place deserve;
> Her forehead high and faire of comely moulde;
>   Her wordes are musicke all of silver sounde;
>   Her wit so sharpe as like can scarce be found;
> Each eyebrowe hanges like Iris in the skies;
> Her Eagles nose is straight of stately frame;
> On either cheeke a Rose and Lillie lies;
> Her breath is sweet perfume or hollie flame;
>   Her lips more red than any Corall stone;
>   Her neck more white than aged swans that mone;
> Her breast transparent is, like Christall rocke;
> Her fingers long, fit for Apolloes Lute;
> Her slipper such as Momus dare not mocke;
> Her vertues all so great as make me mute:
>   What other partes she hath I neede not say,
>   Whose face alone is cause of my decaye.

Here we find the stock ingredients: the lady as inaccessible saint,
incomparable in physical beauty and of inexpressible virtue; the
lover in rapt adoration and decay, locquacious yet mute. The

blazon of the lady's attributes, metonymic and fragmentary, reifies the body in a manner analogous to the visual codes of modern pornography while explicity repressing the unnamable 'other parties' dispersed in the sublimations of Petrarchan discourse. The catalogue follows the established range of imagery – beaten gold, roses and lilies, coral – in everything but the aquiline nose, the beauty of which is confirmed in a footnote citing a Latin source. The metre, varied only in the first foot of the poem, works with the anaphora, the repetition of syntactic patterns and their coincidence with the line, the evident strain for rhyme and metrical regularity in 'as like can scarce be found' and the otherwise superfluous 'aged swans that mone', and the 'poetically' foregrounded syntax of lines 3, 5, 6, 12 and 13 to impose the signature of 'eloquence' and form.

There is much scope, in these very significations of artifice or excess, for the sort of deconstructive reading that would put signifiers themselves at odds with the concept of a consolidated code and the transcendental, ultimately inexpressible signifieds that code postulates – the lady's virtue, the extra-discursive turmoil of 'love' at its most personal and intense. The most promising aporia for such an intervention is, perhaps, the 'mone' of the swansong, which seems to have no place in the poem's conventional schema except to provide a rhyme for 'stone'. But such ingenuity would put at hazard some important formal and historical differences within the broader Petrarchan paradigm, and, if anything exemplifies a restricted code characteristic of late-sixteenth-century English Petrarchism, then Watson's poem does. The important factors here are, relatively speaking, a turning-away from the production of meaning towards an unmediated representation of 'love', its subject and object, a self-consciousness directed, overwhelmingly, towards the experience rather than its signification and constitution in language. The code in this, one of its most straightforward products, remains invisible in the manner of the transparent rendering of seemingly natural truths analysed by Barthes in *Mythologies*, not the crisis and productivity of *écriture* but the routine ideological reproduction of *écrivance* or, in Bakhtin's terms, an almost seamless monologism.[6]

This is the restricted Petrarchan code caricatured in Jaques's third age of man, 'the lover, / Sighing like a furnace, with a woful ballad / Made to his mistress' eyebrow' (*As You Like It*, II.vii.147–9).[7] Earlier, in the sonnet sequence published posthumously in

1591, Sidney's Astrophel protests against the stilted language,
assisted by dictionary alliteration, and the derivative qualities of
the English lyric:

> You that do dictionary's method bring
> Into your rhymes, running in rattling rows;
> You that poor Petrarch's long-deceased woes
> With new-born sighs and denizened wit do sing;
> You take wrong ways . . . .
>
> (*Astrophel and Stella*, xv)

In Sonnet cxxx, 'My mistress' eyes are nothing like the sun',
Shakespeare too subverts conventional Petrarchism in a reversal
of the familiar blazon, denying the applicability of eight stereotyped
comparisons – including hair like gold, lips like coral and breath
like perfume – before concluding sceptically in the couplet, 'And
yet, by heaven, I think my love as rare / As any she belied with
false compare', the 'she' being a standard designation of the
idealised mistress.[8]

In marked contrast to the conventional Petrarchism of Watson
and his like, at once highly codified and reluctant to acknowledge
itself as discourse, such texts display this code as one of the most
familiar instances of the already-written and treat it as a
conventional literary language whose monolithic claims to truth
call for dialogic and intertextual disruption. Drama allowed more
scope than the sonnet for this process. So *The Spanish Tragedy*, for
example, exploits the conventional Petrarchan association of love
and war in a wooing scene which ends in the murder of Horatio,
includes one of Petrarch's most hyperbolic images of the lover's
anguish in Hieronimo's soliloquy after the death of his son – 'O
eyes, no eyes, but fountains fraught with tears' – and divides a
passage from another of Thomas Watson's sonnets between two
speakers to impel it towards conflict and discontinuity.[9] Later, in
The Changeling, Petrarchism is deployed as the idiom of shallow
romantic idealism, and the plot, through a sequence of murders
and adulteries, discloses the folly of Alsemero, who assumes that
his first glimpse of Beatrice–Joanna in church, where Petrarch first
saw Laura,[10] confirms her virtue and the purity of his love. The
period that separates these two plays sees the consolidation on
the English stage of an idiom which, in context, is presented as a
second- or third-hand lover's discourse. In Shakespeare's comedies

this Petrarchism is a common source of reference – from the language of the young men in *Love's Labour's Lost*, for example, through to Jaques's portrait of the lover or Silvius and Phebe's 'pageant truly play'd / Between the pale complexion of true love / And the red glow of scorn and proud disdain' in *As You Like It* (III.iv.47–9). In *Romeo and Juliet*, Mercutio's apprehension at the approach of the lovesick hero makes these familiar literary associations explicit: 'Now is he for the numbers that Petrarch flowed in' (II.iv.39).

The main preoccupation of the late Elizabethan sonneteers has been described as 'love *in vacuo*', a vacuum moreover which 'abhors nature'.[11] Contemporaries who were critical of this brand of Petrarchism focused on its aesthetic exhaustion and its limited emotional and intellectual repertoire. Repressing the body, the social dimension of love and, for the most part, communication between the lover and the object of his love, this discourse constituted a passion easily re-presented as a self-perpetuating literary fiction. By the time Donne too began to address the limitations of the convention, in poems such as 'The Indifferent' and 'Woman's Inconstancy',[12] and Jonson embarked on his career as a lyric poet, the restricted Petrarchism outlined here had a clearly established double life, in its naïve or 'innocent' form as a primary code for the transparent representation of love as a 'natural', given experience, and as a conventional form of writing embedded in other, less homogeneous texts, and acknowledged as a discourse, a code or a dead letter. At times the cohabitation and overlapping of these two modes present problems that demonstrate the inseparability of formal considerations from the more obviously material determinants of literary production. There are two love poems by Shakespeare, for example, which, in the dramatic context of *Love's Labour's Lost*, are clearly satirical versions of Petrarchism. Printed in *The Passionate Pilgrim*, an anthology by different authors published by William Jaggard in 1599 and attributed to Shakespeare, the same texts appear no more absurd than the other, presumably 'straight', poems around them.[13]

II

During his visit to William Drummond of Hawthornden at

Christmas 1618, Ben Jonson shocked his host by cursing Petrarch, deriding his English imitators, including Spenser, and informing Drummond himself that his poems, which owed much to this tradition, 'were not after the Fancy of ye time'.[14] So Jonson too, like Sidney, Shakespeare and Donne, adopts a stance which is in a sense anti-Petrarchan.

There is, however, another sense in which work by all these poets remains fundamentally indebted to the Petrarchan tradition. In Sidney's sonnet sequence the striken lover Astrophel meditates on the distant, unattainable Stella in a way that suggested the 'English Petrarke' as a suitable appellation for the poet.[15] Sonnet xv, which comments on 'poor Petrarch's long-deceased woes', concludes by advising his imitators to behold Stella and then begin writing with originality and truth. This gesture of rejecting the letter for the spirit, or the appearance for the reality – also employed by Sidney in sonnet i – was not uncommon. The lover in sonnet xx of Thomas Lodge's sequence *Phyllis* (1593), for example, dissociates himself from poets 'in love with curious words' who praise 'the looks', 'the locks' and 'the eye' of their 'fair queens', rioting 'in pompous style' on these frail and unstable beauties when he, in contrast, values the faith and virtue of his mistress. The convention of being unconventional and therefore unique, in Sidney as in Lodge, only boosts the expected hyperbole and adds another twist to the spiral. Thus Petrarchism, in a broader sense, could accommodate a critique of its own more restricted code, and such anti-Petrarchan poems as Shakespeare's Sonnet cxxx occupied a conventional slot in this paradigm, one established by Du Bellay and other poets writing in Europe earlier in the sixteenth century.[16] Such critiques of Petrarchism in Shakespeare are often equivocal. In the early plays immature and idealist lovers employ the code of goddesses, tears and sighs, but the more flexible language of 'true love' is, as Leonard Foster argues, still at root Petrarchan.[17] In comedy the Jacks do, by and large, love their Jills, who remain incomparable in the eyes of the lover and whose dramatic function is to bestow wisdom and grace. In *Romeo and Juliet* the satire on the conventional idiom at the beginning of the play, in Romeo's yearning for the indifferent Rosaline, is framed by a number of standard Petrarchan images later taken to a boldly literal extreme and given central structural importance. The sonnet that forms the prologue incapsulates the whole action of the play, which issues from the fact that the mistress, conventionally the 'dear enemy', is precisely that in the case of the Capulet Juliet. The traditional lover 'died' at his lady's kiss, Romeo's actual fate in the vault at the end of the play. Similarly Donne, while rejecting the narrower English Petrarchism, exploits its framework and conventions, and even Jonson is indebted in his lyric verse to the model he cursed in the hearing of Drummond. The best known of his short poems, the song to Celia 'Drinke to me, onely, with thine eyes', for example, is based on the Petrarchan conceit of the object which has been touched by the deified mistress and transformed by her grace.

The various critiques and interrogations of Petrarchism at its most conventional constitute an expanded code which functions by disrupting or transforming its own inner, restricted code. The permutations of basic moves in this system include the anti-conventional convention and the convention of being anti-conventional in a genuinely inconventional way. Love and sincerity are the elusive transcendental signifieds that call for the horizon of language to be continually pushed back. Each new inscription demands a newer inscription to contain it and recognise that, being inscribed, it can no longer be true. Even at the limit of restricted Petrarchism the imperative to signify love and beauty beyond languages can lead in the direction of a self-reflexivity which, at its most intense, borders on a semiotic delirium or *jouissance*. In *Diana* (1592) Henry Constable seeks an origin which will halt the play of texts, revisions and misreadings, to find only another Petrarchan hyperbole, albeit one that turns the whole history of Petrarchism on its head and finds its true origin here and now, at the moment of seeking:

> Thy coming to the world hath taught us to descry
>   What Petrarch's Laura meant, for truth the lips bewrays.
>   Lo! why th' Italians yet which never saw thy rays,
> To find out Petrarch's sense such forged glosses try.
> The beauties, which he in a veil enclosed beheld,
>   But revelations were within his secret heart,
> By which thy coming he in parables foretold.

This twist which abolishes Petrarch as the effective source of the poem's own Petrarchism does hit on the truth of the matter in a suitably paradoxical way. Petrarch's presentation of love drew on a wide variety of sources, from Propertius and Ovid to the troubadours, the *Roman de la Rose*, Dante and the *dolce stil novo*. In over 300 lyrics written between his first glimpse of Laura in 1327 and his death in 1374, the variety of his themes – including a concern with the problems of writing love poetry – and of his formal and rhetorical repertoire exceeds that of any of his imitators.[18] In the more limited sense of the term, Petrarch himself was not Petrarchan.

Petrarchism, in its broader sense, was a sufficiently flexible mode to survive changes in literary and aesthetic taste. It moved through a mannerist period of ornamentalism, distortion and idealisation to its baroque phase, adding a heightened realism, drama and 'metaphysical' wit, best exemplified as a European phenomenon by Donne, Marino and Gongora. Donald L. Guss examines, alongside this 'extravagant' baroque strain, a 'humanistic' strand of the tradition – characterised by neoclassical decorum and a sober recycling of eternal verities – which informed the work of Jonson and the 'Sons of Ben'.[19] This complex and multifaceted poetic language was, in Guss's terms, a primary channel through which Italian influence reached transalpine Europe', affecting the work of poets in places as far apart as England and Hungary.[20] As a formal system this broader, flexible Petrarchism tends to function by disrupting its own embedded, more restricted code to the point where disruption becomes the norm and 'innocent' Petrarchism the exception – a process which anticipates historically the 'defamiliarisation' described by Victor Shklovsky as a defining characteristic of the novel.[21] But its scope is much more than just that of a literary convention. Petrarchism was as all-embracing as the modern 'lovers' discourse' analysed by Barthes, a language still haunted by distraught lovers and Venuses in blue jeans. ('Inflatable doll / Lover ungrateful / I blew up your body / But you blew my mind'[22]). Petrarchism became, in Leonard Foster's phrase, a 'great international system of love' a cohesive and tenacious cultural paradigm comparable to the chivalric love of the Middle Ages or the romantic love of the eighteenth and nineteenth centuries.[23]

III

After distinguishing two Petrarchisms, the restricted and the expanded code, there remains another problem of definition. If

Petrarchism is so pervasive in late-sixteenth- and in seventeenth-century love poetry, what then is not Petrarchan or at least shadowed by Petrarchism in one sense or another? And, since many of the gestures and images that could be cited to draw a poem within the scope of Petrarchism can be traced to poets who influenced Petrarch, what is distinctive to his work and to its influence during this period? What attaches his name to the paradigm and marks it off from the wider current of a loose romantic tradition which extended from courtly love to the lyrics of modern popular songs?

Beyond the narrower, mannerist Petrarchism self-consciously ornate language ceases to be a distinguishing criterion. To define the larger tradition it is necessary to turn to particular constructions of 'love' and its relationship to the body. Here the clearly non-Petrarchan would be an unashamed, unsublimated acceptance of the physical – an attitude rarely struck in the poetry of the period.

In the poem xxii of his *Canzoniere*, 'A qualunque animale alberga in terra', Petrarch imagines sexual fulfilment with Laura:

> Might I be with her when the sun departs
> and no other see us but the stars,
> just one night, and let the dawn never come!

But in vain: 'I will be under the earth in dried wood, / and the day will be lit by the tiny stars, / before the sun arrives at so sweet a dawn'.[24] In ccxxxvii 'Non a tanti animali il mar fra' l'onde', he wishes that Laura should come to him while he sleeps, but again without satisfaction. For one unique moment, in poem xxiii 'Nel dolce tiempo de la prima stade', he sees Laura naked. She responds with a gesture which, in any other semiotic system, might be construed as flirtation: 'I, who am not appeased by any other sight, stood to gaze on her, when she felt shame and, to take revenge or to hide herself, sprinkled water in my face with her hand.'[25] Petrarch withdraws in panic to be left, like Actaeon, on the verge of being torn to pieces by unfulfilled desires. This, the closest he comes to consummation, only emphasises an uncrossable gulf between the lover and the body of the fair enemy. This frustration of sexual desire brings the sublimation alternately welcomed and suffered in the *Canzoniere*.

This repression decisively marks the border between medieval chivalric love and Petrarchism. Common to both is the lady installed on a pedestal and the suitor's woes, but the existence in troubadour poetry of the *alba*, the song of lovers parting at dawn, indicates the possibility of sensual gratification in the code of courtly love.[26] Sexual fulfilment is also a useful criterion for determining the limits of Petrarchism in the late sixteenth and seventeenth centuries. Within the broader Petrarchan tradition it may be longed for, dreamt about or even defended but never simply enjoyed, described, dramatised or celebrated as a source of mutual pleasure. According to the Neoplatonism with which Petrarchism was aligned, an appreciation of physical beauty and even a tentative defence of the carnal could be countenanced. The *locus classicus* for this is Bembo's ladder in *The Courtier*, where attention to the physical beauty of the loved one may be a step towards the contemplation of an ideal beauty and truth to be reached through successive grades of love and refinement of the feelings.[27] But this appreciation of the physical necessarily excluded an Epicurean celebration of the senses and their gratification. Through the Horatian *carpe diem* theme and the influence of Anacreon, Ovid and Catullus, elements of Epicureanism were incorporated into the work of some late-sixteenth- and seventeenth-century English poets, from Marlowe's translation of Ovid's *Amores* to lyrics by Jonson and his followers, including Abraham Cowley, whose two short poems 'The Epicure' and 'Another', although not dealing directly with love, gave direct expression to the philosophical stance taken in the love poetry of a number of his contemporaries. In some ways this Epicurean or Ovidian strain constitutes an alternative paradigm to the Petrarchan and Neoplatonic. But it is testimony to the centrality of Petrarchism that it exacts its dues from the opposed tradition – in terms of apologies, acknowledgements, and a continuing use of Petrarchan forms and conventions as, fragments of a well-known code to be reworked in the process of defamiliarisation.

By placing the restricted Petrarchan code popular in the 1580s and 1590s at one end of the spectrum and Epicureanism at the other, it is possible to sketch some gradations within the broader Petrarchism of the seventeenth century and attempt to indicate its limits. At one end of this spectrum the lady remains on high and the lover still speaks of his unworthiness. The conventional images reappear, to be supplemented by conceits in the style of Donne, Marino or Guarini. A good deal of minor metaphysical verse falls into this category – for example, Sir Henry Wotton's

'On his Mistris, the Queen of Bohemia', Henry King's 'Sonnet' and 'Sonnet: The Double Rock', Lord Herbert of Cherbury's 'A Vision', and Aurelian Townshend's poem for his patron's daughter-in-law, 'To the Countess of Salisbury':

> Victorious beauty, though your eyes
>   Are able to subdue an hoast,
>   And therefore are unlike to boast
> The taking of a little prize,
> Do not a single heart dispise.

A second category of poems employs this discourse as a stylised foil for what is presented as a more immediate or authentic experience, extending into new areas the convention of scoring off the conventions. This type of intensification by overlaying the familiar with the unexpected is evident in a variety of poems, ranging from Donne's 'The Apparition' to 'A Feaver' and 'A Nocturnall upon S. Lucies Day', in which the loss or threatened loss through death of the lady accounts for the lover's confusion, and on to Milton's sonnet 'Methought I saw my late espoused saint', in which the Petrarchan associations of 'saint' are set against the soul of the dead wife, and the concluding conventional paradox about waking to the darkness of day and solitude is transformed by the implicit reference to the actual blindness of the poet, who has seen his wife only in a dream. King's 'The Exequy' signifies a similar intensification of grief and resolution by transforming the conventional pairing of lover and saint, but this category is by no means limited to elegiac verse. George Herbert's 'Love (III)' for example, concerned with divine grace and redemption, simultaneously deploys and discards the Petrarchan code that shadows its theological discourse:

> Love bade me welcome: yet my soul drew back,
>   Guiltie of dust and sinne.
> But quick-ey'd love, observing me grow slack
>   From my first entrance in,
> Drew nearer to me, sweetly questioning,
>   If I lacked anything.
>
> A guest, I answer'd, worthy to be here:
>   Love said, You shall be he.

I the unkinde, ungratefull? Ah my deare,
    I cannot look on thee.
Love took my hand, and smiling did reply,
    Who made the eyes but I?

Truth Lord, but I have marr'd them: let my shame
    Go where it doth deserve.
And know you not, sayes Love, who bore the blame?
    My deare, then I will serve.
You must sit down, sayes Love, and taste my meat:
    So I did sit and eat.

Here an anticipated pattern is reversed as the suitor's own feeling of unworthiness, rather than the unattainability of the divine loved one, frustrates the desired union. Love has in superabundance the qualities conventionally attributed to the Petrarchan mistress but lacks her scorn and aloofness, substituting for the formal trappings of disdain the informal 'sweetly questioning' attitude of the first stanza, the reassuring smile and touch of the second, and the host's invitation to 'taste my meat' in the third. As a love poem, this alludes persistently to the Petrarchan code only to transgress at every turn, culminating in the invitation to a displaced carnality in the penultimate line and the consummation of the last. The theological discourse which emphasises grace and the forgiveness of sins sets mercy above the code which determines the lover's unworthiness, a law which coincides, in this context, with Petrarchan dictates. Love redeems the poem's protagonist from both the law and the literary convention, and the final invitation, while pitched much lower than anything the unapproachable Petrarchan goddess has to offer, also alludes to the sacrament that embodies a love which makes that of the Petrarchists seem perverse and self-lacerating. Nor is the love figured in the Sacrament altogether separable from the more mundane construction of human love constituted by the colloquial scene and language of the poem. The relationship between the two is too close to dismiss, in the name of allegory, signifiers that bring together sacred and profane love. The question at the end of the second stanza, 'Who made the eyes but I?', presents human love as an expression of the divine which is, in turn, perceptible to human beings only through love.

This second category of poems permits some intriguing slippage and play between the Petrarchan paradigm and the sexuality it represses and sublimates. In Donne's 'The Apparition', for example, the scornful murderess who will cause the lover to die of grief is now the unchaste mistress, and Herbert's 'Love (III)', with its connotations of premature detumescence in the first stanza and fellatio in the third, disrupts not only the sensitised celibacy of Petrarchism but also, through the polymorphous figure of the lady/Lord, its characteristic construction of gendered subject positions.[28]

The third category of poems stages this confrontation of sublimation and sexuality in a much more explicit way. In Donne's 'The Canonization' and 'The Exstasie' and Lord Herbert of Cherbury's 'Ode upon a Question Moved', sexual love is vigorously defended as a necessary part of spiritual love. 'Love's mysteries in soules do grow / But yet the body is his booke', and without physical union the soul can only be a great prince imprisoned ('The Exstasie'). But the defence and rationalisation of the physical in these poems extend and reinforce the Petrarchan and Neoplatonic traditions as much as they challenge them.[29] Even Donne's most Ovidian and erotic work, Elegy XIX, 'To his Mistris Going to Bed', pivots on the homiletics of idealised love. After twenty-six lines that re-present the Petrarchan blazon as striptease, and the plea 'Licence my roving hands to go, / Before, behind, between, above, below', the apostrophe to nakedness turns to souls and casuistry:

> Full nakedness! All joys are due to thee,
> As souls unbodied, bodies uncloth'd must be
> To taste whole joyes. Gems which you women use
> Are like Atlanta's balls, cast in men's views,
> That when a fool's eye lighteth on a Gem,
> His earthly soul might covet theirs, not them.
> Like pictures, or like books' gay coverings made
> For lay-men, are all women thus array'd;
> Themselves are mystic books, which only we
> (Whom their imputed grace will dignifie)
> May see reveal'd. Then since that I may know;
> As liberally, as to a Midwife, shew
> Thy self: cast all, yea, this white lynnen hence,
> Here is no pennance, much less innocence.

The 'witty' celebration of the flesh is overladen here by the cerebral register of mystic books and covers, imputed grace and justification, calling for a negotiation of guilt and a gesture of establishing credentials. The overall effect evokes all the thrills and spills of *coitus interruptus*, or a telephone call from the Dean of St Paul's which catches reader and text *in flagrante dilecto*. If this sequence is not enough to distance the poem from the Epicureanism of its earlier lines, the setting of the whole scene in 'A heaven like Mahomets Paradice' puts the issue beyond doubt, recalling the dreamed and imagined consummations in Petrarch.

Closer to the Epicurean end of the spectrum, but still heavily dependent on Petrarchism, is the fourth category of seventeenth-century lyrics, in which courtly compliment to the idealised lady is so exaggerated that an underlying Ovidian purpose, most commonly seduction, is inescapable. In such poems as Thomas Carew's 'A flye that flew into my Mistris her eye' and Richard Lovelace's 'A Black Patch on Lucasta's Face', the insect's point of view exaggerates the conventional unworthiness of the suitor and the sublimity of the mistress. It also affords opportunities for close-up shots of the body, and for overwhelming experiences of smell, touch and taste that anticipate the poet's reward from his sophisticated mistress, co-sharer in this game of love, should his complimentary move be appropriately reciprocated.

John Cleveland's brilliant satire on this sub-genre, 'Fuscara; or the Bee Errant', draws on both its Petrarchism and its barely concealed eroticism. The bee leaves his garden for Fuscara, 'a more fragrant Paradise', who is the epitome of wisdom and beauty. At her pulse he can tell 'Whether the world's long-liv'd or no', and her hand contains 'mystick figures', at which he 'tipples Palmistry and dines / On all her fortune telling lines'. The ecstatic journey of this 'bold Columbus' around the body of the idealised mistress is touched throughout by sexual fantasy. The privileges of the bee, the fertilising organ of the plant world, fulfil the desire of the lover for penetration:

> Arm'd like a dapper Lance-presade
> With *Spanish* pike, he broacht a pore,
> And so both made and heal'd the sore:
> For as in Gummy trees there's found
> A salve to issue at the wound,
> Of this her breach the like was true,
> Hence trickled out a balsom too.

This burlesque of courtly Petrarchism is also, ultimately, a travesty of its concealed eroticism. The sexual imagery culminates in the orgasmic death of the king bee on stinging Fuscara, but long before this the sensuality is tinged with fear and disgust. The bee's perceptions of magnified veins like violets and a hand 'Tender as 'twere a jelly gloved' are finely poised between an ultimate patriarchal fantasy of acquiescent female flesh without bone or sinew, and a revulsion at the body prefiguring that of Gulliver among the giantesses of Brobdingnag.

Cleveland's bee focalises idealisation, sensuality and a satirical inversion and exaggeration of both, while still taking its cues from the more flexible and persistent type of Petrarchism. The bee in Thomas Carew's 'A Rapture', in contrast, appears to have crossed the Petrarchan frontier and entered a world of physical indulgence limited only by a resolute androcentrism and a continuing objectification and fragmentation of the feminine body. In prolonged metaphorical foreplay, he tastes 'the ripened cherry' and 'The warme, firme Apple, tipt with corall berry', before his lips slide 'Downe these smooth Allies' between 'two milkie wayes' to the 'grove of Eglantine', where, 'with Chimique skill', he distils 'From the mixt masse, one soveraigne balme . . . the great Elixir'. There remains the idealisation and also the blazon, although this more sensual catalogue may owe less to Petrarch than to the biblical Song of Songs. But the course is clearly set here – in spite of the further Petrarchan echoes of galleys, tempests and pilots – not only for intercourse but also for mutual pleasure:

> Now in more subtle wreathes I will entwine
> My sinewie thighes, my legs and armes with thine;
> Thou like a sea of milke shalt lye display'd,
> Whilst I the smooth, calme Ocean invade
> With such a tempest, as when Jove of old
> Fell downe on Danae, in a storme of gold:
> Yet my tall Pine, shall in thy Cyprian straight
> Ride safe at Anchor, and unlade her fraight:
> My Rudder, with thy bold hand, like a tryde
> And skilfull Pilot, thou shalt steere, and guide
> My Bark into Loves channell, where it shall
> Dance, as the bounding waves do rise or fall:
> Then shall thy circling armes, embrace and clip
> My willing bodie, and thy balmy lip

Bathe me in juice of kisses.

While C. S. Lewis called Donne's Elegy XIX, 'pornographic',[30] Earl Miner describes 'A Rapture' as 'genuinely erotic' and also 'genuinely poetic'.[31] But even here there is an imperative to distance the experience and affirm its unreality. These things take place in 'Love's Elizium', where the 'Gyant Honour' is recognised for the idol he is. Although a less immediately suspect place than Donne's 'Mahomet's Paradice', this is still not the world. Nor is Petrarch finally banished. Carew signifies his continuing influence in a fiction which underlies the imaginary nature of the vision as a whole. Last in a catalogue of virtuous women who yield up their bodies in this Elizium is the unattainable mistress par excellence:

> Laura lyes
> In Petrarch's learned armes, drying those eyes
> That did in such sweet smooth-pac'd numbers flow,
> As made the world enamour'd of his woe.

In this poem and others like it – for example, Lovelace's 'Love Made in the First Age: To Chloris' and, to some extent, Donne's Elegy XIX – an Epicureanism that can be relatively untrammelled in, say, Ovid's *Amores* is acted out only in a dimension acknowledged as imaginary and in a way that still recognises an inhibiting Petrarchism or Neoplatonism. To this fifth category of poems may also be assigned such bizarre productions as Robert Herrick's 'The Vine', in which the phallocentrism of the poet's contemporaries runs riot in a dream about his 'mortal part'. This item, transformed into a creeping plant, 'crawling one and every way' enthralls the poet's 'dainty Lucia' by wrapping itself around legs, thighs, buttocks, waist, neck and tying up her arms – an instance of the harmless perversion which frequently crops up among the Anglican clergy, from Herrick to Thomas Kilvert and later in the popular 'kinky vicar' theme cherished by the English tabloid press.

The Petrarchan influence is never fully expunged in the bulk of English love poetry during the first half of the seventeenth century. It is from this tradition that poets continue to take their bearings, and rejection, as in the 1580s and 1590s, is often shadowed by a form of collusion. Nowhere is this clearer than in the cynical dismissal of belief in virtue and truth in such poems as

Donne's 'Song' ('Goe and catch a falling starre') or Waller's 'Song', and in the 'Antipatonicks' written by a number of the Cavalier poets. The norm is also acknowledged in the grotesque snook-cocking of Suckling's 'The Deformed Mistress', where the carnivalesque blazon includes missing teeth, a nose a foot long decorated with pimples and 'a comely Pearl of Snot', ant's thighs, eagle's feet, legs dripping with 'Love's issues', and the belly: 'As for her Belly, 'tis no matter, so / There *be* a belly, and a Cunt below'. Even the Horatian *carpe diem* theme, employed by Waller, Carew, Herrick, Jonson and others, is difficult to separate altogether from the dominant paradigm of sexuality contained and displaced from primary physical experience. Because of its reliance on classical models Earl Miner describes such poetry as 'pre-Petrarchan', but in the seventeenth-century context the basic stance of the lover, as yet unfulfilled, calling on the lady for satisfaction could not function as if Petrarch had never written.[32] As an international lovers' discourse during this period, the Petrarchan text, to apply Derrida's phrase, has no outside.

IV

> Think you, if Laura had been Petrarch's wife,
> He would have written sonnets all his life?
> (Byron, *Don Juan*, iii.viii)

Don Juan's solution to Petrarchism is a reassuringly simple one, and Petrarch's own poems trace the detours of writing around desire founded on a lack:

> The dilemma of the poet is expressed in doubly paradoxical form: he is unable to write, yet forced to write; he finds writing therapeutic, and yet it is writing that creates the suffering – love – for which only writing can provide the cure. The difficulty of matching words to things, expression to emotion, even the purported impossiblity of writing, are themes introduced early in the *Canzoniere*.[33]

This is the basis of a textuality which becomes increasing convoluted as the tradition expands both by redefining the absent object whose full presence will end complaint and make praise superfluous, and then by negating or problematising the code to postulate a different sort of presence – that of a reality, experience or truth constituted as prior to signification and therefore more authentic than the products of literary convention.

But any explanation of this major and lasting international system of love would have to go beyond one poet's alleged sexual repression and consider, in conjunction with its formal characteristics, the historical dimension of that system. A possible point of access to more fundamental cultural and economic considerations is the Petrarchan idealisation of women, the concomitant of which is the disgust and degradation evinced by Suckling in 'The Deformed Mistress'.[34] Leonard Foster explains the conventional elevation of the lady in the chivalric code of the Middle Ages as 'a literary fiction to compensate for a real state of affairs in which it was a man's world and a violent one at that'.[35] Such an analysis could also be applied to Petrarchism in the sixteenth and seventeenth centuries, although only with stringent qualifications. English Petrarchism had an important political dimension in the cult of Elizabeth as fount of wisdom and beauty, at the centre of the revival of chivalry at court and a secular equivalent of the Mariolatry suppressed under Protestantism. It was popular with poets seeking patronage or preferment,[36] and directly employed by the queen, as Foster himself shows, in designating Petrarchan imagery for royal portraiture.[37] The restricted Petrarchan code survives into the Jacobean and Caroline periods largely in the praise of women who are either patrons, potential patrons or their relatives. These particular instances of the real power of royal and aristocratic figures proves nothing about the condition of women in general, of course, and the type of functionalist analysis employed in Foster's comment on the medieval idealisation of women poses serious problems. This approach can be used to prove anything, as the literary 'fiction' may be seen either to reflect or to compensate for the underlying reality, depending on what one perceives that reality to be.

A second, equally problematic, entry to the social and ideological determinants of this literary convention is through the question of sexual repression itself. Here a functionalist account might locate the basis of Petrarchism in a more fundamental historical process, the rise of capitalism, and discover some correlation between the literary convention and the sexual ethic of Puritanism:

if sex is so rigorously repressed, this is because it is incompatible
with a general and intensive work imperative. At a time when
labour capacity was being systematically exploited, how could
this capacity be allowed to dissipate itself in pleasurable
pursuits, except in those – reduced to a minimum – that enabled
it to reproduce itself? . . . The seventeenth century, then, was
the beginning of an age of repressing emblematic of what we
call the bourgeois societies, an age which perhaps we still have
not completely left behind. Calling sex by its name thereafter
became more difficult and more costly. As if in order to gain
mastery over it in reality, it had first been necessary to subjugate
it at the level of language, control its free circulation in speech,
expunge it from the things that were said, and extinguish the
words that rendered it too visibly present.[38]

Foucault here is writing 'as if', deploying a discourse superseded
not only by his own method of analysis but also by the Gramscian
concept of hegemony, for example, or Althusser's theory of the
relative autonomy of ideology and its determination *only in the last
instance* by the economic base. But since it serves Foucault's
rhetorical strategy in *The History of Sexuality* (vol. 1) to begin with
this last instance, it may be useful, if only for a preliminary
gathering of materials to be considered later in a different light, to
examine Petrarchism briefly from this perspective in which 'the
minor chronicle of sex and its trials is transposed into the
ceremonius history of the modes of production'.[39]

In 1599 the episcopal authorities of London and Canterbury,
concerned for most of the decade about a proliferation of licentious
literary works, gathered up volumes of erotic verse to be burned.
These included Marlowe's translation of Ovid's *Amores*. The
century that followed was a period of gradual, uneven but major
change in the treatment of sex in literature. The easy acceptance
of the body, desire and consummation which characterises the
work of such classical poets as Ovid and Catullus, persists in
Boccaccio and Chaucer, and is still apparent at times in
Shakespeare's work, no longer appeared as an officially sanctioned
part of literature in the eighteenth century, when canons of
decorum imposed stricter limits on what could be discussed or
represented and the first legal prosecutions of obscenity in printed
works took place. Restoration texts such as the comedies of
Wycherley and his contemporaries and the poetry of Rochester

are some of the last expressions of the earlier attitude to the body
before it is consigned to the special category of pornography. By
1800 there had taken place a fundamental transformation of the
sexual ethic in which Erasmus could casually offer advice to a
disciple on the choice of a good prostitute, the young women in
Campion's songs could wish for sexually active husbands, Juliet's
nurse would make jokes about infant sexuality, and Sir John
Harrington, in 'The Author to his Wife', could request, among
other household comforts, that in bed she remain 'as wanton,
toying as an ape'.[40]

The role of Protestantism in these changes is complex and often
contradictory. It challenged Roman Catholicism's high valuation
of celibacy by redefining chastity as fidelity within marriage.
Some more radical sects, such as John of Leyden's Münster
commune in the 1530s and Ranters in England in the late 1640s,
even practised free love along with the sharing of property. Alan
Sinfield argues that, in the writing and discussion of love poetry,
orthodox English Protestantism, although basically Calvinist in
theology, was a moderating influence: 'Protestants legitimized
sexual expression but without the male bravura of Ovidian love,
and promoted idealism but without the frustration of romatic
love.'[41] For poets such as Carew, Suckling, Lovelace and Waller,
however, sexual pleasure was a value to be affirmed against a
repression and containment sustained not only by Petrarchism
but also by their Puritan political opponents. Characterised by
their enemies as 'Cavaliers', to signify swaggering and dissolution,
these poets incorporated the equivocal sensuality of their work in
a broader discourse on 'the good life', which set itself against
repression not only in matters of love, but also in opposing
Puritan attitudes to relaxation, drink and festivity.[42] The considered
moral strand of this discourse was manifested under the pressure
of civil war and defeat in such poems as Lovelace's 'To Lucasta,
Going to the Warres' and 'To Althea, from Prison'.

It would, of course, be grossly reductive to claim that the sexual
repressions of Petrarchism and Puritanism are identical. But there
are aspects of the treatment of sexuality in both that imply a
concealment, containment and sublimation of the body which
also extends to Neoplatonic philosophy and even to manuals on
polite behaviour such as della Casa's *Gallateo*, which presupposes
a standard of manners spectacularly indecent according to modern
tastes and encourages its readers to desist from such activities as

revealing the sexual parts in public, picking up excrement from the roadside for friends to smell, and opening handkerchieves 'to glare upon thy snot as if gems and rubies had fallen from thy skull'.[43] The ideas of Weber and Tawney on the relationship between Protestantism and the rise of capitalism are too well known to be rehearsed again here, and Christopher Hill, more recently, has pointed to the remarkable coincidence of social class and religious affiliation in England during the first half of the seventeenth century. The fact that Cromwell and his supporters wrote in religious language, Hill maintains, should not prevent us from realising that they represented a definite secular class, the industrial and commercial bourgeoisie.[44] There are also broad links between Petrarchism and capitalism, both establishing a hold first in the Italian city states in the late Middle Ages and spreading, as the feudal order broke up, to the new nation states of Europe. A pursuit of Petrarchan eloquence, which played a part in the process of 'refining' the European vernacular languages, was also instrumental in constituting the heightened national consciousness that accompanied the economic changes of the sixteenth century.

It is still a large step from this to the claim that Petrarchism was the ideological reflection of a growing economic need to channel the unproductive energies of the workforce by prohibiting sexual pleasure, and Foucault is right in criticising as reductive the wider repressive hypothesis: 'By placing the advent of the age of repression in the seventeenth century, after hundreds of years of open spaces and free expression, one *adjusts* it to coincide with the development of capitalism'.[45] But Foucault is also right in refusing to abandon the analysis of the basic historical determinants of discourses concerned with sexuality. He goes as far as to concede major changes in such discourses in the modern (post-Renaissance) world, but emphasises that the supposed 'repression' is a fiction: 'What is peculiar to modern societies, in fact, is not that they consigned sex to a shadow existence, but that they dedicated themselves to speaking of it *ad infinitum*, while exploiting it as *the* secret.'[46] Foucault does not deal with Petrarchism directly, tending to overlook texts that would now be regarded as 'literature',[47] but illustrates his thesis with reference to the revised sacrament of penance in the Catholic pastoral of the Counter-Reformation, with its emphasis on 'all the insinuations of the flesh – thoughts, desires, voluptuous imaginings, delectations, combined movements of the body and the soul';[48] eighteenth- and nineteenth-century accounts of deviation and the dangers of masturbation and sexual excess; and modern psychoanalysis, viewed by Foucault not as a liberation following three centuries of repression, but as a continuing 'institutional incitement to speak about [sex], and to do so more and more; a determination on the part of the agencies of power to hear it spoken about, and to cause it to speak through explicit articulation and endlessly accumulated detail'.[49]

This formulation, still rooted in the exercise of power, undermines the reductive model which would see Petrarchism simply as an instance of the widespread sexual repression associated with the coming to power of the bourgeoisie. But Foucault's theory throws into an interesting new light the whole range of lyric poetry which draws on Petrarchan conventions. From the work of Petrarch himself to Carew's 'A Rapture', where Laura lies in his learned arms, there is an inexhaustible discourse centred on the secret of sex and the basic theme of its repression in which 'the perpetual spirals of power and pleasure' contribute to the process described by Foucault as 'a proliferation of discourses . . . tailored to the requirements of power.'[50] This spiral, which is an instrument of control, is not necessarily repressive in the crude sense of the functionalist model. It is also a stimulant or, rather, stimulation and repression are inextricably entwined in the exercise of power. This is not to suggest that Petrarchism can bide on the techniques and pleasures of intercourse; like the Catholic confession, it is a recounting of feelings, experiences, fantasies and dreams to a silent listener qualified to judge – confessor, lady or reader. But this type of discourse, Foucault suggests, may be considered not only as a yielding of pleasure to power, but also as 'an extraordinarily subtle form of *ars erotica* . . . the Western, sublimated version of that seemingly lost tradition'.[51] In this sublimated discourse, the *Canzoniere* takes the place of Ovid's *Amores* and *Ars Amatoria*. And, while agreeing with Stephen Minta's observation that Petrarch's work, by anticipating the 'talking cure' becomes an earlier equivalent of psychoanalysis,[52] one might equally conclude from this perspective that psychoanalysis is a late form of Petrarchism.

There is a coda. In *The 120 Days of Sodom*, the Marquis de Sade gives directions for an erotic narrative which closely follow the instructions in some Roman Catholic manuals on the confession of sexual misdemeanours:

> Your narrations must be decorated with the most numerous and searching details; the precise way and extent to which we may judge how the passion you describe relates to human manners and man's character is determined by your willingness to disguise no circumstance; and what is more, the least circumstance is apt to have an immense influence upon the procuring of that kind of sensory irritation we expect from your stories.[53]

But in Sade the 'perpetual spirals of power and pleasure' that characterise Petrarchism and related discourses are not embedded but, as Foucault shows, displayed – here 'sex is without any norm or intrinsic rule that might be formulated from its own nature; but it is subject to the unrestricted law of a power which itself knows no other law but its own'.[54] The implications of this recognition were revolutionary. In prison in 1794, writing *Philosophy in the Boudoir*, Sade urged all Frenchmen to fight for a true republic, in which incest would be permitted, homosexuality and heterosexual sodomy considered normal conduct, and prostitution enforced on all women from childhood. Perhaps here we have at last reached the annihilation of Petrarchism, the idealised alabaster lady finally displaced by a Sadean mistress trussed, whipped, sodomised, occupied in every available orifice. But the whore and madonna, proverbially, are different sides of the same discursive coin. And there is another connection between these two figures. In 1764–7 the Marquis's uncle, the Abbé J. F. P. A. de Sade, wrote his *Mémoires pour la vie de François Petrarque*, in which he states that Petrarch 'dispersed the shadows of barbarism that covered Europe' and brought to Italian poetry 'a sweetness, a harmony, graces – with the result that it has no cause to envy the poetry of Greece and Rome'.[55] There was also a family tradition that an ancestor, whose given name was Ugues, married an acquaintance of Petrarch's in 1325. Laura's full name was Laura de Sade. During his imprisonment the Marquis was consoled by Laura's appearance to him in a dream.[56] The encounter, unlike her similar meetings with Petrarch, was unsullied.

V

Here is a catalogue suggested by this fortunate and fortuitous conjuncture of Petrarch and de Sade.

- The blazon: '1. A shield used in war. 2. A shield in heraldry; armorial bearings, coat of arms; a banner bearing the arms. 3. Description or representation, according to the rules of Heraldry, of armorial bearings. 4. A description or record of any kind; esp. a record of virtues or excellencies. 5. "Show, divulgation, publication" (Johnson)' (*OED*). Medieval blazons, 'solemn, tumultuous, or monumental enumerations' (Julia Kristeva), were proclaimed in public squares to give official details on matters of moment, including troop movements and battle or the price of commodities – an early form of constructing and managing 'the news'. In the plebeian carnival, as Mikhail Bakhtin shows, official blazons were travestied, with sugar-coated strawberries, for example, being advertised at give-away prices and last week's rotten herring priced as a luxury item. The topsy-turvy, grotesquely physical blazon became a familiar rhetorical form, employed by Rabelais among others: 'The bakers not only turned a deaf ear to our shepherds' request, but worse, insulted them outrageously. Apparently our men were waifs, snaggleteeth, red-headed Judases, wastrels and shitabeds; they were stinkers and fly-by-night smoothsters – idlers, too, yet nicksters – belly-busters, proudsters, badsters, clots, sharpers, puts, scabbard-dragglers and sweets. [The latter mild epithet applies to one whose fly is lined with silk and satin.] Joke-smiths, they were, yet lazy, riffraff oaves, louts, wompsters, tonies, wonglers, fops and rattletooth almsters, and, for occupation, they herded petrified turds and shepherded stillicidious excrement' (*Gargantua*, 1.25). The blazon: also a stock device of Petrarchan discourse.

- 'When the table is cleared and the guests get up to leave, take advantage of the general confusion to approach her unobtrusively and pinch her bottom, or press your thigh against hers. . . . You must, of course, put on an act of being desperately in love; and please do all you can to make it convincing. Not that you will have much difficulty in getting her to believe you. Every woman feels potentially lovable: even the most unattractive find themselves irresistible.'   (Ovid, *Art of Love*)

– Note on Petrarch and the Marquis de Sade as unlikely bedfellows:

Lucien Goldmann proposes 'a history of literary wear-and-tear' to deal not only with the creation but also the 'aesthetic disqualification' of symbols: 'it is not enough, perhaps, to say that the symbols are worn out; we must prove, first, that the symbols are recognised as worn out – and no one can tell us if it is after ten years, or twenty, or thirty or seventy years that symbols appear to be exhausted – and secondly, that one must say something new. And it's to say this that one legislates certain symbols, certain forms, and that invention is born.'

– 'For Sade, there is no eroticism unless the crime is "reasoned"; *to reason* means to philosophize, to dissertate, to harangue, in short, to subject crime (a generic term designating all the Sadian passions) to a system of articulated language; but it also means to combine according to a system of precise rules the specific actions of vice, so as to make from these series and groups of actions a new "language", no longer spoken but acted; a "language" of crime, or new code of love, as elaborate as the code of courtly love.'   (Roland Barthes)

– An open book with D. H. Lawrence passages underlined. The 'healthy naturalness' and 'natural fresh openness' about sex in Boccaccio and his contemporaries contrasted with the masturbatory 'dirty little secret' of degraded sex in modern pornography. The latter wholly complicit with images of the chaste mistress: 'Away with such love lyrics, we've had too much of their pornographic poison, tickling the dirty little secret and rolling the eyes to heaven' ('Pornography and Obscenity'). Masturbation, for Lawrence, was compulsive, secretive and obviously well-researched.

– The concluding poem of Petrarch's *Canzoniere*, where the lover, contemplating the approach of death, turns to the Virgin Mary in the hope that she will save him from the consequences of his obsessions with Laura.

– Associated terms centred on English Petrarchism: (1) the body – the vernacular – the 'vulgar' or unlettered classes; (2) refinement – 'literature' – the divided unity of a hegemonic 'national' language.

– Touchstone's carnivalesque equation of Petrarchan discourse and masturbation (*As You Like It*, ii.iv.46–7). Le Roy Ladurie shows that, in Romans at least, festive courtship games and the idealisation of the mistress were exclusive to the rich man's carnival. The plebeian carnival, in contrast, was 'resolutely masculine' and an occasion when a young man's fancy might turn to physical gratification, and specifically to rape. The currently fashionable idealisation of carnival, and particularly its sexual release, needs careful reappraisal.

– 'The victim of a sexual assault is generally delighted, for she takes your audacity as a compliment; whereas the girl who could have been raped but was not is bound to feel disappointment, however pleased she may try to look.' (Ovid, *Art of Love*)

– 'Patriarchy is the power of the fathers: a familial–social, ideological, political system in which men – by force, direct pressure or through ritual, tradition, law, and language, etiquette, education and the division of labour, determine what part women shall and shall not play, and in which the female is everywhere subsumed under the male. It does not necessarily imply that all women in a given culture may not have certain powers.'   (Adrienne Rich)

– More watersheds in the history of sexuality: 'Woman is a temple built over a sewer' (Tertullian, third century AD); 'The real masturbation of Englishmen began only in the nineteenth century'   (D. H. Lawrence, 'Pornography and Obscenity').

– 'Pornography is the eroticism of others' (Alain Robbe-Grillet).

– 'Thy Nobler Part(s), which but to name
  In our Sex would be counted shame
  By Age's frozen grasp possessed,
  From their ice shall be released
  And soothed by my reviving Hand,
  In former Warmth and Vigor stand.
  All a Lover's Wish can reach
  For thy Joy my Love shall teach,
  And for thy Pleasure shall improve
  All that Art can add to Love.
      Yet still I love thee without Art
      Ancient person of my heart.'

(Rochester, 'A Song of a Young Lady to her Ancient Lover')

More bedfellows: Rochester, like the poet in the *Canzoniere*, renounces his past preoccupation with profane love on facing death. The exemplary Restoration libertine and atheist died in July 1680 soon after 'the Hand of God touched him. . . . It was a most penetrating, cutting Sorrow . . . all the pleasures he had known in Sin were not worth that torture in his Mind.'

– A still from Jean Cocteau's *Orphée* (1950). Jean Marais as the poet embraces the dark female figure of La Mort. English subtitle reads, 'You burn like ice!'

– 'Have intercourse in whatever position you consider least becoming to the lady in question. It will be quite easy to manage: few women admit the truth about themselves, or think they could fail to look charming in any position. I also recommend you to open the shutters wide, so that you can observe her less attractive features in broad daylight. And when you have come, and are lying in a state of physical and mental exhaustion – when you feel a certain revulsion, so that you wish you had never touched a woman in your life, and cannot imagine touching another for ages – at this point carefully register every spot and pimple, and keep your eyes firmly fixed on all her imperfections.' (Ovid, *Remedies for Love*)

- The oxymoronic (Petrarchan) phallus: 'Its prodigious size made me shrink again; yet I could not, without pleasure, behold, and even ventur'd to feel, such a length, such a breadth of animated ivory! perfectly well turn'd and fashion'd, the proud stiffness of which distended its skin, whose smooth polish and velvet softness might vie with that of the most delicate of our sex, and whose exquisite whiteness was not a little set off by a sprout of black curling hair round the root, through the jetty sprigs of which the fair skin shew'd as in a fine evening you may have remark'd the clear light ether through the branchwork of distant trees over-topping the summit of a hill: then the broad and blueish-casted incarnate of the head, and blue serpentines of its veins, altogether compos'd the most striking assemblage of figure and colours in nature. In short, it stood an object of terror and delight.' (John Cleland, *Fanny Hill*, 1749)

- 'If patriarchy sees women as occupying a marginal position within the symbolic order, it can construe them as the *limit* or borderline of that order. From the phallocentric point of view, women will then come to represent the necessary frontier between man and chaos; but because of their very marginality they will also seem to recede into and merge with the chaos of the outside. Women seen as the limit of the symbolic order will in other words share in the disconcerting properties of *all* frontiers: they will be neither inside nor outside, neither known nor unknown. It is this position that has enabled male culture sometimes to vilify women as representing darkness and chaos, to view them as Lilith or the Whore of Babylon, and sometimes to elevate them as representatives of a higher and purer nature, to venerate them as Virgins and Mothers of God. In the first instance the borderline is seen as part of the chaotic wilderness outside, and in the second it is seen as an inherent part of the inside: that part that protects and shields the symbolic order from the imaginary chaos. Needless to say, neither position corresponds to any essential truth of woman, much as the patriarchal powers would like us to believe that they did.' (Toril Moi)

- 'I used to be lunatic from your precious face,

I used to be woebegone and so restless nights,
My aching heart would bleed, for you to see,
Oh! But now . . .
No more 'I Love You's;'
A language is leaving me'.

(Snatch of a lyric on BBC Radio 1, 7 August 1986, by The
Lover Speaks)

Still in love, with curious words.[57]

NOTES

1. See for example D. L. Guss, *John Donne, Petrarchist* (Detroit: Wayne State University Press, 1966); Leonard Foster, *The Icy Fire* (Cambridge: Cambridge University Press, 1969) *passim*; R. G. Cox, 'A Survey of Literature from Donne to Marvell', in B. Ford (ed.), *The Pelican Guide to English Literature: Donne to Marvell* (Harmondsworth: Penguin, 1960) p. 51; Earl Miner, *The Cavalier Mode from Jonson to Cotton* (Princeton: Princeton University Press, 1971) p. 102.
2. See G. Hammond (ed.), *Elizabethan Poetry: Lyrical and Narrative*, Casebook series (London: Macmillan, 1984), particularly the editor's introduction and extracts from the work of C. S. Lewis and Yvor Winters.
3. R. Barthes, *A Lover's Discourse*, tr. R. Howard (New York: Hill and Wang, 1978).
4. Cited in D. L. Peterson, *The English Lyric from Wyatt to Donne* (Princeton: Princeton University Press, 1967) pp. 45–7.
5. Barthes, *A Lover's Discourse*, pp. 3–6.
6. See R. Barthes, *Mythologies*, tr. A. Lavers (London: Paladin, 1973); T. Todorov, *Mikhail Bakhtin: The Dialogic Principle*, tr. W. Godzich (Manchester: Manchester University Press, 1984) pp. 60ff.
7. All references to Shakespeare are to *William Shakespeare: The Complete Works*, ed. P. Alexander (London: Collins, 1951).
8. This sonnet reads like an inversion of Petrarch's *Canzoniere*, poem xc. See A. Mortimer (ed.), *Petrarch's Canzoniere in the English Renaissance* (Rome: Minerva Italica, 1975) p. 22.
9. See ii.iv, iii.ii.1ff. and ii.i.3–10 respectively.
10. See i.i. There is also an allusion to Dante in the choice of the name 'Beatrice'.
11. W. W. Greg, *Pastoral Poetry and Pastoral Drama* (London: Bullen, 1906) p. 411; R. B. Young, 'English Petrarke', *Yale Studies in English*, 138 (1958) 12.
12. See Peterson, *The English Lyric*, p. 293.

13. *Love's Labour's Lost*, iv.ii.99–113; iii.56–68.
14. Ben Jonson, *Works*, ed. C. H. Herford and P. and E. Simpson (Oxford: Clarendon Press, 1925–52) i, 132–3.
15. Young, in *Yale Studies in English*, 138.
16. See Mortimer, *Petrarch's Canzoniere*, pp. 21–2.
17. For this, and points that follow, see Foster, *The Joy Fire*, pp. 10, 51.
18. See R. M. Durling, in *Petrarch's Lyric Poems*, ed. Durling (Cambridge, Mass.: Harvard University Press, 1976) p. 9.
19. See Guss, *Donne, Petrarchist*, p. 18.
20. See ibid., pp. 16–18.
21. On defamiliarisation, see Hawkes, *Structuralism and Semiotics* (London: Methuen, 1977) pp. 65–7.
22. From Bryan Ferry's lyric 'In Every Dream Home a Heartache', Roxy Music, *For your Pleasure*, Island ISLPS 9232 (1973).
23. Foster, *The Joy Fire*, p. 2.
24. *Petrarch's Lyric Poems*, p. 58.
25. Ibid., p. 66.
26. Foster, *The Joy Fire*, p. 2.
27. See ibid., p. 27; and J. Briggs, *This Stage-Play World* (Oxford: Oxford University Press, 1983) p. 127.
28. But the Petrarchan lady could be referred to as the 'lord', as she is in Wyatt's translation of Petrarch in 'My galley . . .'.
29. See A. J. Smith, *John Donne: The Songs and Sonnets* (London: Arnold, 1964) *passim*.
30. See J. Lovelock (ed.), *John Donne: Songs and Sonets*, Casebook series (London: Macmillan, 1973) p. 113.
31. Miner, *The Cavalier Mode*, p. 81.
32. Ibid., p. 118.
33. S. Minta, *Petrarch and Petrarchism: The English and French Traditions* (Manchester: Manchester University Press, 1980) p. 62.
34. On this and the points that follow, see also M. Evans, *Signifying Nothing: Truth's True Contents in Shakespeare's Text* (Brighton: Harvester, 1986) pp. 174–7.
35. Foster, *The Joy Fire*, p. 2.
36. See A. F. Marotti, '"Love is Not Love": Elizabethan Sonnet Sequences and the Social Order', *ELH*, 49 (1982) 396–428.
37. Foster, *The Joy Fire*, p. 122ff.
38. Michel Foucault, *The History of Sexuality*, vol. i, tr. R. Hurley (Harmondsworth: Penguin, 1981) pp. 6, 17.
39. Ibid., p. 5.
40. See ibid., p. 27; and Briggs, *This Stage-Play World*, p. 47.
41. A. Sinfield, *Literature in Protestant England, 1550–1650* (London: Croom Helm, 1983) p. 62.
42. Miner, *The Cavalier's Mode*, p. 216.
43. G. della Casa, *Galateo*, tr. R. Peterson (1576), ed. H. J. Reid (London: no publisher, 1892) p. 73.
44. C. Hill, *The Century of Revolution, 1603–1714*, 2nd edn (Wokingham: Van Nostrand Reinhold, 1980) pp. 12, 63–4, 107–9, 141–4.
45. Foucault, *History of Sexuality*, i, 5.

46. Ibid., p. 35.
47. Cf. Evans, *Signifying Nothing*, pp. 241–2, 261.
48. Foucault, *History of Sexuality*, I, 19.
49. Ibid., p. 18.
50. Ibid., p. 72.
51. Ibid., p. 71.
52. Minta, *Petrarch and Petrarchism*, p. 63.
53. Cited in Foucault, *History of Sexuality*, I, 21.
54. Ibid., p. 149.
55. Cit. Minta, *Signifying Nothing*, p. 2.
56. D. Thomas, *The Marquis de Sade* (London: Weidenfeld and Nicolson, 1976) p. 7.
57. Ovid passages from *The Technique of Love and Remedies for Love*, tr. P. Turner (London: Panther, 1968) pp. 44, 46, 123. D. H. Lawrence extracts from *A Selection from Phoenix*, ed. A. A. H. Inglis (Harmondsworth: Penguin, 1971) pp. 306–26; Robbe-Grillet and Cleland quotes from M. Charney, *Sexual Fiction* (London: Methuen, 1981) pp. 1, 81 (Charney notes the Petrarchan qualities of the second passage, p. 80). Other references, in sequence: J. Kristeva, *Desire in Language*, tr. L. S. Roudiez *et al.* (New York: Columbia University Press, 1980) p. 53; M. Bakhtin, *Rabelais and his World*, tr. H. Iswolsky (Cambridge, Mass.: MIT Press, 1968) p. 430; R. Macksey and E. Donato (eds), *The Structuralist Controversy* (Baltimore: Johns Hopkins University Press, 1972) pp. 35–6; R. Barthes, *Sade/Fourier/Loyola*, tr. R. Miller (New York: Hill and Wang, 1976) p. 27; E. Le Roy Ladurie, *Carnival in Romans*, tr. M. Feeney (Harmondsworth: Penguin, 1980) pp. 179, 200–2, 211–13; A. Rich, *Of Woman Born* (London: Virago, 1977) p. 57: *Poems by John Wilmot, Earl of Rochester*, ed. V. de Sola Pinto (London: Routledge and Kegan Paul, 1953) pp. xxxvi, 20; T. Moi, *Sexual/Textual Politics* (London: Methuen, 1985) p. 167; 'No More "I Love You's"' from *The Lover Speaks*, A&M Records, AMA 5127 (1986). With thanks to David Freeman, a co-sharer in this work.

9

The White Devil and the Fair Woman with a Black Soul

SYLVIA FREEDMAN

In 1612 John Webster published his first great tragedy, *The White Devil*, with its powerful heroine and its dramatic central scene of her arraignment as a whore. He had taken a long time writing it, as he tells us in his preface, and it had already received its first performance. Though the events of the play were based on a true Italian story, the pivotal trial scene has no parallel in any of the accounts of the real Vittoria's life but is Webster's own imaginative invention.[1] That it owes something to a contemporary English trial has not previously been suggested. And yet only five years earlier the most famous beauty of her day was actually on trial similarly accused.

The woman was Lady Penelope Rich. Her trial took place in 1607 in the Court of Star Chamber, where she was charged with fraud and forgery of the will of her second husband, the Earl of Devonshire.[2] It was the prosecution's case that she could not inherit his vast estate since she was not the 'Earl's lawful wife but an Harlot, Adulteress, Concubine and Whore'. She had married the Earl only three months before his death, though as Lord Mountjoy he had been her lover for many years. A month before the wedding her first husband, Lord Robert Rich, had finally divorced her, but the terms of the divorce did not permit remarriage.[3] The criminal proceedings in Star Chamber were the culmination of a series of legal actions designed to prevent her from inheriting the Devonshire fortune.

Penelope Rich was not only the most celebrated beauty of her day; she led an eventful life, full of violent changes. When she was thirteen her father had arranged a marriage for her to Philip Sidney, but the plan fell through when her father died.[4] The family's poverty necessitated she should marry a rich man, and against her will she was married off to Lord Rich, with Penelope protesting at the ceremony itself.[5] Immortalised as Sidney's Stella, virtuous and demure, she was to undergo a complete reversal in her public persona when, after her second husband's death, she was depicted in scurrilous lampoons as a lustful woman.[6] Sister to the Earl of Essex, the Queen's favourite, she was protected by her brother's position, enjoying a remarkable measure of freedom, only to be imprisoned and tried for her part in the Essex rebellion. She had survived to win back a place for herself at the court of King James, to be reunited with Mountjoy on his triumphant return from Ireland, to marry her lover and be elevated to the grand title of Countess of Devonshire, only to have all her good fortune snatched away again.

It is now reasonably certain that John Webster the dramatist was the same John Webster who enrolled as a student at the Middle Temple in August 1598 and is described in its records as the son of John Webster gentleman.[7] Webster the dramatist's father was indeed also called John and the plays reflect a keen interest in and knowledge of the law. Many of Webster's literary associates were members of the Middle Temple, in particular John Ford, John Marston and Sir Thomas Overbury. The Middle Temple adjoined Essex House in the Strand, its gardens sweeping down to the Thames alongside the extensive gardens of Essex House, each with its own landing-stage, Temple Stairs and Essex Stairs. Students at the Middle Temple therefore lived in immediate proximity to Essex House and could not have failed to observe the daily activities of their great neighbours.[8] Penelope Rich had her own apartment at Essex House, on the east side next to Middle Temple, and it was there that she and her lover, Lord Mountjoy, met and that their children were born and baptised.[9] There Penelope, her brother and her lover formed the centre of the most brilliant circle of its day. There the Earl offered lavish hospitality, with great banquets and theatrical entertainments. Middle Temple students could hardly have missed the comings and goings, by river and by coach, at Essex House.[10] Like Vittoria's, Penelope's

> Gates were chok'd with coaches, and her rooms
> Outbrav'd the stars with several kind of lights

When she did counterfeit a prince's court.
In music, banquets and most riotous surfeits
This whore, forsooth, was holy.

(III.ii.72–7)[11]

The residents of both establishments shared a love of plays and at Christmas-time the aristocrats visited their legal neighbours for the Revels, with Lady Rich a brilliant central figure in the audience. Bartholomew Young confessed that at the 1597–8 Revels, when he played the part of a French orator, it was she, of all the audience, with her 'perfect knowledge' of the language, of whom he was most in awe.[12]

Although *The White Devil* is based on historical sources, it draws its vitality, I would suggest, not from the bare bones of an Italian revenge story but from nearer home, from people and events Webster had himself observed. Webster drew attention, in the arraignment scene itself, to the practice of using the current scandal of the day as material for a play, when Monticelso says,

I make but repetition
Of what is ordinary and Rialto talk,
And ballated, and would be play'd a' th' stage,
But that vice many times finds such loud friends
That preachers are charm'd silent.

(III.ii.246–50)

Webster himself helped to write at least one such play, *The Late Murder in Whitechapel, or Keep the Widow Waking*, a low-life drama that led to the authors being accused in Star Chamber of libel.[13] Where the events concerned the great, the risks were proportionately higher, as Samuel Daniel found in 1604 when he was called before the Privy Council to explain the similarities between his play *The Tragedy of Philotas* and the Essex débâcle.[14] With his legal connections and fascination with momentous lawsuits Webster must have known of the Penelope Rich trial and have wanted to write about it. The choice of a historical Italian plot would reduce the chances of a connection being made, whilst at the same time the parallels would give the play topical significance. Like Hamlet's presentation of 'The Mousetrap', Webster could use the historical original as a shield, pointing out that 'the story is extant, and written in very choice Italian'.

The following parallels of situation may be drawn between *The White Devil* and the life of Penelope Rich.

1 (a)   Vittoria, a famous beauty but poor, has been married off when very young, for money, to the ridiculous Camillo, who is unworthy of her and whom she will cuckold.

(b)   Penelope, outstandingly beautiful but of an impoverished family (her brother was left 'the poorest Earl in England'[15] when their father died) was similarly married off, to the wealthy but foolish Lord Rich ('that rich fool', as Philip Sidney called him).[16]

2 (a)   At the opening of *The White Devil* the Duke of Brachiano, a powerful nobleman, has fallen in love with Vittoria and with the assistance of her brother seduces her, promising her 'to seat you above law and above scandal'. Brachiano puts his love for Vittoria above everything. She is 'Dukedom, health, wife, children, friends and all'. For him she loses her reputation. Because society condemns their love, Brachiano enters upon a criminal path to preserve it. For her he discards his wife and has her and Vittoria's husband murdered. His responsibilities of government take second place.

(b)   Lord Mountjoy, Earl of Devonshire, a powerful nobleman, had been deeply in love with Penelope Rich for many years. During the earlier years of their relationship, her brother's position had been her safeguard. He had made it possible for his friend Mountjoy and his sister to meet by opening up his home to them. There the lovers could meet privately, in Lady Rich's chamber with its sumptuous black and gold bed. There their children were born and baptised. After her brother's death and Mountjoy's return from Ireland as a great national hero, to be created Earl of Devonshire, it was her lover's power that protected her from scandal. Like Brachiano, the Earl tried to regain her reputation for his mistress by marrying her. ('You are blemish'd in your fame, / My lord cures it.') Penelope's 'crime' was adultery, and it is this that Vittoria is charged with, not murder. As Monticelso says, 'Next the devil adultery / Enters the devil murder'. In Penelope's case the further accusations were merely of forgery and fraud. Just as Brachiano had vowed,

> nor shall government
> Divide me from you longer than a care
> To keep you great
>
> (i.ii.263–5)

so Mountjoy, as Earl of Devonshire one of King James's close advisers, had put affairs of state second when he married Penelope. He incurred the King's anger, who told him 'that he had purchased a fair woman with a black soul',[17] a White Devil in fact.

3 (a)   The historical husband of Vittoria was not the ineffectual fool Webster presents. Gunnar Boklund has suggested that Webster took the stock stage cuckold and made him a butt for bawdy humour.[18] Webster depicts Camillo as pompous and self-important, a man whom 'by his apparel / Some men would judge a politican', but in reality is 'an ass in's footcloth'. Without dignity, when openly called a cuckold he feebly replies

> Is it given out so?
> I had rather such reports as that my Lord
> Should keep indoors.
>
> (ii.i.329–31)

(b)   Lord Rich had much in common with Camillo. Openly cuckolded, he was too cowardly to do anything about it, lacking the courage to challenge Mountjoy to a duel. Instead he confined himself to snide remarks, bleating to his brother-in-law about 'Lords of the Council [who] are freely privileged to receive writing from other men's wives without any further question and have full authority to see every man's wife at their pleasure'[19] – a veiled complaint about his wife's lover. Without the abilities to make his mark at court, he enjoyed small-time power as a justice of the peace, relishing the dignity of office without bringing to it any of his own. Like Camillo he took care to wear the right apparel: the correct dress for meeting the new King James was a matter of deep concern to him.[20] He was as weak and ineffectual as Camillo, leaving his wife to obtain favours at court and exert the influence he coveted but lacked.[21] Just as Camillo knows that 'A man may be made cuckold in the day-time / When the stars' eyes are out' (ii.ii.74–5), so Lord Rich must have known what was happening at Essex House.

4 (a) Both stories are about the court and its corruption, as a breeding-ground for discontent and ambition. Vittoria's last words sum it up:

> O happy they that never saw the court
> Nor ever knew great men but by report.

Cornelia, their mother, regards Flamineo's pandering as the beginning of the fall of their house. She puts a curse on Vittoria:

> If thou dishonour thus thy husband's bed,
> Be thy life short as are the funeral tears
> In great men's.
>
> (ii.ii.293–5)

and

> May'st thou be envied during his short breath,
> And pitied like a wretch after his death.
>
> (i.ii.297–8)

(b) Penelope had been brought up in the north, arriving at court when she was eighteen. All her disasters resulted from events at court and her brother's ambitions centred there. Whilst the power and corruption of court life might be said to be a commonplace of the time, the Devereux family was the most notorious example of a meteoric rise and fall from favour at court. The Earl of Devonshire lived for only three months after their marriage and there was indeed cause to pity Penelope when she found herself unprotected, not recognised as his widow, prosecuted in the Court of Star Chamber for criminal acts she had not committed, followed swiftly by her own death. The 'funeral tears' shed for England's recent hero were certainly scant. Two days after his death a court gossip was writing, 'happy had he been if he had gone two or three years before the world was weary of him, or that he had left that scandal behind him'.[22]

5 (a) Vittoria and Brachiano's is a great and all-consuming love. Flamineo may seek to degrade it into lust, whilst at the opposite end of the spectrum Cornelia conventionally condemns it from the strict moralist's viewpoint. Neither extreme should prevent our recognition that this is a love on the same plane as Antony and Cleopatra's. At the start of the play Brachiano is 'Quite lost' for Vittoria. At the end, as he is dying, he wants only her, brushing aside his son to call for her:

> Where's this good woman? Had I infinite worlds
> They were too little for thee. Must I leave thee?
> (v.iii.18–19)

He dies calling her name. When Brachiano declares his love, Vittoria accepts it directly, reciprocating with a candour and lack of flirtation that cuts through and belies all that her brother has been saying. 'O my loved lord', she calls him (v.iii.8). As he dies, she too is 'lost for ever' (v.iii.35). Even her enemy Francisco remarks on her grief: 'How heavily she takes it' (v.iii.182).

(b)   Penelope and Mountjoy's relationship was the great illicit love story of its day. They were constant to each other for sixteen years without marriage before they were finally able to wed. Their love ended only with his death and he died 'in the embrace of his dearest wife, who kissed his face and hands, amidst praise and tears'.[23] It inspired poets, including the very first effort of Webster's collaborator John Ford, who, in his elegy on Mountjoy's death, 'Fame's Memorial', staunchly defended Penelope and tried to rescue her reputation, placing her 'above fame'.[24]

But it is above all in the arraignment scene that Vittoria begins to take on a striking resemblance to Penelope Rich. To compare the two, we need to look first at the relevant parts of Penelope Rich's life. She was no stranger to the law, even before her Star Chamber trial. Her first interrogation was about a letter she wrote to the Queen in January 1600,[25] an impassioned plea on her brother's behalf (imprisoned after his hasty return from Ireland and intrusion into the royal presence) in which she accused her brother's enemies of conspiracy, regardless of her own safety. Francis Bacon denounced this letter as 'an insolent, saucy, malapert action'.[26] Called before the Privy Council to explain herself, she took up the letter and added a postscript: 'What I meant I wrote and what I wrote I meant.'[27] Vittoria demonstrates a similar ability to cut through verbiage into plain speaking when she takes on the lawyer who insists on speaking Latin.

Penelope was again in trouble over this same letter when it was published, though without her consent. Webster would have been about twenty at the time and may have already discontinued his legal studies. In any event the letter was common knowledge, copies of it being publicly sold. On this occasion Penelope was interrogated by the Lord Treasurer Lord Buckhurst, for whom she proved more than a match. She had no difficulty in convincing him of her innocence, much to the anger of Sir Robert Cecil, the Queen's chief adviser. Cecil believed she had shown 'a proud disposition and not much better than a plain contempt of her Majesty and yourself that was used in the cause'.[28] The Queen herself had been highly displeased that Penelope, 'being a lady to whom it did not appertain so to meddle in such matters, would be so bold to write in such a style to her, especially when . . . her former careless and dry answers showed how little she valued her Majesty's commandments'.[29] Penelope, like the White Devil, could, in Charles Lamb's phrase, plead with 'innocence-resembling boldness'.

She was next called to account over her part in the Essex rebellion. She had been at the conspirators' supper the night before, the only woman present.[30] Later that night and again the next morning she was busy rounding up supporters for her brother. She was at Essex House during its siege and her name appeared in the list of protagonists of those involved.[31] She was imprisoned during the period of her brother's trial and later learnt how he had betrayed her, seeking to blame her for goading him on and calling him a coward for holding back. His sister, he said, 'must be looked to, for she had a proud spirit'.[32] Strange as it seemed, her brother, it appeared, had envied her: 'so strangely have I been wronged, as may well be an argument to make one despise the world, finding the smoke of envy where affection should be clearest'[33] – just as Flamineo grows to envy his 'rich sister'. When Penelope herself was examined by the Privy Council she did not reveal the weakness of her brother but 'used herself with that modesty and wisdom'[34] – just as Vittoria tendered her modesty to her judges – so as to be released. It is this mixture of modesty and wisdom on the one hand, scorn and defiance on the other, that is peculiarly characteristic of both Penelope and Vittoria.

The last occasion on which Penlope came before a court was the

Star Chamber trial of 1607 when she was accused of forgery and fraud and branded a whore. Long before their marriage her lover had set up a trust for Penelope and their children, determined that she should inherit his fortune, to the exclusion of his common-law heir, of whom he 'made little account'. When in March 1606 he suddenly fell ill he spent his last energies in completing the arrangements. After his death several distant cousins came forward to claim the estate and a series of legal battles began, culminating in Star Chamber. When Penelope came to make her answer to the charges she did so with dignity and self-possession, denying them all but not deigning to reply in kind to the defamatory allegations. Three weeks later she made a second answer. She had been named as Lady Rich in the suit, a name she no longer recognised as hers, and her first answer had been as Countess of Devonshire. Forbidden to use that name, she gracefully conceded the dignity of that title, so long as she was not called Lady Rich. Courageously standing up to the attack, she retaliated by observing that the plaintiff had not taken his case further, as the court had ordered him to do, and she attributed his omission to fear. In this last answer she called herself 'the right honourable the Lady Penelope'. As an earl's daughter she was so entitled, an honour reconferred on her by King James in her own right. But she no longer had a surname, only her title and her personal name.

Penelope shared with Vittoria a range of emotional reserves that enabled her to confront her accusers and retain her dignity and self-possession: courage, defiance, wit, resilience, resourcefulness. Neither of them was necessarily more wicked than other remarkable women, only more famous for wickedness. Flamineo's farewell to his sister is equally appropriate to Penelope:

> Know many glorious women that are fam'd
> For masculine virtue, have been vicious,
> Only a happier silence did betide them.
> She hath no faults, who hath the art to hide them.
> (v.vi.242–5)

They also share an ambiguity as to the extent of their guilt.
The masculine aspect of Penelope's character was noted by

John Ford and admired by him in his elegy 'Fame's Memorial' (dedicated to Penelope as Countess of Devonshire) in which he celebrated her as 'a creature of a more than female spirit'.[35] Vittoria too has, or, as she suggests, for her own protection can assume, 'masculine virtue'.

Just as Vittoria refuses to recognise anything of herself in Monticelso's ravings against whores, so Penelope, though technically an adulteress, could justify in her own eyes the love to which she and Mountjoy had remained constant for sixteen years.

There are verbal references suggesting images associated with Penelope Rich, and a separate investigation would be needed to explore them. I limit myself here to one strand of imagery. Penelope Rich had been celebrated as Sidney's Stella and later poets continued to associate her with stars. Thomas Campion, for example, in one of his Latin poems,[36] called her 'Stella Britannica', the Star of Britain, giving her pride of place amongst a host of beautiful women, ancient and modern: 'Penelope, whose face will one day set on fire the passions of Astrophel [i.e. Sidney] and who with her sweet voice will enchant the conqueror of the Irish [i.e. Mountjoy, as Vittoria captivated Brachiano "with music"]'. After her death she was compared to a falling star or comet.

Webster emphasises this imagery in relation to Vittoria. She has 'been styl'd / No less in ominous fate than blazing stars / To princes'. Her brother's death, she says, 'Shall make me like a blazing ominous star, / Look up and tremble' (v.vi.130–1). She has 'been a most prodigious comet'. It is imagery that was associated at the time with Penelope Rich above all other women.[37]

Like the earlier play, *The Duchess of Malfi* was based on a historical Italian story. Though not published until 1623 it was written much earlier and was first acted no later than December 1614.[38] In the interval between the two tragedies there had been yet another lawsuit concerning the Devonshire fortune, this time in Chancery, in 1612.[39] It was there alleged that there had been a plot to obtain the fortune, concocted by Lady Rich and 'her servant John Wakeman'. Wakeman, it was said, had sought to 'gratify the said Lady' and 'insinuate himself into her favour' and 'to bring profit to himself had devised this plot'. In fact John Wakeman had been one of the Earl of Devonshire's legal advisers and the story that he was Lady Rich's servant and of a plot was a complete fabrication. Though the two stories of a great lady and her servant are very different, it is not inconceivable that Webster found in this lawsuit a seed for his play.

Penelope Rich shared certain characteristics with both of Webster's heroines. All three were unable to choose freely whom to marry – the Duchess's remark on how 'The birds live . . . Happier than we; for they may choose their mates' applied to all of them. All entered upon a second marriage in doubtful circumstances. All lost their reputation and became the subject of notorious scandal. They were women of passion, made 'of flesh and blood, not alabaster', whose 'greatest sin lay in [their] blood', and all were accused of being whores. Each had a strong practical sense and 'masculine' side to her nature that led her to take the initiative in a man's world and challenge traditionally defined roles. Each faced her enemies alone with courage and dignity, without vindictiveness, living and dying 'like a prince'. Whilst all three attained the highest titles, Penelope shared with the Duchess the distinction of a title in her own right. Both died clinging with great dignity to their identity. In Star Chamber shortly before her death, Penelope, deprived of her married title and of a surname, had simply identified herself by her own personal name and title. The Duchess, who, in a curious reversal, has no personal name, dies powerfully affirming her identity: 'I am Duchess of Malfi still'.

Thomas Middleton, in his commendatory verse for the 1623 publication of *The Duchess of Malfi*, called it 'this masterpiece of tragedy'. Middleton's collaboration with Webster went back over twenty years, and if anyone had special inside information it was he. The first line of his tribute is 'In this Thou imitat'st one Rich, and Wise'.[40] Penelope's surname had been the most popular pun of its day.[41] 'Rich' in the line is spelt with a capital R, though this in itself is inconclusive since other words are similarly treated. The addition of the comma – coming before the conjunctive 'and' – causes the reader to pause, and think. Wasn't Middleton indicating, discreetly, that he recognised Webster's model?

NOTES

Spelling has been modernised in the quotations.

1. See Gunnar Boklund, *The Sources of 'The White Devil'* (Uppsala: University of Uppsala Press, 1957) pp. 111–12.
2. Public Record Office, STAC 108.10. All quotations from the case are from this source.
3. British Library Add. MS 38170.82–4.
4. A. Collins, *Sydney Papers* (London, 1746) i, 147.
5. British Library, Lansdowne MS 885.86.
6. See *The Poems of Sir Philip Sidney*, ed. W. A. Ringler (Oxford: Clarendon Press, 1962) p. 559.
7. *Middle Temple Records*, ed. C. H. Hopwood (London, 1904) i, 388.
8. M. C. Bradbrook in *John Webster: Citizen and Dramatist* (London: Weidenfeld and Nicolson, 1980) has suggested that Webster saw Penelope when she was at St Bartholomews, Lord Rich's London home, but she was rarely there. On the two recorded occasions when she was – once when she had smallpox, and once when she was placed in custody there – she would not have been much in evidence. For my comments on this book see *English*, 140 (1982) 188–90.
9. Baptism records for their first daughter and second son, who was baptised at Essex House, in the register of St Clement Danes church (opposite the site of Essex House), now in Westminster City Archives.
10. No doubt of special interest to Webster. Through Mary Edmond's discoveries we know that Webster's father was a coachmaker: 'In Search of John Webster', *The Times Literary Supplement*, 24 Dec 1976, pp. 1621–2.
11. All quotations taken from *John Webster: Three Plays*, ed. D. C. Gunby (Harmondsworth: Penguin, 1972).
12. *Diana of de Montemayor*, translated out of the Spanish by B. Yong (1958), in British Library.
13. See C. J. Sisson, *The Lost Plays of Shakespeare's Age* (Cambridge: Cambridge University Press, 1936) p. 20 ff.
14. Ibid., p. 3.
15. Letter from Sir Francis Knollys (his grandfather) to the Earl of Essex, 14 Nov 1585, quoted in W. B. Devereux, *Lives and Letters of the Devereux, Earls of Essex* (London, 1853) i, 178.
16. *Astrophel and Stella*, sonnet xxiv.
17. Peter Heylyn, *Aulicus Coquinariae* (1650) p. 112, in British Library.
18. Boklund, *The Sources of 'The White Devil'*, p. 152.
19. Warwickshire County Archives, Aylesford Papers, Letter no. 53.
20. *Transactions of Essex Archaeological Society*, n.s., vii: *History of the Barrington Family* (1884) p. 14.
21. British Library, Lansdowne MS 57.51; Historical Monuments Commission, Salisbury Papers, xv. 179. Both quoted in *The Poems of Philip Sidney*, p. 445.
22. *Memoirs of the American Philosophical Society*, 12: John Chamberlain, *Letters*, ed. N. E. McClure (Philadelphia, 1939).
23. Robert Johnston, *Historia Rerum Britannicarum* (Antwerp, 1655) p. 443.
24. See note 35.
25. British Library, Stowe MS 150.140.

26. Fynes Moryson, *An Itinerary* (Glasgow, 1907) II, 314.
27. Quoted in M. S. Rawson, *Penelope Rich and her Circle* (London, 1911) p. 228.
28. Calendar of State Papers Ireland 1600, p. 346.
29. Hatfield House, Cecil Papers, 181.62.
30. Calendar of State Papers Domestic 1598–1601, p. 572.
31. Ibid., p. 546.
32. G. Goodman, *The Court of King James I* (London, 1839) II, 17.
33. Bodleian Library, Tanner MS 114.139.
34. Goodman, *The Court of King James I*, p. 17.
35. Three stanzas of Ford's elegy, including these words in praise of Penelope, were omitted from the published version and only appear in the manuscript copy at the Bodleian Library. Bertram Lloyd has pointed out that from a literary point of view these stanzas are no worse than the rest and attributes their suppression to the dictates of prudence, as being too fervent in their defence of the disgraced Penelope: 'An Inedited Ms of Ford's Fame's Memoriall', *Review of English Studies*, I (1925) 93–5.
36. *The Works of Thomas Campion*, ed. W. R. Davis (London: Faber and Faber, 1969) p. 394. Translated from Latin.
37. A great deal has been written about star imagery in relation to Penelope Rich: see in particular H. H. Hudson's article in the *Huntington Library Bulletin*, VII (1935) 89–129.
38. William Ostler, who first played Antonio, died on that day: see C. W. Wallace in *The Times*, 2 and 4 Oct 1909, quoted by John Russell Brown in his edition of *The Duchess of Malfi*, Revels Plays (London, 1964) p. xvii.
39. Public Record Office, Chancery 2.19.56.
40. Taken from the 1623 edition at the British Library.
41. Beginning with three sonnets of *Astrophel and Stella*, nos XXIV, XXXV and XXXVII, omitted from the first publication in 1591 but included in the 1598 edition and from then on imitated extensively.

10

A King and No King: Monarchy and Royalty as Discourse in Elizabethan and Jacobean Drama

ROBERT GIDDINGS

The kingly office is in truth a kind of generalship, irresponsible and perpetual . . . a generalship for life: and of such royalties some are hereditary and others elective. . . . There is another sort of monarchy not uncommon among barbarians, which nearly resembles tyranny. But even this is legal and hereditary.

(*Aristotle's Politics*, III. 14, tr. Benjamin Jowett)

In *The Reign of Elizabeth 1558–1603* (1936) J. B. Black cautions us against too readily assuming that the literature of an age is necessarily a mirror of its history. In his view this is particularly the case in the literature of the Elizabethan period. In the works of Shakespeare and his contemporaries we find much about contemporary life in its social aspect, but political power struggles, administrative machinery and legal and political institutions held little fascination for the writers of the time, who were as little interested in these matters as the multitude in the streets:

> Politics and literature had not yet come together, but ran their courses in entirely different channels. As for the truly great writers, they are less parochial and more universal in their appeal than at any other period. Those who search for 'political allusions' in their works do not find much to reward them for their pains, and the little they do find is of comparatively small value.[1]

164

It is worth ignoring this advice, for, while it is true that there is very little evidence in Elizabethan prose fiction, drama and poetry of direct contemporary political content – Shakespeare for example, does not once locate action in Elizabethan London, preferring Rome, Athens, Illyria, Vienna, Venice or the fourteenth or fifteenth centuries – political and ideological discourse is manifestly present in Elizabethan imaginative literature and frequently makes a major contribution to works' thematic coherence. This is certainly the case with the long debate about the nature of government, the notion of the state and theories of monarchy and succession. These themes seem all-pervasive in Elizabethan literature. Elizabethans seemed very interested indeed in those matters which focus themselves in the question 'Why should I obey the State?' and very willing to canvass the various answers put up in more recent times by Brian Redhead:

> The Pragmatic – *'Because if I don't they will cut my head off'*.
> The Theological – *'Because it is God's will'*.
> The Contractual – *'Because the State and I have done a deal'*.
> The Metaphysical – *'Because the State is the actuality of the ethical idea'*.[2]

To draw our evidence from our greatest dramatist alone, a perceptive reading of the plays will show that each question is fully developed somewhere. The first cycle of history plays explores the realities of the pragmatic approach with all its horrors. *Richard II* discusses the theological case fully and the two great plays which deal with the reign of Henry IV reveal the consequences of the contractual arrangement. The entire action of *Henry V* is based on the metaphysical case, which is also discussed in several key moments of *Henry VIII* (as will be evaluated in a moment).

It has been a sorry consequence of the Freudian–mythical approach to Shakespearean drama (King Lear as 'Everyman' and all the rest of it) that the writer's very obviously powerful attraction to political ideas has been masked. During the period when new ideas from the past were being absorbed and new areas of debate were being opened up, in the course of which the basic political assumptions which had endured so long were to be totally rearranged – culminating in the English revolution of the mid seventeenth century – political themes in Shakespeare stand out like brass in an orchestra: not always dominant, but adding weight and sonority, and from time to time blazing out above everything else. The medieval idea of degree is beautifully expressed in *Troilus and Cressida*:

> Degree being vizarded,
> The unworthiest shows as fairly in the mask,
> The heavens themselves, the planets, and this centre
> Observe degree, priority, and place,
> Insisture, course, proportion, form,
> Office, and custom, in all line of order. . . .
>   . . . O! when degree is shak'd,
> Which is the ladder to all high designs,
> The enterprise is sick. How could communities,
> Degrees in schools, and brotherhoods in cities,
> Peaceful commerce from dividable shores,
> The primogenitive and due of birth,
> Prerogative of age, crowns, sceptres, laurels,
> But by degree, stand in authentic place?
> Take but degree away, untune that string,
> And, hark! what discord follows.
>
>   (I.iii.83–110)[3]

Julius Caesar and *King Lear* body forth in the most frightful terms the manner in which demogogues and tyrants seize upon the opportunities offered when a political vacuum is created at the centre of power. It is even possible to read *Macbeth* is this developing discourse as evidence of the preparation in the national political consciousness for that final act of regicide on 30 January 1649.

The seeming stability of the kingdom at the death of Queen Elizabeth I in 1603 has tended to give the Elizabethan age in the popular historical imagination a stability wholly at variance with the facts. Elizabeth's early life was spent in an atmosphere of intrigue and constant danger in which she narrowly escaped being executed. Many of her countrymen disputed her own claim to the throne, and for many years the glory of her reign was shadowed by the threat of rebellion at home, invasion from abroad (particularly from her brother-in-law, Philip II of Spain) and endless plots and intrigues. The matter of the succession was a constant nagging question, frequently aired and invariably avoided until the very end. Thus her portrait as Gloriana in Spenser's *The Faerie Queene* is one which requires considerable qualification. Although she was constantly the subject of praise and flattery from the poets of the day, Shakespeare was seemingly reticent.

There is a truly grand moment in *Henry VIII* when Cranmer speaks at Elizabeth's baptism, claiming that he does so at heaven's bidding:

> and the words I utter
> Let none think flattery, for they'll find 'em truth.
> This royal infant – heaven still move about her! –
> Though in her cradle, yet now promises
> Upon this land a thousand thousand blessings.
> Which time shall bring to ripeness: she shall be –
> But few now living can behold that goodness –
> A pattern to all princes living with her,
> And all that shall succeed: Saba was never
> More covetous of wisdom, and fair virtue
> Than this pure soul shall be: and princely graces,
> That mould up such a mighty piece as this is,
> With all the virtues that attend the good,
> Shall still be doubled on her; truth shall nurse her;
> Holy and heavenly thoughts still counsel her;
> She shall be lov'd and fear'd; her own shall bless her;
> Her foes shake like a field of beaten corn,
> And hang their heads with sorrow; good grows with her;
> In her days every man shall eat in safety,
> Under his own vine what he plants; and sing
> The merry songs of peace to all his neighbours.
> God shall be truly known; and those about her
> From her shall read the perfect ways of honour,
> And by those claim their greatness, not by blood.
>
> (v.v.15–39)[4]

It may well be significant that the majority of Shakespearean textual scholars believe that these lines are, in fact, by John Fletcher. Cranmer's speech goes on to prophesy that this state of affairs will not end when she dies, because from her ashes phoenix-like will rise 'another heir' who will be as admirable as she was:

> So shall she leave her blessedness to one, –
> When heaven shall call her from this cloud of darkness, –
> Who, from the sacred ashes of her honour,
> Shall star-like rise, as great in fame as she was,
> And so stand fix'd. Peace, plenty, love, truth, terror,
> That were the servants to this chosen infant,
> Shall then be his, and like a vine grow to him:
> Wherever the bright sun of heaven shall shine,
> His honour and the greatness of his name
> Shall be, and make new nations; he shall flourish,
> And, like a mountain cedar, reach his branches
> To all the plains about him; our children's children
> Shall see this, and bless heaven.
>
> (v.v.43–56)

This is certainly a form of the wisdom of hindsight, perceived through roseate glasses. A brief glance through the headlines of history easily displaces Fletcher's glowing phrases.[5] Stability and harmony seem qualities very seriously lacking while Elizabeth occupied a place on the stage of politics and statecraft.

In January 1554 Sir Thomas Wyatt gathered an army of two thousand at Rochester in Kent in rebellion against Mary's Spanish marriage.[6] Wyatt reached Southwark but was unable to force a passage over London Bridge; he crossed Kingston Bridge but was defeated on 9 January. Three days later Lady Jane Grey was executed. Edward Courtenay, the Earl of Devon, was imprisoned in the Tower, and Henry Grey, Duke of Suffolk, Lady Jane's father, was executed for complicity in the rebellion. On 18 March, Elizabeth was sent to the Tower for suspected complicity in the affair, and on 11 April Sir Thomas Wyatt was executed. Wyatt had hoped to involve her substantially in this undertaking and attempted to persuade her to marry Edward Courtenay, who was the son of a cousin of Henry VIII and of the blood royal. He had at one time hoped to marry Mary, but being disappointed in these ambitions had formed the plan of marrying Princess Elizabeth and making her queen, believing that popular disaffection with the proposed marriage with Philip of Spain would gain him support. This was not an auspicious beginning to Elizabeth's career. Nor was the fact that when she was proclaimed queen on

17 November 1558 (the same year that Mary Queen of Scots married the Dauphin, future King Francis II of France) the bishops did not recognise her as head of the Church. When she was barely three years old her father, Henry VIII, divorced and beheaded her mother, Anne Boleyn, which made her illegitimate until the Succession Act of 1544. The Catholic consciences of her bishops were very delicate, and this condition no doubt pertained to many of her clergy and population. In Catholic eyes she was not legitimate nor the rightful Queen, and the Pope was the head of the Church. Matters were resolved by the Act of Supremacy, passed in April 1559, which undid Mary's reconciliation with Rome and declared the Queen in Parliament to be Supreme Governor of the Church. The Act of Uniformity, passed a month later, enforced the Protestant Prayer Book of Edward VI, modified in a Catholic direction in certain parts (for instance, in the Communion Service and in the matter of clerical vestments).[7]

In January 1559 the Count de Feria, the Spanish ambassador, pressed Philip II's suit for the Queen's hand in marriage, and in July, when Henry II of France was killed in a tournament and Francis II became king, his wife, Mary Queen of Scots, assumed the title Queen of England. It was in this year that Elizabeth launched the greatest dilemma of her reign – the question of the succession – when she assured her Parliament that she had no intention of marrying. The question of Mary's title to the succession was the dominant interest of her life.[8] She could reckon on the support of a large and influential section of the nation. She was a great-granddaughter of Henry VII, as she was the daughter of James V of Scotland and his second wife, Mary of Guise – James V was the son of James IV and Margaret Tudor, who was the eldest daughter of Henry VII and Elizabeth of York (daughter of Edward IV and Elizabeth Woodville). It was Mary Stuart's wish to be designated 'heir presumptive' to the English crown. Her ambitions seemed to be checked by the Treaty of Edinburgh between England and Scotland, signed on 6 July 1560. By this treaty French troops were evacuated, a Protestant Council of Regents was appointed, Queen Elizabeth's sovereignty to England was recognised and the claims to the English throne by Mary Stuart were annulled. The 'Auld Alliance' between Scotland and France was at an end – but Mary refused to ratify the treaty, and the succession question and Mary's claim rumbled on in diplomatic activity and covert intrigue.

Matters were again brought to a crisis in October 1562, when Elizabeth suffered a severe attack of smallpox. An unconditional Catholic succession by Mary Stuart was clearly on the cards. Protestants canvassed support for Lady Catherine Grey, daughter of Henry Grey, Duke of Suffolk, and sister of Lady Jane Grey, who was descended from Mary Tudor, daughter of Henry VII. Failing Henry VIII's line, those descended from Mary 'had the remainder' in the succession by Act of Parliament.[9] Others supported the claims of Henry Hastings, third Earl of Huntingdon, who was heir presumptive to the crown through his mother, Catherine Pole, who was descended from George, Duke of Clarence, brother to Edward IV and Richard III. Others supported Edward Seymour, Earl of Hertford and Duke of Somerset, who was descended from the same family as Jane Seymour, third wife of Henry VIII. Catholics favoured the Stewart line. This picture of politicking and intrigue hardly bodies forth the glowing predictions of Cranmer in *Henry VIII*.

In January 1563 the English Parliament met and pressed the Queen to marry and resolve the succession problem. Elizabeth was evasive to the point of finesse. She assured them that she could not embark on such a matter without much advice and consideration; she needed no reminders from them as her recent illness had brought her own mortality home to her; she would not marry in haste; even if she married late in life, God would provide her with children as he did St Elizabeth. 'Though after my death you may have many stepdames, yet you shall never have a more natural mother than I mean to be unto you all'.[10] After the prorogation of Parliament in April 1563, John Hales, who had pamphleteered against the Stuart claim and in support of that of Lady Catherine Grey, was imprisoned, and his patron, Sir Nicholas Bacon, former Lord Keeper of the Great Seal and Privy Councillor, was exiled from court.

On 29 July 1565 Mary Stuart married Henry, Lord Darnley, in Edinburgh. The succession question was about to enter a new and more dangerous phase, with the expulsion of the Protestant lords in Scotland, Mary's machinations with the Pope and the King of Spain and the birth of Prince James on 19 June 1566. These events served to spotlight the essential fragility at the heart of the realm's seeming stability – the succession question was unsettled and the Queen was unmarried.

At the Parliament which was called at the end of September

1566 these matters became explosive. It seemed in vain for Elizabeth's Lord Chamberlain and Secretary to assure the members that she was now moved to marry and that she would prosecute this matter 'for the weal of her Commons'. These assurances were met with a barrage led by Sir Robert Bell (MP for Lyme Regis), Robert Monson (MP for Lincoln) and Paul Wentworth (MP for Buckingham): monarchs should make known their successors, and, if Queen Elizabeth refused to do this she was no mother to her country but a stepmother, even a parricide, for she preferred that England should expire with her than that it should survive her. Princes have never stood in awe of their successors: this was the behaviour of cowards and timorous women – the wrath of God and the alienation of her subjects' hearts would be her reward.[11]

Elizabeth's counterblast was equally sulphurous. On 5 November 1566 (the coincidence of the date has not escaped notice) she summoned thirty members of both Houses and harangued them. Her policy, she told them in unmistakable terms, was aimed at avoiding chaos, for should policy-makers be at liberty to treat about her succession then it would lead to rivalry; 'As soon as there may be a convenient time . . . I will deal therein for your safety, and offer it unto you as your prince and head, without request; for it is monstrous that the feet should direct the head'.[12] The bodily imagery is striking, and is worth further deliberation. The central plank of her policy was clear: while the succession was open, she was safe – Protestants, inspired by hope, and Catholics, motivated by fear, were both for her; and successors, once announced, were in danger. These remarks could not possibly fall on deaf ears, as the historical precedents were as numerous as they were frightening.[13] Indeed, the whole matter has considerable historical importance, providing, as it does, very interesting early evidence of the power struggle between sovereign and Parliament which was to erupt in the English revolution of the mid seventeenth century. As A. L. Rowse has observed,

It is strange that not until our own day have people begun to appreciate the significance of the Parliamentary struggle under Elizabeth. It was already on: only the unfolding success of her policy and the increasing evidence that it was in line with the will of her people, the national unity imposed by the war and, it must be added, her incomparable skill in handling Parliaments

. . . only this prevented conflict reaching deadlock and postponed it until she was under her marble stone.[14]

Events in the north now moved towards a climax. David Rizzio, Secretary to Mary Queen of Scots, had alienated the Scottish lords by the influence he exerted over Mary and in particular had annoyed her husband, Henry Stuart, Lord Darnley. Darnley had been refused the crown matrimonial and felt he had been ousted altogether from political influence by Rizzio. The Scottish nobles exploited his jealousy of Rizzio to make him join their conspiracy to murder Rizzio in 1566. In return for the crown matrimonial and the right of succession he promised to re-establish Protestantism. But after Rizzio's murder on 9 March 1566 he betrayed the nobles to Mary and helped her to escape to Dunbar. Relations between them deteriorated and he refused to attend the baptism of the future James VI. He was himself murdered at Kirk o'Field, near Edinburgh, on 10 February 1567 on the orders of James Hepburn, Earl of Bothwell. On 15 May, Mary married Bothwell and a month later the Lords of the Covenant defeated Bothwell's forces at the Battle of Carberry Hill. Bothwell fled to Norway but Mary was taken prisoner and held at Lochleven Castle. On 24 July 1567 she was compelled to abdicate, and her stepbrother, the Earl of Moray, was appointed Regent for the infant James.

These events are echoed in Shakespearean drama. It was voiced abroad all over Edinburgh that Mary had been involved in the murder of her husband; besides talk in taverns, there were numerous placards exhibited in public places. The most famous of these was the so-called 'Mermaid and Hare', which showed Mary as a mermaid, with a whip, protecting the hare – Bothwell – from the hounds which were chasing him. The family crest of Bothwell was a hare. In Act II of *A Midsummer Night's Dream* (1595) Oberon says to Puck,

> Thou remember'st
> Since once I sat upon a promontory,
> And heard a mermaid on a dolphin's back
> Uttering such dulcet and harmonious breath,
> That the rude sea grew civil at her song,
> And certain stars shot madly from their spheres

To hear the sea-maid's music.
(ii.i.148–54)

Mary had been given the opportunity to choose between a divorce, a trial (at which the Casket Letters, implicating Mary in the murder of Darnley, would be produced) and abdication.[15] Her reputation was now severely traduced: as Antonia Fraser points out in *Mary Queen of Scots* (1969), the implication behind the use of the mermaid was not romantic, but deliberately insulting, as the word was commonly used at the time to denote a siren and, by analogy, a prostitute. She escaped from Lochleven with George Douglas to Hamilton Palace. There she was joined by Scottish nobles and 6000 men. After the defeat of her forces at Langside by the army of the Earl of Moray on 13 May 1568 she fled to England.

Mary was to spend the rest of her life confined in a series of English castles: Carlisle, Tutbury, Wingfield, Coventry, Fotheringhay. She was immediately made the focal point of a series of plots and abortive rebellions. She had the support of many English Protestants who were alarmed at Elizabeth's inability to resolve the succession question. It was the ambition of sections of the nobility to get Mary Stuart married to Thomas Howard, fourth Duke of Norfolk. This, it was believed, would guarantee the succession. Mary herself was supported by the English Catholics. The Earls of Northumberland and Westmoreland led the Revolt of the Northern Earls in November and December 1569. These were the northern stars who shot madly from their spheres to hear the sea-maid's music.[16] The revolt was sternly put down and every village and town that sent men to support the northern earls was punished – over 600 were hanged.

In February 1570 Elizabethan was excommunicated and deposed by papal bull, at the same time the French were trying to re-establish themselves in Scotland and the relationship between Spain and England was rapidly deteriorating. The Ridolfi Plot (1571–2), the Throckmorton Plot (1582) and the Babington Plot (1586) were all attempts to depose Elizabeth and replace her with Mary. Mary Stuart was tried by a commission at Fotheringhay Castle in Northamptonshire in October 1586 for her part in the Babington Plot and found guilty. Elizabeth postponed signing the death warrant for four months, but Mary Stuart was finally beheaded on 8 February 1587. Contemporaries could not fail to catch the echoes in Shakespeare's *Richard II* (1595) and *King John* (1598). Henry Bolingbroke fully realises that he can never be safe while the deposed Richard lives, longs for his death and yet deplores it. The parallels in *King John* are even nearer home. Arthur, Duke of Brittany, was the posthumous son of Geoffrey, third son of King Henry II. His uncle, Richard I, declared him heir to the throne. He was captured by John at Mirabel in 1202. While he lived John's ambitions were thwarted:

> He is a very serpent in my way;
> And whereso'er this foot of mine doth tread
> He lies before me.
>
> (III.iii.61–3)

The murder of Arthur is undertaken at John's command, but he is anxious and perplexed when he learns that his orders have been executed. Salisbury says of him,

> The colour of the king doth come and go
> Between his purpose and his conscience,
> Like heralds 'twixt two dreaful battles set:
> His passion is so ripe it needs must break.
>
> (IV.ii.76–9)

John denies he has such powers of life and death and yet inwardly is racked with remorse:

> They burn in indignation. I repent:
> There is no sure foundation set on blood,
> No certain life achiev'd by others' death.
>
> (IV.ii.103–5)

Similar anguish comes through very powerfully in those extraordinary lines given to Henry V before the Battle of Agincourt:

> Not today, O Lord!
> O! not today, think not upon the fault
> My father made in compassing the crown.
> I Richard's body have interred anew,
> And on it have bestow'd more contrite tears
> Than from it issu'd forced drops of blood.

Five hundred poor I have in yearly pay,
Who twice a day their wither'd hands hold up
Toward heaven, to pardon blood; and I have built
Two chantries, where the sad and solemn priests
Sing still for Richard's soul.

(*Henry V*, iv.i.288–98)

Edmund Spenser's unfinished masterpiece, *The Faerie Queene* (1589–96), also contributed considerably to the political and ideological discourse, containing as it does such indelible portraits of the protagonists: Mary Stuart (Duessa), Queen Elizabeth (Belphoebe, Mercilla, Britomart, Cynthia and Gloriana), Philip II (Grantorto, Geryoneo) and Henry of Navarre (Byrbon). The political thrust of the allegory is strong and it is particularly valuable in giving modern readers some idea of how contemporaries viewed Mary Queen of Scots before the Romantic revolution and the energies of Sir Walter Scott constructed the more familiar model.[17] Duessa is the daughter of Deceit and Shame and represents falsehood in general. She attempts to seduce Redcrosse and make him an easy prey to his enemies. At her trial Duessa is found guilty of adultery, murder and treason, but Mercilla does not have her executed. This portrait of Mary Queen of Scots caused much offence north of the border but represents the standard English Protestant view:

Then there was brought, as prisoner to the barre,
A Ladie of great countenance and place,
But that she it with foule abuse did marre;
Yet did appear rare beautie in her face,
But blotted with condition vile and base,
That all her other honour did obscure,
And titles of nobilitie deface:
Yet in that wretched semblant she did sure
The peoples great compassion unter her allure.[18]

The Armada of 1588 was the climax of Spanish and Catholic antagonism against Elizabeth and England, aimed at deposing the Queen of England even though she could no longer be replaced by Mary Stuart. From the Spanish point of view England was a heretic country ruled by an illegitimate sovereign who had no right to the crown. There were also obvious commercial, imperial and political reasons why Spain wished to replace Elizabeth. In the event, the Armada's destruction boosted the morale of the Protestant nations of Europe for generations, but only slightly diminished Philip II's ambitions against England.[19] The ultimate aim of the Armada was to replace Elizabeth with the Infanta of Spain, Isabella, Philip II's daughter. This policy had been prefigured in the writings and propagandising of the Jesuit Robert Persons, who published his notorious *Conference about the Next Succession* in 1594.[20] Three Catholic claimants were supported. The leading candidate was the daughter of Philip II. The King of Spain believed his title to the English throne was a sound one, as he could claim descent from the House of Lancaster and that Mary Stuart had made a will ceding her right to it to Philip II.[21]

It was part of Spain's intended strategy to use Ireland as a jumping-off point for an invasion of the English mainland. Stability and order in Ireland were much more than just a matter of domestic policy. Persons argued that Isabella's was the best claim to the succession. Hers was followed by that of James VI and finally that of Arabella Stuart, who was the daughter of Charles Stuart, Earl of Lennox, younger brother of Lord Darnley, who was next in line to the throne after James. Persons' *Conference* was the manifesto of a Catholic conspiracy to put Isabella on the throne and thwart all attempts to impose the unconverted King of Scotland on the nation.

Queen Elizabeth's insecurity made her very aware of the parallels between events of her reign and those recounted in Shakespeare's *Richard II*, which was acted the following year. The deposition scene in particular deeply offended her, and was published for the first time only in the Fourth Quarto of 1608, 'With new additions of the Parliament Sceane, and the deposing of King Richard, As it hath been lately acted by the Kinges Majesties seruants, at the Globe'.

It is, in the true sense of the term, remarkable that, in a period marked by unrest in Ireland, the Gowrie conspiracy in Scotland and the revolt led by the Earl of Essex, so many Shakespearean dramas – *Richard II*, and then 1 and 2 *Henry IV* (1597), *Julius Caesar* (1599), *Henry V* (1599) and *Hamlet* (1602) – developed a discourse centred on the socio-political crises of succession, usurpation, divine right and anarchy. These are all deeply political plays written by a dramatist with his hand on the pulse of the society which produced him. Read in their historical context, their qualities are dazzling.

The mind that conceived *Richard II* and *Julius Caesar* understood the dangers of divine right on the one hand and of mob rule on the other, as well as the terrible abyss which seemingly stable and organised societies could hurl themselves into when a power at the centre was suddenly removed. Into such a vacuum all manner of socially destructive evil could be drawn. But, as the writer of the two *Henry IV* plays shows us, order and equilibrium cannot simply be purchased by violence.

The parallels with the Essex revolt are impressive. Robert Devereux, Earl of Essex, was appointed Lord Lieutenant of Ireland in March 1599. He signed a truce with the Irish rebel leader, Tyrone, in September, disobeyed the Queen by leaving Ireland, and was arrested at the court at Nonesuch on 28 September 1599. Early the next year the Earl of Tyrone resumed his rebellion against Elizabeth. Essex was tried for his misdemeanours in Ireland in June 1600 and lost his offices at court. On 7 January 1601 he led a revolt in London against the Queen. It failed and he was tried for treason and executed on 25 February 1601.[22] On 4 August 1601 the historian William Lambarde presented the Queen with a copy of the records of the Tower of London, and in conversation she talked about the recent revolt and Essex's attempts to depose her. In Lambarde's account,

> So her majestie fell upon the reign of King Richard II, saying, 'I am Richard II. Know ye not that?'
> W. L. Such a wicked imagination was determined and attempted by a most unkind Gent. the most adorned creature that ever your Majestie made.
> *Her Majestie* He that will forget God, will also forget his benefactors; this tragedy was played 40 times in open streets and houses.[23]

Shakespeare has given us two detailed studies of Essex, in *Troilus and Cressida* and *Hamlet*. In *Troilus* he is Achilles, a Greek general who is torn by two conflicting loyalties. On the one hand he is in love with Polyxena, the sister of Hector, the Trojan hero. On the other hand he is a Greek military commander, continually reminded of his duties by Ulysses. Achilles is blamed for the sluggish Greek war effort. It is claimed that he would rather lie in his tent all day in convivial company – that of Patroclus and the foul-mouthed Thersites – than give the lead expected of him. Priam's son, Hector, sends a challenge to any 'that holds his honour higher than his ease'. Ulysses realises that this is aimed at Achilles, but sends the dull-brained Ajax, as this will provoke Achilles. Hector realises that Ajax is related to the Trojan royal family and their fight is discontinued. When his friend Patroclus is killed by Hector, Achilles slays Hector and drags his body around behind his horse.

The situation presented here is much closer to recent political and military affairs than it is to Homer's *Iliad*. Towards the end of 1600 Essex and his followers – the Earl of Southampton (Shakespeare's patron) and the notoriously malcontented Henry Cuffe – were railing and plotting against the Queen's privy councillors. George Chapman, on whose translation of Homer Shakespeare based *Troilus and Cressida*, dedicated his work to the Earl of Essex, as 'Most true Achilles whom by sacred prophecy Homer did but prefigure in his admired object'. A. L. Rowse suggests in *William Shakespeare: A Biography* (1963) that Shakespeare is reflecting the shattering events of the past two or three years. The Trojan War, like the long war with Spain, is drawing to an end. The similarities between Achilles and Essex are very strong, as sulking in his tent – withdrawing from court and duty when he did not get his own way – had regularly been Essex's way of putting pressure on Elizabeth. Like Shakespeare's Achilles, Essex had a habit of making things small as nothings seem of overriding importance:

> Possessed he is with greatness
> And speaks not to himself but with a pride
> That quarrels at self-breath; imagined worth
> Holds in his blood such swollen and hot discourse . . . .[24]

Thersites is Henry Cuffe, Essex's irascible but scholarly secretary, and the glittering Patroclus is Henry Wriothesley, third Earl of Southampton, who ordered a performance of *Richard II* at the Globe on the eve of the Essex revolt to incite public opinion.[25]

In the famous description of Hamlet, 'The courtier's soldier's, scholar's eye, tongue, sword, the expectancy and rose of the fair state, the glass of fashion . . .', there is much of Essex. The little patch of ground that hath in it no profit but the name refers to the siege of Ostend during the summer of 1601. The eclipses of the sun mentioned refer to eclipses recently observed in England and, as Rowse maintains in *William Shakespeare: A Biography*, there are very strong political parallels. There was a cloud over the public scene. The people's hero was in disgrace, withdrawn into an inner world of resentment, meditation and treason, yet – like Hamlet – for long undecided on any course of action. It is a fact that in 1600, the probable time of *Hamlet*'s composition, Essex was suffering from melancholia and depression, such as is portrayed in Hamlet's character. Even more striking is the extraordinary coincidence that, when Robert Devereux's father, Walter Devereux, the first Earl of Essex, died of dysentry in the autumn of 1576, it was widely rumoured that he had been poisoned at the instigation of Robert Dudley, Earl of Leicester, who married his widow, Lettice, the eldest daughter of Sir Francis Knollys – a set of relationships closely paralleling the Hamlet–Claudius–Gertrude set. Robert Devereux, the young Earl of Essex who died at the executioner's hands in 1601, was 'the observed of all observers' and, in the popular mind, 'was likely, had he been put on. / To have prov'd most royal' (v.ii.411–12).

Even in the autumn of her old age Queen Elizabeth felt insecure. Sir John Harington, the wit and scholar who was Elizabeth's godson, has left a moving portrait of her at this time:

She disregardeth every costly dish that cometh to the table. . . . Every new message from the City doth disturb her . . . the many evil plots and designs hath overcome all her Highness' sweet temper. She walks much in her chamber, and stamps with her feet at ill news; and thrusts her rusty sword at time into the arras in great rage. . . . But the dangers are over, and yet she always has a sword by her table . . . .[26]

William Camden, the antiquary and historian, recorded that, weeks before the Queen died (on 24 March 1603), Puritans, Papists, ambitious people of all sorts posted to Scotland by land and sea to adore 'the rising sun and gain his favour'. When she was asked about the succession she replied, 'I have said that my throne was the throne of kings, and I would not that any base should succeed me.' When she was asked what these words meant she replied, 'I will that a king succeed me, and who but my kinsman the king of Scots'. James acceded as James I of England

on the day Elizabeth died and reached London on 7 May 1603. In
July a plot was uncovered involving Lords Cobham and Grey to
dethrone James and replace him with Arabella Stuart. Sir Walter
Ralegh was arrested on 17 July for complicity in this plot and
James's coronation was held on the 25th of the same month.
Ralegh was reprieved in November but did not regain royal
favour until 1618.

James's tendencies towards absolutism were soon to make
themselves plain. On 14 January 1604 the Hampton Court
Conference brought together the English bishops and leading
Puritans, and, though James and Archbishop Whitgift supported
the request for a new English translation of the Bible, the
appearance of harmony was deceptive. Two months later James's
first Parliament met and he found his plans for a union with
Scotland opposed. The Commons indicated its claim to free
elections (Goodwin's case, 5 April) and its right to protect
members from arrest (Sherley's case, 15 May). On 7 July, James
prorogued Parliament.

It was around this time that Shakespeare brought forth *Macbeth*.
This extraordinary play is full of contemporary references, dating
it to about 1605. The very brevity of the drama – which has often
brought critical acclaim for the masterly precision and coherence
of its symbolism – is owing to the fact that it was written for
performance at court. It might have been one of the entertainments
organised for the visit of King Christian IV of Denmark in the
summer of 1606. Although the farmer, referred to in Act II, who
hanged himself in the expectation of plenty is a stereotypical
figure, we know that there was serious speculation on the price of
wheat that year and that this brought financial ruin to many.[27]

The Porter has one of the most terrible references to recent
events when he declares, 'Faith, here's an equivocator, that could
swear in both scales against either scale; who committed treason
enough for God's sake, yet could not equivocate to heaven; O,
come in, equivocator . . . ' (II.iii.10–14). This refers to the notorious
Gunpowder Plot and the trial of the conspirators. Guy Fawkes
was arrested in the cellars of Parliament on 4 November 1605, and
the Gunpowder Plot – to blow up the House of Lords during
James's state opening of Parliament on the 5th, was discovered.
Robert Catesby and other conspirators made their escape but
were later caught. The reference to the 'equivocator' is clearly to

Henry Garnett, a Jesuit, who was professor of Hebrew at the English College in Rome. He was arrested after three days' search at Hindlip Hall and imprisoned in the Tower. He was examined twenty-three times before the Privy Council. He admitted that he had lied at his trial but attempted to justify his deceit by appealing to the doctrine of equivocation, which – it was held – was justified under certain circumstances when a witness saved himself by hiding the truth by dissimulation. The Jesuits were notorious equivocators, according to Elizabethan and Jacobean street mythology.

Shakespeare's major historical source for the story of Macbeth was Holinshed's *Chronicles of England, Scotlande and Irelande* (1577). But the dramatist altered the details in some very interesting ways. In the murder of Duncan he changes Holinshed's version of the killing of an earlier King Duff by Donwald. It was here he found the intoxication of the chamberlains and the signs and omens in the natural world which parallel the horrors on earth. Donwald, like Shakespeare's tragic hero Macbeth, was urged on to his crime by the ambitions of his wife. It seems clear that Shakespeare, in trying to please James I, substituted the crime of Donwald for the historical Macbeth's, so as to make Duncan's murder more like the shocking murder of Darnley, the father of King James. By these means he would be more assured that James would respond to the dreadful crime of Duncan's bloody murder.

Another of Shakespeare's striking moments seems to have been plucked from the air. Matthew Gwinne, the distinguished physician of St John's College, Oxford, who was also a poet and playwright, presented a pageant in honour of James I, his Queen and the Prince of Wales on the occasion of their visit to Oxford in August 1605. When the royal party appeared at the gates of St John's College they were accosted by three boys dressed 'like nymphs or sybils'. These declaimed that once in the past they had prophesied power without end to the successors of Banquo and that they had returned now in order to predict the same for King James and his descendants:

First Sibyl.   Hail, thou who rulest Scotland!
Second Sibyl.   Hail, thou who rulest England!
Third Sibyl.   Hail, thou who rulest Ireland!

These lines are echoed in *Macbeth*:

> *First Witch.*   All hail, Macbeth! hail to thee, thane of Glamis!
> *Second Witch.*   All hail, Macbeth! hail to thee, thane of Cawdor!
> *Third Witch.*   All hail, Macbeth, that shalt be king
>   hereafter! (I.iii.48–56)

Writing about the frightening but arresting manner in which the German cinema between the wars and before the rise of Hitler seems to rehearse the darker and deeper subconscious themes and motifs of the time which was to bring forth such monsters, Siegfried Kracauer wrote,

> What films reflect are not so much explicit credos as psychological dispositions – those deep layers of collective mentality which extend more or less below the dimension of consciousness. Of course, popular magazines and broadcasts, bestsellers, ads, fashions in language and other sedimentary products of a people's cultural life also yield valuable information about predominant attitudes, widespread inner tendencies.[28]

We must therefore seek to find in the popular dramas of Elizabethan and Jacobean times, 'the abstract and brief chronicles of the time' (*Coriolanus*, I.i.74–5), some similar continuing political discourse deeply buried in the subconscious. It would seem we have a nation which is already beginning to entertain the idea of putting the tyrannic sovereign to death – Shakespeare's plays are full of the murders of kings and rulers, and the action of *Macbeth* strikes very near the political truths of the period. King James's conception of the nature of kingship is quite closely mirrored in *Coriolanus* (1608) and *King Lear* (performed at court in 1606). Both plays stress the paternal nature of the ideal ruler and are full of physical imagery and references to the human body and its various parts which are strongly reminiscent of James's own published comments on kingship. Menenius refers directly to the 'helms of the state' who care for the people 'like fathers'. His celebrated analogy of the body–state – with its references to 'the kingly crowned head', 'the vigilant eye', 'the counsellor heart' and 'the arm our soldier' (*Coriolanus*, I.i.113–16) – echo that discourse on the body politic as a natural, organic, God-given system which we have already seen so well articulated by Queen

Elizabeth and which was to find such a literate champion in James. In *The True Law of Free Monarchies* (1598) James asserted,

> And the general agreement of the law of nature in this our ground with the laws and constitutions of God and man already alleged will by two similitudes easily appear. The king towards his people is rightly compared to a father of children, and to a head of a body composed of divers members. For as fathers the good princes and magistrates of the people of God acknowledged themselves to their subjects. . . . And the proper office of a king towards his subjects agrees very well with the offices of the head towards the body and all members thereof. For from the head, being the seat of judgement, proceedeth the care and foresight of guiding and preventing all evil that may come to the body. . . . The head cares for the body, so doth the king for his people. . . .
>
> And now first of the father's part . . . consider, I pray you, what duty his children owe to him, and whether upon any pretext whatever it will not be thought monstrous and unnatural for his sons to rise up against him . . . and when they think good to slay him, or cut him off. . . .
>
> And for the similitude of the head and the body, it may very well fall out that the head will be forced to gar[29] cut off some rotten member . . . to keep the rest of the body in integrity: but what state the body can be in, if the head for any infirmity that can fall to it be cut off, I leave it to the reader's judgement.[30]

Explicitly and implicity these themes run through the literature of the period and are found most noticeably in the dramas. Shakespeare's histories and Roman plays provide excellent examples of this discourse explicitly rehearsed, but it finds equally strong implicit treatment in the tragedies and romances. In *King Lear* we have the theme of children against parents in both the Lear–daughters and Gloucester–sons narrative, and in *The Tempest* the monster, Caliban (remember James's words 'monstrous and unnatural'), rises against his father-figure, Prospero. *Macbeth* above all plays shows the terrors which are let loose when subjects raise their hands against their natural masters, but the theme is very strong in *Hamlet* also. The discourse here embedded in the literature of the early seventeenth century miraculously shadows forth the cataclysmic political events of the English

revolution. Slightly to paraphrase a celebrated statement of
Ernesto Laclau, we are looking at the ensemble of the phenomena
in and through which social production of meaning takes place,
which is an ensemble which constitutes a society as such. The
discourse discussed here, then, is not to be seen as a level or a
dimension of the social, but on the contrary, as being coextensive
with the social as such.[31] As Janet Wolff says, 'Meaning,
consciousness and even the objects of thought are perceived as
constructed in discourse . . . .'[32]

That great moment of fracture in English history, after which
nothing would ever be the same again, when the sovereign and
his Parliament were locked in war, when the king was brought to
trial and beheaded and the attempt was made to govern the
country by man-made laws, was prefigured in Jacobean drama.
As Christopher Hill has written, the Civil War brought intellectual
changes: 'Though everything was done to obliterate the memory
of that epoch, ways of thinking would never be the same
again . . . .'[33] The modern age dates from the middle of the
seventeenth century. As Dr Johnson commented, 'The civil wars
have left in this nation scarcely any trace of more ancient
history . . . .' The philosophy of the Levellers that the old
constitution had broken down in the war and that the state must
therefore be consciously reconstructed is surely just an extreme
instance of the awareness that England had finally left behind the
Middle Ages. The language and imagery used to express this
thesis is of immense interest:

> In the beginning of time, the great Creator Reason made the
> earth to be a common treasury, to preserve beasts, birds, fishes,
> and man, the lord that was to govern this creation; for man had
> domination given to him, over the beasts, birds, and fishes; but
> not one word was spoken in the beginning, that one branch of
> mankind should rule over another.
>
> And the reason is this. Every single man, male and female, is
> a perfect creature of himself; and the same spirit that made the
> globe dwells in man, to govern the globe: so that the flesh of
> man being subject to Reason, his Maker, hath him to be his
> teacher and ruler within himself, therefore needs not run
> abroad after any teacher and ruler without him . . . .[34]

Thus (and more) Gerrard Winstanley. The imagery and iconography drawn from the body–state analogy are gone for ever: the creative rationality of man has replaced the faith in organic nature – the great and continuing debate as to how we should govern ourselves has been opened. In Christopher Hill's view this appeal to conscience against authority is an appeal to the present against the past, 'For the society in which men live forms their consciences, whereas authority gets fossilized in a set of institutions or writings'.[35]

Monarchy had gone for ever. In 1660 royalty was restored. Monarchy and royalty are vastly different things, and this, too, was explored in Jacobean drama. *A King and No King*, a tragicomedy by Francis Beaumont and John Fletcher, is one of the most curious dramas of the time. Even more curious was its reception when first performed by the King's Men at court, Blackfriars and the Globe in 1611. It was frequently revived throughout the 1630s and was immensely popular during the Restoration. Dryden praised it lavishly in his *Essay of Dramatic Poesy*, referring to it as 'that excellent play' and comparing it favourably with dramas by 'the ancients' and asserting that the play's authors had the advantage of Shakespeare's wit as their precedent as well as their own 'great natural gifts, improved by study'. According to Dryden, Beaumont was considered so accurate a judge of plays that the great Ben Jonson submitted all his writings for Beaumont's censure and had help from the same quarter in contriving his plots. The author of *An Essay of Dramatic Poesy* almost runs out of superlatives in his attempts to localise and characterise the genius of Beaumont and Fletcher:

> Their plots were generally more regular that Shakespeare's, especially those which were made before Beaumont's death: and they understood and imitated the conversation of gentlemen much better; whose wild debaucheries, and quickness of wit in repartees, no poet before them could paint as well as they have done . . . . they represented all the passions very lively, but above all, love. I am apt to believe the English language in them arrived to its highest perfection. . . . Their plays are now the most pleasant and frequent entertainments of the stage; two of theirs being acted through the year for one of Shakespeare's or Jonson's . . . .[36]

Even when due allowance is made for the fact that the 'national greatness of Shakespeare' is a fairly recent construction in our culture,[37] the praise lavished on Beaumont and Fletcher is still breath-taking. It seems to me that *A King and No King* must have meant more in the century which experienced the English revolution and the Restoration, that in some strange way it prefigured realities and subliminally fingered some very delicate political nerve-endings.

On the face of it, *A King and No King* is a fairly straightforward Beaumont and Fletcher tragicomedy. If read innocently, removed from its historical and political context, it even seems as vacuous as the libretto of a Rossini *opera seria* – the obvious comparison would be with *Semiramide* (1823).[38] *A King and No King* inhabits the familiar exotic no-place of so many Elizabethan and Jacobean poetic dramas, although technically it is located in Armenia. A war has just ended, and peace will bring happy days: 'the King has made a fair hand on't; he has ended the wars at a blow. Would my sword had a close basket-hilt, to hold wine, and the blade would make knives! for we shall have nothing but eating and drinking.'[39]

The war has been a long and contentious one between Arbaces, King of Iberia, and Tigranes, King of Armenia. Arbaces has defeated Tigranes in single combat, thus physically and symbolically defeating the Armenian nation. While Arbaces has been away at the war, his sister Panthea has grown to beautiful womanhood. To seal the peace between them, Arbaces offers Tigranes Panthea's hand in marriage. Unfortunately Tigranes' affections are already engaged to an Armenian beauty, Spaconia. He declines the offer of freedom thus held out to him and sends Spaconia to enlist Panthea's help in opposing the match proposed by Arbaces. Arbaces regards himself as a master of statecraft and diplomacy and is full of admiration for his own tolerance of stupidity:

> By Heaven and earth,
> I were much better be a king of beasts
> Than such a people! If I had not patience
> Above a god, I should be called a tyrant
> Throughout the world: they will offend to death
> Each minute.[40]

The drama moves smoothly through its *epitasis* to its *catastasis*:

when Tigranes, Arbaces and Panthea meet, Tigranes is so smitten
by Panthea's beauty that his resolve to remain loyal to Spaconia is
severely shaken; and, much to his surprise, Arbaces is strangely
and deeply drawn to his own sister by the most unbrotherly
sexual attractions and desires. His conscious mind rejects the fact
that Panthea is his sister:

> Here I pronounce him traitor,
> The direct plotter of my death, that names
> Or thinks her for my sister: 'tis a lie,
> The most malicious of the world, invented
> To mad your King. He that will say so next,
> Let him draw out his sword, and sheathe it here:
> It is a sin fully as pardonable.
> She is no kin to me, nor shall she be . . . .[41]

But he is drawn to her as to a magnet:

> Why should there be such music in a voice,
> And sin for me to hear it? all the world
> May take delight in this; and 'tis damnation
> For me to do so. You are fair and wise,
> And virtuous, I think; and he is blest
> That is so near you as your brother is;
> But you are naught to me but a disease,
> Continual torment without hope of ease.
> Such an ungoldly sickness I have got,
> That he that undertakes my cure must first
> O'erthrow divinity, all moral laws,
> And leave mankind as unconfined as beasts,
> Allowing them to do all actions
> As freely as they drink when they desire.[42]

The material is excellently worked up by Beaumont and Fletcher
in an obvious and direct manner which cries out for operatic
treatment that fully deserves the definition Dryden gives to *status*:

the height and full growth of the play: we may call it properly
the counter-turn, which destroys that expectation, embroils the
action in new difficulties, and leaves you far distant from that
hope in which it found you; as you may have observed in a

violent stream resisted by a narrow passage, – it runs round to an eddy, and carries back the waters with more swiftness that it brought them on.[43]

And so to the *dénouement*, which is equally masterly. The situation appears to be deadlocked: Arbaces cannot control his passionate love for Panthea, who in turn, loves him; Tigranes, against his better judgement, is also drawn to Panthea and fears he may lose his love for Spaconia. We now come to the discovery, or the unravelling of the plot. Gobrias has been Lord Protector of Iberia since the death of the late King. He now reveals that Arbaces is in truth his son, and that the Queen Mother has adopted him secretly, and passed him off as her own child when it seemed she would have no issue herself. Panthea was born six years later. Therefore, Arbaces is no relative of Panthea, and may love her and be loved by her in honourable fashion. Tigranes repents his temporary loss of loyalty to Spaconia and is reunited with her. The play ends with the union of Arbaces and Panthea as the King who is now No King blesses Tigranes:

> Mayst thou be happy
> In thy fair choice, for thou art temperate!
> You owe no ransom to the state! Know that
> I have a thousand joys to tell you of,
> Which yet I dare not utter, till I pay
> My thanks to Heaven for 'em . . . .
> 　　　　　　　. . . and you, queen
> Of goodness and of us, oh, give me leave
> To take your arm in mine! Come, every one
> That takes delight in goodness, help to sing
> Loud thanks for me, that I am proved no King![44]

The *dénouement* is perfect: after a long and terrible war further chaos was threatened by an apparently uncontrollable mutual sexual attraction which was incestuous. But peace and harmony are restored when the real truth is revealed: Arbaces is the honourable son of the Lord Protector.

Oliver Cromwell, Lord Protector, died on 3 September 1658. His son Richard succeeded him as Lord Protector. On 22 April 1659 Richard dissolved Parliament after a peaceful *coup d'état* staged by the Army to prevent Parliament from gaining control over it. The constitutional crisis between the Army and Parliament, it was hoped, would be settled permanently by the Derby Petition, framed by John Lambert. But on 25 May Richard Cromwell resigned and the Rump Parliament re-established the Commonwealth. There was a Royalist uprising in Cheshire in August, which was put down by Major-General Lambert, and on 12 October the Army expelled the Rump Parliament. A week before Christmas, General Monck in Scotland called for a free Parliament, and the Long Parliament met again on 26 December, excluding only those members who had been purged in 1648.

Events now moved swiftly towards a conclusion. Monck entered England in January with an army and on 16 February 1660 declared for a free Parliament. On the 21st the Long Parliament recalled those who had been purged in 1648 (the Presbyterians). On 16 March the Long Parliament (elected November 1640) dissolved itself. The State of Virginia declared Charles II King and restored its former Governor, Sir William Berkeley. On 4 April, Charles issued the Declaration of Breda, which promised an amnesty and religious toleration. The Convention Parliament met at Westminster on 25 April, and Charles was invited to return to England. On 29 May, Charles entered London. A king was restored. And yet he was not really king. The true course of events is summarised by that great mythologiser of the nation's history, Thomas Babington Macaulay:

> The history of England, during the seventeenth century, is the history of the transformation of a limited monarchy, constituted after the fashion of the middle ages, into a limited monarchy suited to that more advanced state of society in which the public charges can no longer be borne by the estates of the crown, and in which the public defence can no longer be entrusted to a feudal militia.[45]

In Macaulay's view the politicians who led the Long Parliament in 1642 attempted to accomplish this change themselves by transferring to the estates of the realm the choice of ministers, the command of the Army and the running of the entire state administration. This enterprise was wholly shaken by the course taken by the Civil War, which invoked a power they could not control, and for a time the evils of military government were only mitigated to a degree by the personal power and authority of Oliver Cromwell himself as Lord Protector. When he passed from the scene there was the danger that order and liberty would perish in ignominious ruin. That catastrophe was averted by the Restoration, by inviting Charles to return, as King but No King.

Beaumont and Fletcher's well-crafted play fascinatingly drew on political currents latent at the time and put before theatre-goers of the Restoration recent political events and crises in the form of a dream with a happy ending. As Bernard Shaw wrote in 'Maxims for Revolutionists' in *Man and Superman*, 'Kings are not born: they are made by artificial hallucination. When the process is interrupted by adversity at a critical age, as in the case of Charles II, the subject becomes sane and never completely recovers his kingliness'.

Sir John Reresby, baronet, who died in 1689, knew King Charles II well. He had travelled on the continent during the Commonwealth, but returned at the Restoration and entered Parliament as the representative for Aldborough as a supporter of the court. In his *Memoirs*, published in 1734, he described Charles thus: 'He was not an active, busy, or ambitious prince, but perfectly a friend to ease, and fond of pleasure; he seemed to be chiefly desirous of peace and quiet for his own time.'

Times had changed.

NOTES

1. J. B. Black, *The Reign of Elizabeth 1558–1603* (1936; Oxford: Oxford University Press, 1985) pp. 280–1.
2. Brian Redhead, *Political Thought from Plato to NATO* (London: BBC, Ariel Books, 1984) p. 9. Cf. also A. L. Rowse, *The England of Elizabeth* (London: Macmillan, 1953) p. 297ff.; and J. D. Mackie, *The Early Tudors 1485–1558* (1952; Oxford: Oxford University Press, 1985) p. 188ff.
3. The musical imagery is noteworthy. Shakespeare constantly associates stability with harmony and anarchy with discord. See B. L. Joseph, *Shakespeare's Eden: The Commonwealth of England 1558–1629* (London: Blandford, 1971) p. 154ff.; and Caroline Spurgeon, *Shakespeare's Imagery and What It Tells Us* (1935; Cambridge: Cambridge University Press, 1971) pp. 74–8, 269–71 and 280. At the end of *3 Henry VI*, King Edward looks forward to peace in musical terms:

   Sound, drums and trumpets! Farewell sour annoy!
   For here, I hope, beings our lasting joy.

Richard of Gloucester, on the other hand, speaks sneeringly of 'this weak and piping time of peace' and likens himself 'to a chaos'. The Archbishop of Canterbury in eulogising the qualities of King Henry V draws the parallel between war and peace in musical terms:

> List his discourse in war, and you shall hear
> A fearful battle render'd you in music.
> (*Henry V*, i.i.43–4)

4. See A. C. Partridge, *The Problem of Henry VIII Re-opened* (1949); and J. Spedding, 'On the Several Shares of Shakespeare and Fletcher in the Play of Henry VIII', *Gentleman's Magazine*, n.s., xxxiv (Aug–Oct 1850) 115–24, 381–2.
5. Cf. Ferdinand Braudel, *Civilization and Capitalism*, vol. ii: *The Wheels of Commerce*, tr. Sian Reynolds (London: Collins, 1983) p. 472ff.
6. Mackie, *The Early Tudors*, p. 557ff.
7. Philip Hughes, *The Reformation* (London: Burns and Oates, 1960) p. 260ff.
8. Black, *The Reign of Elizabeth*, p. 69ff.
9. In 1553 Catherine Grey married Henry Herbert, afterwards second Earl of Pembroke, but was divorced after the execution of her sister, Lady Jane Grey. She secretly married Edward Seymour, Earl of Hertford, and was in consequence imprisoned in the Tower under the Act of 1536 which made it treason for persons of royal blood to marry without the sovereign's consent.
10. Black, *The Reign of Elizabeth*, p. 96; and cf. J. E. Neale, 'Parliament and the Succession Question in 1562–3 and 1566', *English Historical Review*, 1921, pp. 497–520.
11. Rowse, *The England of Elizabeth*, p. 336ff.
12. Black, *The Reign of Elizabeth*, pp. 96–8.
13. The Wyatt rebellion had obviously threatened Elizabeth. Roger de Mortimer (1287–1330) had more or less ruled the realm through his liaison with Isabella, wife of Edward II, whom he probably had murdered. Edward III was in the meantime a mere figurehead. William de Montacute joined forces with Edward III, and Mortimer, after being tried for usurping royal power and for other crimes, was hanged, drawn and quartered in 1330. See May McKisack, *The Fourteenth Century 1307–1399* (1959; Oxford: Oxford University Press, 1985) pp. 90–102.

    John de la Pole, Earl of Lincoln (1464–87), is another example of one who suffered from close association with the centre of state power. He was the son of the Duke of Suffolk and Elizabeth, sister of Edward IV, and was recognised heir presumptive during Richard III's reign. He supported Lambert Simnel's plot and was killed at Stoke Field, Nottingham, in 1487.
14. Rowse, *The England of Elizabeth*,
15. The Casket Letters were a notorious collection of documents. The Earl of Morton claimed to have found them in a silver casket in June 1567. If they were genuine they proved Mary's responsibility for Darnley's murder. The manuscripts included letters from Mary to

Bothwell, French sonnets, a signed (but undated) promise to marry Bothwell and a marriage contract between the two. At subsequent inquiries Mary asked to see the documents but her request was not granted. The Casket Letters were lost after the execution for high treason of William Ruthven, fourth Baron Ruthven and Earl Gowrie in 1584. See Black, *The Reign of Elizabeth*, p. 102ff.; Andrew Lang, *The Mystery of Mary Stuart* (1912); W. Goodall, *Examination of the Letters Said to be Written by Mary Queen of Scots to James, Earl of Bothwell*, 2 vols (1754); T. F. Henderson, *The Casket Letters and Mary Queen of Scots* (1890); and M. H. Armstrong Davison, *The Casket Letters* (London: Vision Press, 1965. An excellent brief account of the matter will be found in J. E. Neale, *Queen Elizabeth I* (Harmondsworth: Penguin, 1971) p. 158ff.

16. Neale, *Elizabeth I*, pp. 177–193
17. See A. L. Rowse, *The Elizabethan Renaissance: The Cultural Achievement* (London: Macmillan, 1972) p. 53ff.
18. See Alan Bold and Robert Giddings, *Who Was Really Who in Fiction* (London: Longman, 1987), entries for Duessa, Grantorto, Una. See also A. C. Hamilton, *Allegory in 'The Faerie Queene'* (London: Hutchinson, 1961); and K. Williams, *Spenser's 'Faerie Queene': The World of Glass* (London: Routledge and Kegan Paul, 1966).
19. Black, *The Reign of Elizabeth* pp. 396–405.
20. Robert Persons (or Parsons, 1546–1610) was a Jesuit and controversialist, associated with Edmund Campion. Persons had his own printing-press and was involved in intrigues in England and in Spain, where he fiercely advocated the cause of Philip II. He was rector of the English College at Rome, where he died. He published over thirty polemical pamphlets, the most notorious being his *Conference about the Next Succession* (1594). See *Letters and Memorials of Robert Persons*, ed. Leo Hicks (London: Catholic Record Society, 1942).
21. Black, *The Reign of Elizabeth*, pp. 390–1.
22. Neale, *Elizabeth I*, pp. 356–81.
23. Wiliam Lambarde (1536–1601) was the author of several legal and historical works. This conversation is quoted in Oscar James Campbell and Edward G. Quinn, *The Reader's Encyclopedia of Shakespeare* (New York: Thomas Y. Crowell, 1966) p. 445.
24. See A. L. Rowse, *William Shakespeare: A Biography* (London: Macmillan, 1963) pp. 344–5.
25. Henry Cuffe, author and politician (1563–1601) was professor of Greek at Queen's College, Oxford, and accompanied Essex to Cádiz as his secretary in 1596. He was faithful to Essex during his period of disgrace. He was tried for complicity in Essex's treason and executed in 1601. For a biography of Southampton, see A. L. Rowse, *Shakespeare's Southampton* (London: Macmillan, 1965).
26. Quoted in Black, *The Reign of Elizabeth*, p. 494.
27. See *Macbeth*, II.iii.5–6.
28. Siegfried Kracauer, *From Caligari to Hitler: A Psychological History of the German Film*, 5th edn (Princeton: Princeton University Press, 1974) p. 6.

29. 'Gar': verb, 'to make, cause, induce or compel' – *Chambers's Scots Dictionary* (Edinburgh: Chambers, 1974).
30. James I, *The True Law of Free Monarchies* (1598), in *The Norton Anthology of English Literature*, 3rd edn, M. H. Abrams *et al.* (New York: Norton, 1974) I, 1640–1.
31. Ernesto Laclau, 'Populist Rupture and Discourse', *Screen Education*, no. 34 (1980) 87–93.
32. Janet Wolff, *Aesthetics and the Sociology of Art* (London: Allen and Unwin, 1983) p. 91ff.
33. Christopher Hill, *Reformation to Industrial Revolution* (Harmondsworth: Penguin, 1969) pp. 198–9.
34. Gerrard Winstanley, *The True Leveller's Standard Advanced* (1649), in *The Norton Anthology*, I, 1657.
35. Hill, *Reformation to Industrial Revolution*, p. 199.
36. John Dryden, *An Essay of Dramatic Poesy* (1668), in D. J. Enright and Ernst de Chickera (eds), *English Critical Texts, Sixteenth to Twentieth Century* (London: Oxford University Press, 1966) pp. 78 and 89–90. By 'lively' Dryden meant life-like. See also Arthur Miziner, 'The High Design of *A King and No King*', *Modern Philology*, XXXVIII (1940).
37. See Terry Hawkes, *That Old Shakespeherian Rag* (London: Methuen, 1986); and Robert Giddings, 'Mythologising Old Bill', *Listener* 17 April 1986.
38. See T. B. Tomlinson, *A Study of Elizabethan and Jacobean Tragedy* (Cambridge: Cambridge University Press, 1964) p. 242ff.; and Una Ellis-Fermor, *The Jacobean Drama*, 5th edn (London: Methuen, 1965) p. 201ff.
39. Beaumont and Fletcher, *A King and No King*, I.i, in *Beaumont and Fletcher*, ed. J. St Loe Strachey (London: Ernest Benn, 1950) p. 5.
40. Ibid, p. 12.
41. Ibid., p. 44 (III.i).
42. Ibid. p. 45.
43. Dryden, *Essay* in Enright and de Chickera, *English Critical Texts*, p. 62.
44. *Beaumont and Fletcher*, p. 108 (*A King and No King*, V.iv).
45. T. B. Macaulay, *The History of England* (1849–60) (London: Longman, 1862) I, 72.

11

Masques and Murderers: Dramatic Method and Ideology in Revenge Tragedy and the Court Masque

DARRYLL GRANTLEY

Jacobean revenge tragedy, with its turbulent, bloody and uncertain topos, might be thought to have little relationship in terms either of dramatic method or of philosophical concerns with the masque of the court of James I, a dramatic genre of ceremonial serenity and metaphysical certainties. The origins of these two forms of drama were different, as were the purposes they were designed to serve and the audiences for which they were written. Masques were the highly wrought and visually splendid creation serving a celebratory and idealising function within the narrow confines of the court, while revenge tragedy, though also sometimes performed at court, had to satisfy the demand for popular, frequently satirical drama of the broader audiences in the public and coterie theatres. However, they were both ultimately the products of the same political state and literary culture, and many of the writers of tragedies in the period were also writers of royal masques.[1] There is also the fact that many tragedies contain masques as part of their action, either dramatised within the plays or at least referred to as an integral part of the narrative. As products of the royal court, masques were narrowly engaged in constructing a particular view of the political *status quo*, while the protagonists of revenge tragedy were almost invariably individuals with power in the state; the exercise of power in or the running of the state featuring substantially in this drama. Some sort of

common ground and a relationship, however oblique, might thus
be seen to exist between the two forms in terms of subject matter.
However, what is common to both may perhaps best be sought in
the dramatic principles adopted by the Jacobean playwrights.
These principles may be regarded as furnishing the particular
identity of drama at this period, certainly distinguishing it from
the dominant forms of Renaissance drama which preceded it and
having implications for the type of plays that were to be written in
the Caroline period and after the interregnum later in the century.

Masques have until recent years received scant attention from
scholars of the Renaissance theatre and, aside from the
insubstantiality of their written texts, the reason is possibly that
they might be regarded as peripheral to the concerns of the
theatre historian, in the sense both of not being in the mainstream
of the theatrical life of the time and, more profoundly, of not even
being drama in every sense of the word. Stephen Orgel has
pointed to the nature of masques as being something other than
pure representation:

> To the Renaissance, appearing in a masque was not merely
> playing a part. It was, in a profound sense, precisely the
> opposite. When Inigo Jones and Ben Jonson presented Queen
> Anne as Bel-Anna, Queen of the Ocean, or King James as Pan,
> the universal god, or Henry, Prince of Wales as Oberon, Prince
> of Faery, a deep truth about the monarchy was realized and
> embodied in action, and monarchs were revealed in roles that
> expressed the strongest Renaissance belief about the nature of
> kingship, the obligations and perquisites of royalty. Masques
> were games and shows, triumphs and celebrations; they were
> for the court and about the court, and their seriousness was
> indistinguisable from their recreative quality.[2]

A little further on he continues, 'the Renaissance ruler went on [in
the masque] to create an alternative heaven, asserting his control
over his environment and the divinity of his rule through the
power of art at his command'.[3]

Instead of constructing a mimetic relationship with the real
world of the audience, the masque thus becomes a metaphor,
reinterpreting reality in terms partly of analogy but also by
dissolving the boundary between reality and representation. In
doing this it creates a sealed, hermetic world of reference; in a

sense the world it represents is entirely and self-consciously a theatrical one, not purporting to be anything else. Attention is constantly called to the devices of the spectacle and the ways in which the drama makes its revelations: it is overtly emblematic. Jacobean tragedy can be seen as adopting a similar approach to the process of representation. Of course, the nature of this tragedy produced by a range of dramatists with individual styles is widely divergent, but a distinct tendency towards a similar approach to that outlined above manifests itself: schematic, self-displaying, metaphoric rather than mimetic theatre creating an entirely theatrical frame of reference. Attributes such as these, which might be regarded as characteristically Jacobean, in fact are first found in Thomas Kyd's prototype revenge play, *The Spanish Tragedy* (1587–8), and it is a particularly interesting phenomenon that this form of arguably crude drama should not only have persisted but actually have evolved further after the developments in dramaturgical sophistication of the 1590s. It is clear from comparison with the tragedy predominating in the 1590s that the characterisation and dramatic devices of revenge tragedy were old-fashioned by the early seventeenth century, and the continued use of them by a number of competent dramatists has to be seen as a deliberate feature of a specific genre. Revenge drama is, of course, not the only form of tragedy in this period, but it was extremely popular and the qualities which it exemplifies are to be found to a greater or lesser extent in many other Jacobean tragedies. Revenge tragedy is a rather loosely defined genre, and 'the threate of blood' is sometimes preferred as including plays with similar attributes but without a dominant revenge motif. This discussion will consider not only significant revenge plays proper, such as *The Revenger's Tragedy* (1607), Webster's *The White Devil* and *The Duchess of Malfi* (1613), and Middleton and Rowley's *The Changeling* (1622), but also Marston's slightly pre-Jacobean two-part revenge drama, *Antonio and Mellida* (1601) and *Antonio's Revenge* (1601), as well as related non-revenge plays: John Marston's tragicomedy *The Malcontent* (1604), Middleton's *Women Beware Women* (1609–27), Beaumont and Fletcher's *The Maid's Tragedy* (1610–11) and Tourneur's *The Atheist's Tragedy* (1611), all of which are conceived very much in terms of revenge drama or 'theatre of blood'.

An autoreferential focus on the process of dramatic representation was present in the genre right from the beginning, as Kyd in *The Spanish Tragedy* not only put a frame of the audience-within-the-play in the figures of the ghost of Andrea and the spirit of Revenge, but also located the effective climax of his play in a play-within-a-play in which the boundaries between represented events and real events are dissolved. Perhaps the best-known instance of this theatrical self-consciousness occurs in *Hamlet*, in the ambiguity of Hamlet's 'antic disposition', which is as problematic for the audience as it is for the characters in the play, or in the self-reflexivity of the players scene (II.ii) and in the play-within-a-play (III.ii). *Hamlet* is a play in which Shakespeare toys with the various formulae of revenge tragedy in the process of constructing a play which is essentially about not taking revenge. Among the Jacobean revenge plays, the idea of some form of drama within drama is almost a *sine qua non*, and it has the inevitable effect of foregrounding self-consciously the dramatic medium as a medium and throwing up questions about the nature of representation. In Marston's *Antonio and Mellida* the emphasis on the theatrical nature of the work is even more pronounced, as the Induction, rather in the fashion of the opening of Jonson's comedy *Bartholomew Fair*, has the actors in the play discussing their parts as actors. The second half of this tragedy, *Antonio's Revenge*, makes use of two dumbshows in the course of the action, one in III.i and one in v.i; *The Revenger's Tragedy* has a dumbshow in v.iii speeding the narrative to its climax; and Webster's two classic tragedies both have dumbshows integral to the action, *The Duchess of Malfi* in III.iv and *The White Devil* in II.ii. These shows are used in various ways in these plays, to compress the narrative, to isolate and highlight certain important sequences in it or to prepare for the action to follow. Whatever their function, they were old-fashioned devices even by the time Kyd was writing *The Spanish Tragedy* in the 1580s, having first made their appearance in native English tragedy in *Gorboduc* in 1561. In each case the use of this device in the plays is also avoidable: the information or effects which these dumbshows convey to the audience are either not strictly necessary or could easily be arrived at by other means. They might thus be regarded as a part of a deliberate theatricalist intention in these plays. In each instance of their occurrence the drama changes gear and thus draws attention to the theatrical medium through which the narrative is being presented. As with the masque, there is a far from straightforward relationship between the audience and the plays here. This by itself is not of any major significance but becomes more important when viewed in the context of a broader consideration of the approach adopted by the Jacobean revenge tragedians, a consideration which involves examining the patterns of reference and meaning which are created in these plays.

Another important feature which the revenge tragedy shares with the masque is the creation of a hermetic theatrical world which is its own frame of reference and which seeks less to the mimetic than to be metaphoric theatre. In each case the worlds presented are ones in which normal expectations do not obtain. An interesting contrast can be made here between theatrical metaphors in, one the one hand, two plays by Shakespeare, the well-known comparison in *As You Like It*, ii,vii ('All the world's a stage / And all the men and women merely players') or the similar theatrical metaphor in *Macbeth*, v.v ('Life's but a walking shadow; a poor player, / That struts and frets his hour upon the stage, / And then is heard no more'), and, on the other, the Duchess's weary exclamation in *The Duchess of Malfi*, iv.i, 'I account this world a tedious theatre / For I do play a part in't against my will'. The difference is that Shakespeare's metaphors are just that, rhetorical observations. The Duchess's, however, has far more immediate resonances within the play, since it is uttered at a point at which the play has become most overtly theatrical; the events in which she is an unwilling participant are deliberately staged like theatre and the world of the Duchess is the world of melodrama. This is accounted for by deliberate design on the part of other protagonists who are torturing her, but it is generally a feature of the macabre theatrical world of the play.

The theatricalism of revenge tragedy manifests itself in several aspects of this genre and is particularly to be seen in the works of John Webster. As with the masque, the world portrayed by this drama has its own rules which bear little relation to the real world; it sets up a self-contained, closed-off system of values and ideas which might be said to have a validity in the theatre alone. This principle is illustrated in the construction of dramatic character. Psychological subtlety and complexity of motivation are less important than clarity of dramatic type and forcefulness in self-revelation. There are some variations between dramatists, though the effect is broadly similar in that what finally emerges in each case is a certain one-dimensionality of character and fixity of type which is determined more by the exigencies of narrative and dramatic effect than anything else. Marston, in his *Antonio* plays, written for performance by the boys of St Paul's, uses the ranting declamatory style of Kyd's drama to establish his characters. The chacterisation of *The Revenger's Tragedy* uses this too but to a lesser extent, and resorts to allegorical names for the characters to express their moral types or roles in the drama: thus 'Lussurioso' is a lecher, 'Ambitioso' an ambitious younger half-brother, 'Spurio' a bastard and 'Vindice' the revenger. Tourneur in *The Atheist's Tragedy* bases particularly his central character on an explicitly stated idea which is then carefully worked out as the basis of that character's behaviour and motivation.

Webster's characters are to some extent individualised but in his two major plays he uses a similar formula in terms of the dominant characters. Both *The Duchess of Malfi* and *The White Devil* contain among their central figures scheming dukes, corrupt cardinals, powerful and attractive female victims and, at the very heart of the action, the malcontents who manage it all: Bosola and Flamineo. The scenes are so arranged as to place a focus on various of these characters, not to develop them psychologically but to exploit their dramatic potential. The best examples are the scenes involving the principal women characters in each play: in *The Duchess of Malfi*, iv.i and ii, in which the Duchess endures mental torture and death, and, in *The White Devil*, the arraignment of Vittoria Corombona in iii.ii. These are scenes the principal interest of which is not so much narrative or character development, though these may naturally be present too, but the display of a victim under persecution. The victimhood is what is essential, just as the lycanthropy of Duke Ferdinand and the melancholy of the Cardinal are in the scenes in which these figures enjoy the dramatic focus in *The Duchess of Malfi*. It is interesting to note that after the death of the Duchess the dramatic interest of the play shifts squarely to the Duke, the Cardinal and Bosola as the characters offering the greatest possibilities for theatrical exploitation. The rather curious inconsistency of Bosola, who carries out the wishes of the Arragonian brothers even while he appears to switch his sympathies to the Duchess, is a good example of the use of character for theatrical expediency. He will be needed to wreak vengeance on the brothers in the latter part of the play and thus is simply made to change accordingly. As he has already been established as a malcontent and competent Machiavellian, he is the best character to use from the point of

view of dramatic effect.[4] The emphasis is consistently on theatrical
display, and, though the instances cited exemplify this particularly
well, the same principle can be seen to operate in the construction
and use of dramatic character in other Jacobean tragedies,
particularly revenge plays. This places the requirements of theatre
before psychological consistency or complexity, thus separating
off the world of the play, which, rather than being constructed
along mimetic lines, has its own rules and frame of reference. As
in the masque, the emphasis remains on the visual surface of
reality.

Theatricalism is also evident in the narrative construction of
revenge plays. Horatio's account to the ambassador in *Hamlet*,
v.ii, could easily be used to sum up the narrative of one of these
plays:

> So shall you hear
> Of carnal, bloody and unnatural acts,
> Of accidental judgements, casual slaughters,
> Of deaths put on by cunning and forced cause,
> And, in this upshot, purposes mistook
> Fallen on th' inventors' heads.

The world created is one in which perceptions are unreliable,
reality is slippery and almost no relationship of trust may be
relied upon, even ties of blood being very prone to betrayal. It is,
in short, a world in which conventions of realism give way to the
demands of the popular theatre. As in the masque, though with
an effect which is the absolute converse of it, theatre replaces
realism. The structure of action in the masque is based not on the
logical development of a plausible narrative but on a series of
conceits, and in revenge tragedy the equivalent of these are
intrigue strategies producing an equally implausible narrative.
However, while in the masque this distance from realism involves
the almost total negation of irony, at least in the overt intention of
the writing, Jacobean revenge drama goes to the other extreme
and dramatic irony becomes one of the main principles of narrative
construction. In this respect it recalls *The Spanish Tragedy*, in which
all the climactic moments are based on things not being what they
seem – as in the case of the arbour which instead of being a place
of repose and romantic trysts becomes a place of slaughter; the
execution of Pedrigano, where the ironies are hinged on false

expeditions of last-minute release; and the final murder scene, with its complex and multi-layered ironies. In the *The Revenger's Tragedy* there are many ironies, but among the most interesting are the incident in II.iii in which Lussurioso rushes in upon the bedroom of his father and stepmother seeking to uncover incestuous adultery, and Lussurioso's sending the disguised Vindice on a mission to corrupt his own sister in II.ii. Both of these incidents, ironical in themselves, set in train a sequence of ironies which become more dramatically titillating as they descend further into the realms of improbability. In the Webster plays, two classic scenes illustrate the extent to which irony is exploited in the melodramatic universe of this drama. In *The Duchess of Malfi*, v.ii is a complex scene which involves a series of turns-about and double-crossings involving Julia, the Cardinal and Bosola, an unexpected declaration of love and an even less expected murder by bizarre means, all in the space of a few minutes, undermining any attempt by the audience to construe the events in terms of psychological probability. In *The White Devil* a similar scene to this is v.vi, the scene of the pretended suicide pact which Flamineo attempts to impose upon Vittoria and her maid Zanche, which piles twist upon twist and ends in multiple murder. Credibility is not a question here, because what this drama requires of the audience is not simply a suspension of disbelief. Like the masque, it involves the acceptance of a wholly different conception of dramatic representation, one which constructs a world based entirely on theatrical convention.

Another theatricalist feature observable in revenge tragedy is an exaggerated preoccupation with the macabre. This too has its origins in Kydian drama: in *The Spanish Tragedy* Hieronymo's discovery of his son's stabbed and hanging corpse in the arbour and later his quite gratuitous action of biting out his own tongue set the tone for the popular sensationalism of revenge drama. Shakespeare exploited this fully in *Titus Andronicus*, and his incorporation of a graveyard scene and skull in *Hamlet* nods in the same direction; here, though, the skull is a *memento mori* which becomes the basis for a philosophical disquisition. In revenge tragedy the macabre constitutes a major part of the tone of the drama, presenting a world of nightmare in which horror and the grotesque are an accepted part of the frame of reference, and in which distortion rather than naturalism determines the texture of social intercourse and values.[5] The fact that this drama relies heavily on the visual for its impact also contributes to this.

One consistent element in this drama is the device of the ghost, something which in Senecan tragedy is used for a specific dramatic purpose which has as much or more to do with narrative expediency – the exhortation to revenge – as effects of horror. Shakespeare in *Hamlet* and Marston in *Antonio's Revenge* uses the ghost in this way; in both plays the ghosts of murdered fathers enter calling for vengeance, but in other plays the presence of ghosts is gratuitous. In *The Atheist's Tragedy* the appearance of the ghost of the murdered Montferrers on two occasions contributes little if anything to the progress of the narrative. In *The White Devil* the ghosts of Isabella in iv.i and Brachiano in v.iv are similarly, strictly speaking, redundant to the action. There is no ghost as such in the *The Duchess of Malfi*, but the echo scene in the graveyard (v.iii) provides a ghostly touch without affecting the course of the action in any way. Other macabre effects in these plays involve the use of specific stage props, objects which either possess or are invested with qualities of exotic horror. These include the severed head of the executed younger brother and the disguised and poisoned skeleton with which the Duke is murdered in *The Revenger's Tragedy*, the fumed picture and poisoned helmet in *The White Devil*, both unusual murder weapons, the dead man's hand and wax dummies in *The Duchess of Malfi*, the death's head which is used as a pillow in *The Atheist's tragedy* and the murdered man's finger in *The Changeling*. The atmosphere of baroque horror which these images create has its basis in two recurrent ideas. One is the danger which lurks in unexpected places and objects, thus adding to the nightmare unpredictability of the society and life being depicted: terror and death concealed in familiar objects. The other is the stress on bodily dismemberment or destruction: severed heads and limbs and other reminders of physical torture and death. Both of these aspects contrast with the masque's conception of the world, in which uncertainty has no part in the smooth ceremonial nature of the dramatic action, and the bodies of the king and others are invested with either a semi-divine or quasi-mythological property. What is especially evident in this is a removal from the physical to a semi-spiritual sphere, while revenge tragedy by contrast foregrounds the physical, particularly in its more earthy and horrific manifestations. Implications of divinity and immortality are never far away in the masque, whereas revenge drama luxuriates in the horror of mortality. They adopt a fundamentally similar dramatic method to achieve their ends, however. In revenge drama the use of stage props of such potent impact on an otherwise unadorned stage necessarily shifts the attention of the audience from the action and the words to visual images, paralleling to some extent the far more elaborate staging of the masque, in which visual image was all important. In each case the image is a powerful signifier, encapsulating implications far beyond its immediate meaning.

A final significant point relating to the similarity of dramatic method between the masque and revenge tragedy is related to this emphasis which both forms place on visual image. This is the principle of display which is basic to both forms. In the masque this is self-evident, since the genre is essentially ceremonial. However, it can also be discerned as constituting the main organising principle of revenge tragedy. The climactic points of these plays especially are arranged as overt exhibitions of revenge, of persecution or of brutal ironies which have little to do with naturalism and a great deal to do with dramatic effect and show. Examples of various types of display come readily to hand. In *The Atheist's Tragedy* the climax of the play is reached on a scafford upon which the villain, d'Amville, knocks out his own brains in the course of trying personally to execute the hero, his nephew Charlemont. The whole event is a sudden turn-around in events, not a natural conclusion of a narrative development, and above all it is spectacular. Its ironical significance is further elaborated by the accidental suicide himself as he confesses his crimes before dying, and the scene is an example of the overtness of this drama's method. Another instance can be found in the death of the Duke in *The Revenger's Tragedy*, in which the hell of the revenge which is being wreaked on the Duke has to be made minutely plain to the sufferer himself as well as to the audience; in the course of it he learns of the adultery of the Duchess with his eldest son. Another such protracted death is that of Brachiano in *The White Devil*, in which Lodovico and Gasparo reveal to him at length the process of poisoning that is claiming his life and insist that, dying without absolution, he is damned for ever. The death of the Duchess in *The Duchess of Malfi* is preceded by a long and ghastly course of mental torture in which the tyranny of the Arragonian brothers is made explicit beyond the strict requirements of the narrative. Bosola in this occupies a strangely paradoxical role which owes a great deal to do with displaying not only this tyranny but also the pathos of the Duchess's death; he is not only the stage manager of the action but in a curiously detached way is commentator on it at the same time, both in his conversations with the Duchess before the murder and in those with Duke Ferdinand after it. The outward, displaying orientation of revenge drama has something of a morality-play quality about it in its careful tailoring of dramatic method to the conceptual content generated by its narrative.[6] In this respect it corresponds again to the dramatic method of the masque, in which the philosophical and political ends of the drama narrowly define its construction.

The effect of the creation of a hermetic, theatricalist frame of reference in the revenge drama was effectively to distance the political implications which are inherent in it, at least technically. A drama which was so patently constructed to create and satisfy a popular demand for exotic and melodramatic entertainment and whose frame of reference was essentially theatrical would self-evidently be less likely to attract unwelcome official attention than more serious and more overtly topical political drama. One aspect of this was the setting of the plays in the Mediterranean world, which, as conceived by Renaissance Englishmen, was an exotic place whose prevailing values were entirely Machiavellian. For dramatic writers this had the advantage of providing them with a moral and political universe which was sufficiently self-contained and apparently remote to be a relatively safe setting for political tragedy, and at the same time one which by its very nature readily yielded the staff of the most lurid of popular drama. It is fairly obvious that this conception of the Mediterranean world, though probably stimulated by the writing of Machiavelli, owes a lot to the dramatic literature in which it is given imaginative life and which was the most popular medium for its dissemination. The elaboration and use of a histrionic cosmos in this drama goes further in covering its political tracks than the use of allegory or remote settings, such as a classical one, to mask reference to contemporary political conditions and practice. Where the drama extends its material beyond the bounds of psychological and naturalistic probability, its serious allusive potential is called into question. Such an attribute was of immense value under a king whose conception of the position of the monarch was such that his strictures against the negative portrayal of kings in literature and drama extended even to the representation of enemy rulers.[7] James I was a keen patron of drama and, besides his lavish expenditure on masques, commissioned many performances of popular plays at court.[8] The danger of incurring royal displeasure was a longstanding one, even under Elizabeth, and James's readiness to take retribution on writers was evident even before he came to the English throne.[9]

The fact that revenge tragedy was thus apparently removed into the realm of purely sensational popular entertainment did not, however, mean that it was devoid of relevance for contemporary political and social conditions. The very fact that it dealt customarily with covert corruption in the state or in ruling households was highly significant, considering that there was a wide discrepancy between, on the one hand, the image of impeccable paternalistic and divinely ordained rule presented in James's writings and other pronouncements, and promoted and dramatically enacted in the masques and other ceremonial manifestations of royal power, and, on the other, the fact of a considerable amount of corruption behind the scenes, both personal and political.[10] Several of the dramatists of the time, such as Marston, who wrote satirical verse before turning to drama, were avowedly satirical writers, even if their satire tended customarily to eschew political targets in favour of more generalised ones such as moral or psychological types – as, for instance, in Jonson's comedy of honours. A more specific instance of social relevance in this drama is the prevalence of the figure of the malcontent, usually in some way economically deprived or perceiving himself to be wrongfully deprived of position, means or power. There is evidence of considerable discontent among the large number of aspiring graduates in and around James's court and several writers may be numbered among those disappointed in their ambitions and thereby suffering real economic hardship.[11] In various indirect ways, therefore, this form of popular theatre does address issues with significant political implications. However, probably its most trenchant and profound statement lies in its confrontation of the ethos of mystical state power at the heart of James's political philosophy and forming the basis of the conception and construction of the court masque. Though this has already emerged in the comments thus far, these have principally been concerned with dramaturgy, and a number of important points remain to be mentioned in relation to the actual content of the drama.

The first concerns the choice of principal characters in these plays and the dominant ideas attached to them. Since revenge drama is highly formulaic, there is a great deal of correspondence between the plays in terms of the types of figures which populate them. Significant as a type are corrupt rulers, their corruption residing either in the misuse of power or sexual abuse or both, predatory sexuality frequently leading to Machiavellian perfidy. Rulers who resort to foul means to achieve illicit sexual ends include the Duke in *The Revenger's Tragedy*, the Duke of Brachiano in *The White Devil*, the King in *The Maid's Tragedy*, and the Duke of Florence in *Women Beware Women*. The sexual element is significant not only because of the quasi-theological suggestion of sexual impropriety as in a sense emblematic of the soul's corruption, but also because of its relevance to the connection between court politics and James's favourites, though this relevance may have been obscured in the period, at least officially, by the fact that James's preferences were homosexual.[12] Rulers or ruler figures whose corruption is more concerned with power include d'Amville in *The Atheist's Tragedy* and the Arragonian brothers in *The Duchess of Malfi*. D'Amville is not actually a ruler but adopts Machiavellian means to gain control of family wealth. This is perfectly suitable as a metaphor for state politics in terms of the official ideology of the family within the body politic.[13] The Arragonian brothers are principally concerned with the acquisition of hegemony over the Duchess's domain, but sexual corruption is never far away, particularly in the case of the Cardinal. What is important about the portrayal of rulers in all these plays is their direct challenge to the masque's mystification of royal power, since they expose that power as being not only highly political, in the sense that it involves the calculated and cynical manipulation of others, but also consistently corrupt and dangerous. In no case is royal concern shown to extend beyond the immediate self-gratifying aims of the ruler to the state at large.[14]

Another figure with significant political implications in these plays is the malcontent, as exemplified by Malevole in *The Malcontent*, Vindice in the *The Revenger's Tragedy*, Bosola in *The Duchess of Malfi*, Flamineo in *The White Devil*, and Calianax in *The Maid's Tragedy*. Each of these is a figure either disgraced or fallen from some previously more favoured social position or blocked in some way in his ambitions. The important point is that these characters have become malcontents through some observable cause, frequently foul play by others in power. This contrasts with the essentialism of the characterisation in the masque, in which any determination of social position or moral state is fixed and mysterious and in which the fountainhead or moral insight and probity is always the ruler. Furthermore, the role of the malcontent as commentator helps to complicate the moral issues, since he can at once be engaged in activities which are morally dubious or unequivocally evil while being able to comment with insight on the corrupt practices of those in power: Malevole, Vindice, Bosola and Flamineo are all sharp analysts. Further complication is produced by the question of the morality of revenge: the stress on lurid instrumentality obscures the moral issues as persecutor becomes victim and *vice versa*. This complication contrasts markedly with the clear dichotomies to be found in the masque – for instance, in the sharp distinctions between the world of the masque and that of the antimasque, a good example of which is to be found in Jonson's *Masque of Queens* (1609), in which the cacophonous and disordered witches' dance of the antimasque is suddenly silenced and banished by the glorious and harmonious entry of the main masque.

Aside from the characters who populate them, revenge tragedies are distinguished by the convoluted structures of deception and intrigue which constitute their narratives. Sometimes, as with d'Amville's intrigue in *The Atheist's Tragedy*, the ends are nakedly evil; sometimes, as with the Duchess's subterfuge in *The Duchess of Malfi*, deception is a weapon used by the innocent in their own defence; and sometimes, as in Vindice's plot in *The Revenger's Tragedy*, evil confronts evil. It is in a way less dramatically important to what end the intrigue is constructed than how subtle and sophisticated it manages to be. This too provides an interesting counter to the masque, since not only does it undermine the mystification of political power but it has implications for the dramatic method of the masque itself. Jonson discusses the relationship between display and mystification in the masque as follows:

This it is hath made the most royal princes and greatest who are commonly the personators of these actions, not only studious of riches and magnificence in the outward celebration or show, which rightly becomes them, but curious after the most high and hearty inventions to furnish the inward parts, and grounded on antiquity and solid learnings; which, though their voice be taught to sound present occasions, their sense doth or should always lay on more removed mysteries.[15]

As the only fully illusionistic form of theatre in the period, the masque constructed elaborate images while at the same time seeking to collapse the distinctions between those images as constructed representations and the world of actual reality, thus burying the ideology which informed it. Revenge tragedy in its complex intrigue plots demonstrates essentially the methods by which appearances can be made to diverge from reality and how apparent truth frequently has some more subtle political process behind it.

A significant motif in revenge drama which is also of relevance here is madness. In some form or another mental imbalance crops up in many, if not most revenge tragedies.[16] This was, of course, incorporated as a highly successful dramatic device by Kyd in *The Spanish Tragedy*, the madness of Hieronymo providing a good deal of the theatrical interest of the play, to the extent that it was subtitled 'Hieronymo is Mad Again'. It is likely that this accounted for much of the play's success in the theatre, and it is easy to see why madness became part of the formula of this popular form of tragedy. It is never entirely clear whether Hieronymo's madness is genuine or not. Shakespeare in both *Hamlet* and *Titus Andronicus* adopts a Kydian formula in associating madness with the main protagonist of each of these plays in a very equivocal way. Madness clearly has to be treated very carefully, since it threatens always to remove its victim from legitimate consideration as a dramatic figure. A clear example of this is Lady Macbeth, who, as soon as she loses her wits, ceases to contribute motive force to the play and is reduced to an emblem of mental suffering. If madness is introduced into these plays it therefore has either to be in some way in the background or to be connected with the principal protagonists in an ambiguous way, and this appears to be the way in which it is usually handled. Overt manifestations of madness occur in *The Changeling*, the sub-plot of which includes a troupe of madmen practising a dance; *The Duchess of Malfi*, in which the Duchess is tortured mentally by a parade of madmen; and *The White Devil*, in which Cornelia, the mother of the intriguer Flamineo, is seen in a cameo distracted with grief over the murder of her younger son. In each of these cases and particularly the latter two, in which the mad scenes occur near the climax of the action, the atmosphere of the plays is made more nightmarish by the presence of this element. However, more important is the suggestion of madness which is often present in the principal protagonists. In *The Malcontent* Malevole is described by Pietro in these terms: 'th' elements struggle within him; his own soul is at variance within herself' (i.ii) and the manic quality of his machinations and pronouncements in the play bear this out, notwithstanding that the role of a malcontent is a guise. In *The Atheist's Tragedy* d'Amville, though an intelligent philosopher, suffers from a fixation of ambition that compromises the sanity of his actions, and this is intensified towards the end of the play, especially in vi.iii, where he enters 'distractedly'. In *The Revenger's Tragedy* Vindice's obsessional qualities and the baroque nature of his schemes speak for themselves, as do Flamineo's *The White Devil*. In *The Duchess of Malfi* Duke Ferdinand's persecution of the Duchess is associated with the developing disease of lycanthropy, and the Duke's descent into madness corresponds with an increasingly nightmarish complication of horror and guilt towards the end of the play. The presence of this element of madness in revenge tragedy presents another interesting challenge to the assumptions which underlie the masque. While the action of the masque is rarely supported by a process of logical reasoning, the mystification of power summons up a higher motivation for and justification of action. The retreat from reason is thus sanctified and dignified by recourse to a higher authority which takes a divine or mythological form. There is also in the masque a claim to harmony or regulation or both which is associated with royal power or the idealised *status quo*. Hence the chaotic and disordered world of the antimasque can be banished at a stroke by the simple assertion of this order, as in *The Masque of Queens*. The ethos of revenge tragedy, with its implications of a dark irrationality never far from the surface of human behaviour, is a direct challenge to this. Madness is not amenable to authority and undermines any sense of system. Thus the revenge genre offers a view of social relations, order and authority which subverts and undermines that of the masque and the political philosophies which inform it.

A few words might be said in conclusion about the presence of masques within revenge tragedies. It is a curious fact that several tragedies have masques inserted in them, frequently at climactic points of the action.[17] One can turn again to *The Spanish Tragedy* for an early instance of the inclusion of court entertainment in this drama, but the manifestations in later plays show a greater use of music and dance, conventional elements in the Jacobean court masque. The practice of including masques in tragedy has been examined in several studies, from a number of points of view, including the dramaturgical and generic implications and the ideas engendered by the juxtaposition.[18] However, what remains to be considered are the political implications of the conjuction of two forms constructed, as they are, around such fundamentally conflicting notions of power and social relationships. A significant point to be remembered in this is the normal ideological function of the masque. The placing of a form which essentially presents an idealised view of the *status quo* within a theatrical cosmos which exposes the corruption of power in the state cannot but subvert the idealisation and the ideology which sustain it. Of the plays discussed in this essay, six include a masque: Marston's two *Antonio* plays, *The Maid's Tragedy*, *The Atheist's Tragedy*, *The Revenger's Tragedy* and *Women Beware Women*. (Additionally, *The Duchess of Malfi* includes a masque of madmen, although it is not actually referred to as such, and a masque of madmen is prepared for though not executed in *The Changeling*.) In each case the celebratory function of the masque in the context of state in which it occurs becomes heavily ironic, which is interesting since the ideology of the masque itself substantially excludes irony. In the plays considered here, the irony emerges either from a contrast between the ideal harmony connoted by the dramatic entertainment and the corruption behind the scenes (as in *The Maid's Tragedy*, but there is an element of this in all these plays), or from the way the masque conceals the final stages of the murderous intrigue (as in *The Revenger's Tragedy* or *Women Beware Women*). It is not that the inner theatrical episode in some way makes the outer frame of the play appear more valid or real, but rather that the whole basis of trust in representation is undermined and shown to depend purely on an ideological construction of reality. The inclusion of the court masque in the nightmare, Machiavellian world of revenge-theatre *Realpolitik* completes its demolition of the idealised and harmonious world presented by the courtly entertainment.

Antonio's opening speech in *The Duchess of Malfi* restates James's ideology of the royal court as the fountainhead of harmony and order in the state. In talking of the king of France he says,

In seeking to reduce both State and people
To a fix'd order, their judicious King
Begins at home. Quits first his royal palace
Of flattering sycophants, of dissolute,
And infamous persons, which he sweetly terms
His Master's master-piece, the work of Heaven,
Considering duly, that a Prince's court
Is like a common fountain, whence should flow
Pure silver drops in general.

This suggests the ideal, but in the play it remains just that, isolated in a strange world of corruption. The exaggeratedly and theatrically extreme events of the play work to present the diametric opposite of this, thus reducing the sacrosanct political ideal to a dramatic contrast, as remote in its fictional extremity as the baroque world of horror is in opposition to it. As a cultural product, revenge tragedy might be considered to exist in a similar relation to the masque. In terms of simple contrast it exposes the fictiveness of the masque's construction of reality by erecting a contrasting conception of power in the state, and, in terms of dramatic method, it calls into question the reliability of dramatic representation through its own theatricalism, thus undermining the masque's claim to authority.

NOTES

1. Among the writers who produced court masques as well as tragedies for the public theatre were Jonson, Middleton, Beaumont, Chapman and Marston.
2. Stephen Orgel, *The Illusion of Power* (Berkeley, Calif.: University of California Press, 1975) p. 38.
3. Ibid., p. 55.
4. Discussions of this inconsistency in the characterisation of Bosola include C. G. Thayer, 'The Ambiguity of Bosola', *Studies in Philology*, LIV (1957); and I. Ribner, *Jacobean Tragedy: The Quest for Moral Order* (London: Methuen, 1979) pp. 110–16.
5. For an interpretation of the preoccupation with the macabre in one play, see S. Schoenbaum, '*The Revenger's Tragedy*: Jacobean Dance of Death', *Modern Language Quarterly*, xv (1954) 201–7.
6. See L. G. Salingar, '*The Revenger's Tragedy* and the Morality Tradition', *Scrutiny*, vi (1938) 402–24.

212   *Jacobean Poetry and Prose*

7. See G. P. Gooch and H. J. Laski, *English Democratic Ideas in the Seventeenth Century* (Cambridge: Cambridge University Press, 1898) p. 61.
8. Lists of plays performed at court may be found in M. Steele, *Plays and Masques at Court, 1558–1642* (New Haven, Conn.: Yale University Press, 1926); and G. E. C. Bentley, *The Jacobean and Caroline Stage* (London: Oxford University Press, 1941) pp. 94, 173, 194, 213, 249, 299, 322 and 336.
9. Several writers, including Jonson and Marston, either suffered penalties under both Elizabeth and James, or took active steps to avoid it by modifying what they wrote. Fulke Greville destroyed his tragedy *Antony and Cleopatra* for fear of official retribution. For accounts of the sensitivity of Elizabeth and James to the subject matter of literature and drama, see D. Bevington, *Tudor Drama and Politics* (Cambridge, Mass.: Harvard University Press, 1960) pp. 8–9, 12–13; and J. Goldberg, *James I and the Politics of Literature* (Baltimore: Johns Hopkins University Press, 1983) pp. 1–3.
10. An account of the corruption and prodigality of the Jacobean court can be found in G. P. V. Akrigg, *Jacobean Pageant or the Court of James I* (London: Hamish Hamilton, 1962) chs 14 and 17.
11. See L. C. Knights, *Drama and Society in the Age of Jonson* (Harmondsworth: Penguin, 1962) pp. 267–74.
12. A contemporary comment on James's chastity with women and his predilection for handsome young men is to be found in Sir John Oglander, *A Royalist's Notebook*, ed. Francis Bamford (London: Constable, 1936) pp. 174 and 196. Caroline Bingham also discusses James and his favourites in *James I of England* (London: Weidenfeld and Nicolson, 1981) pp. 76–87.
13. See L. Stone, *The Family, Sex and Marriage in England, 1500–1800* (London: Weidenfeld and Nicolson, 1979) pp. 152–4.
14. Jonathan Dollimore discusses the demystification of state power in *The White Devil* in his *Radical Tragedy* (Brighton: Harvester, 1984) pp. 231–46.
15. Quoted in R. Strong, *Art and Power: Renaissance Festivals, 1450–1650* (Woodbridge, Suffolk: Boydell Press, 1984) p. 20. The chapter entitled 'Removed Mysteries' (pp. 20–41) deals with the mystification of power in masques and festivals.
16. That the drive for revenge is in itself a form of madness is argued in C. A. and E. S. Hallett, *The Revenger's Madness* (Lincoln, Nebr.: University of Nebraska Press, 1980).
17. See S. P. Sutherland, *Masques in Jacobean Tragedy* (New York: AMS Press, 1983).
18. Sutherland reviews the work on this (ibid., pp. 1–8).

12

All about Eve: Woman in *Paradise Lost*

JOHN SIMONS

Twist me, turn me,
Show me the elf,
I looked in the mirror
And saw . . . .
    (Traditional)

The text is open, its form invites completion. It waits empty for us to enter it, to insert ourselves, to create it through reading. The text is as a mirror which may contain us. It reflects nothing except what we see in it, and we cannot look into it directly unless we see ourself. The epic text also holds a mirror in its folds, and, as the hero looks into the distorted time which is bounded by his poem, he sees or hears the traces of his past and future. In the self-reflexive epic mode, time and space combine to construct the hero once for the reader and once for himself. Aeneas sees himself on the walls of Carthage; Odysseus hides his head and weeps as he hears the poem of himself in his own poem; Beowulf defends himself against Unferth's assault on his past; while, poised between two traditions, Sir Gawain blushes at the reputation he must keep up.

What of *Paradise Lost*? Adam perhaps hears of himself in the history recounted by Michael. Eve does not hear this – she is silenced in dreams; but she does find herself in the poem, at her entrance. It's on this passage that I should like first to concentrate:

That day I oft remember, when from sleep

I first awaked, and found myself reposed
Under a shade of flowers, much wondering where
And what I was, whence thither brought, and how.
Not distant far from thence a murmuring sound
Of waters issued from a cave and spread
Into a liquid plain, then stood unmoved
Pure as the expanse of heaven; I thither went
With unexperienced thought, and laid me down
On the green bank, to look into the clear
Smooth lake, that to me seemed another sky.
As I bent down to look, just opposite,
A shape within the watery gleam appeared
Bending to look on me, I started back,
It started back, but pleased I thence returned,
Pleased it returned as soon with answering looks
Of sympathy and love; there I had fixed
Mine eyes till now, and pined with vain desire,
Had not a voice thus warned me, What thou seest,
What there thou seest fair creature is thyself,
With thee it came and goes: but follow me,
And I will bring thee where no shadow stays
Thy coming, and thy soft embraces, he
Whose image thou art, him thou shall enjoy.
Inseparably thine, to him shalt bear
Multitudes like thyself, and thence be called
Mother of human race: what could I do,
But follow straight, invisibly thus led?
Till I espied thee, fair indeed and tall,
Under a platan, yet methought less fair,
Less winning soft, less amiably mild,
Than that smooth watery image; back I turned,
Thou following cried'st aloud, Return fair Eve,
Whom fly'st thou? Whom thou fly'st, of him thou art,
His flesh, his bone; to give thee being I lent
Out of my side to thee, nearest my heart
Substantial life, to have thee by my side
Henceforth an individual solace dear;
Part of my soul I seek thee, and thee claim
My other half: with that thy gentle hand
Seized mine, I yielded, and from that time see
How beauty is excelled by manly grace

And wisdom, which alone is truly fair.

(IV.449–91)

Eve is thrown into being and her awakening repays examination since through her a potent analysis of the hierarchies of coding in Milton's text may be developed.

Writing of the same passage Cleanth Brooks pointed out that 'The psychology of Eve is sound and convincing. To the student of Freud it may even seem preternaturally so'.[2] Preternatural indeed. My aim now is to examine the arrival of Eve in the poem and Milton's subsequent presentation of her by reading the text through Lacan's rereading of Freud. Here is Lacan's famous description of the child's passage through what he terms the 'mirror stage', the stage which facilitates the entrance into the symbolic order, an entrance into social life:

> This jubilant assumption of his specular image by the child at
> the *infans* stage, still sunk in his motor incapacity and nursling
> dependence, would seem to exhibit in an exemplary situation
> the symbolic matrix in which the *I* is precipitated in a primordial
> form, before it is objectified in the dialectic of identification with
> the other, and before language restores to it, in the universal,
> its function as subject.[3]

Eve passes through the mirror stage quite literally. She is initiated into the symbolic order of the text as a result of her narcissistic experience which teaches her to separate herself from the world as an individual: to understand the integrity and autonomy of her body and desire, over against the undifferentiated 'liquid plain . . . Pure as the expanse of heaven'. Her initiation comes quickly in the voice of the Father who forbids her play and in her joyful self-recognition. She is led by the forbidding Father to Adam: a being less fair than herself – and she attempts to flee, for already the vision of completion in her early experience becomes an idea to be recaptured and a thing to be repressed. In the order of Eden she is to have an existence as the mirror in which Adam sees himself, to be the Other – yet Adam is 'Less winning soft, less amiably mild'. Eve must learn to repress her first vision of completion and to accept the loss of integrity and the fragmentation consequent on the relationship she is to assume with Adam. In his *Vitis Palatina* Bishop King had the following to say about the Creation:

The woman at her first creation was made to bee a *sicut*. *Sicut* is of similitude, so is a woman. Look back to the first institutions, *Faciamus adiutorium* . . . of what quality? *Simile sui*, like to himselfe: There is the *sicut*. *Simile?* what is that? . . . *Simile sui* that which is *contra ipsum*, not contrary; but *e regione*, face to face, as the Angels stood over the mercy-seat; *coram ipso*, as a glasse that reflecteth and returneth upon a man his owne image, that is, *quasi alter ipse, ipse coram ipse*, an other selfe, himselfe before himselfe.[4]

The woman reflects the self of the man – not her own self. As the mirror waits, signifying nothing till it is filled by our presence, so the woman waits, drained of meaning till she is filled by the signifying presence of the man. She waits to enter the realm of social discourse and literally, in sexual intercourse, to be filled with the penis which is the pole of the phallo-centric codes of patriarchal society.

The woman's body is fragmented in itself but reconstituted by the disciplines of a repressive order: 'He for God only, she for God in him' (IV.299). Or, as Thomas Gataker put it

The man is as the head and the woman as the body. . . . And as it is against the order of nature that the body should rule the head: so it is no lesse against the course of all good order that the woman should usurpe authorite to herself over the husband, her head.[5]

The real Milton was, as we know, something of a heretic in these matters, but in his role as justifying poet he reproduces with a loving precision the hierarchies of his society. There is perhaps a tension between these aspects of his being which contributes towards the subversive presence of Eve in his poem.

The Father forbids incest and threatens castration, the physical fragmentation of the complete self so unstably held in the memory. Yet Eve is bidden to a kind of incest. The incest of Satan and the daughter who sprang from his body produced the formless horror death – what will be produced from the incest of Adam and his 'daughter' Eve? The unfallen pair are forbidden the knowledge of good and evil, but Adam has nothing previous to repress: only Eve has the memory of her own completion. At Adam's birth the psychological process is short-circuited:

As new waked from soundest sleep
Soft on the flowery herb I found me laid
In balmy sweat, which with his beams the sun
Soon dried, and on the reeking moisture fed.
Straight toward heaven my wondering eyes I turned,
And gazed a while the ample sky, till raised
By quick instinctive motion up I sprung,
As thitherward endeavouring, and upright
Stood on my feet; about me round I saw
Hill, dale, and shady woods, and sunny plains,
And liquid lapse of murmuring streams; by these,
Creatures that lived, and moved, and walked, or flew,
Birds on the branches warbling; all things smiled,
With fragrance and with joy my heart o'erflowed.
My self I then perused, and limb by limb
Surveyed, and sometimes went, and sometimes ran
With supple joints and lively vigour led:
But who I was, or where, or from what cause,
Knew not; to speak I tried, and forthwith spake,
My tongue obeyed and readily could name
What e'er I saw.

(viii.253–73)

Unlike Eve, he is

                        without more train
Accompanied than with his own complete
Perfections, in himself was all his state.

(v.351–3)

There is not the lack in Adam which there is in Eve, for Adam's mirror is Eve. Adam's body is already differentiated from the world: 'My self I then perused'. The order of language springs fully formed from his mouth and in himself he contains the codes which will organise Paradise. Eve must enter Adam's order, but Milton is too honest a poet to forget her potential integrity and the threat which her self may pose. Fragmentation may be remedied by completion; castration, or the fear of it, by the acquisition of a phallus. The knowledge which will enable Eve to reconstitute the symbolic order is presented in the flamboyant, phallic vision of the serpent:

> his head
> Crested aloft, and carbuncle his eyes;
> With burnished neck of verdant gold, erect
> Amidst his circling spires, that on the grass
> Floated redundant . . . .
>
> (IX. 499–503)[6]

I do not wish to pursue a fatuous aetiology of prelapsarian neurosis, nor to argue through the text's account of a rejection of the reality principle (in Eve as 'general mother' both ontogenetic and phylogenetic): rather I want to use the powerful models of Freudian and Lacanian psychoanalysis to understand the significance of Eve's actions within the hierarchy of codes which is Milton's epic.

Geza Roheim points out that the Hebrew verb for 'eat' can also refer to sexual intercourse (a fact surely known to Milton) and that 'knowing' in the Bible may be a euphemism for carnal knowledge.[7] Kate Millett makes the point forcibly, though she over-generalises: 'Everywhere in the Bible "knowing" is synonymous with sexual intercourse and clearly a product of contact with the phallus, here in the fable objectified as a snake'.[8] Eve's transgression represents an attempt to reconstitute herself as the subject which was lost by the terms imposed on her by the pre-existent order. It is perhaps inevitable that this reconstitution takes place as an encounter with a talking snake, a code-generating phallus. This is an opportunity to master the dominant signifier in the code which represses her and an ironic reversal of the *bijou indiscret*, the gossiping vagina of the *fabliau*.

'Ici dans le champ du rêve tu es chez toi', said Lacan, and Eve's first temptation takes the form of the dream of flying. Freud's treatment of such dreams stresses their sexual component and Eve's 'tresses discomposed, and glowing cheek' (v.10) appears to bear this out in the poem.[9] Also interesting is a remark of Hélène Cixous: 'It's no accident that *voler* has a double meaning, that it plays on each of them and thus throws off the agents of sense'.[10] The dream is of sexual encounter, surrender, memory. Eve has looked into the mirror; now the dream shows her on the road to becoming Woman, the 'narcissistic master-criminal'.[11] Adam attempts to console her: 'Best image of my self and dearer half' (v.95). A more inappropriate address would be hard to imagine. 'Ici dans le champ du rêve tu es chez toi.' The dream is her true home. Here is a space in which she can contemplate the memory of her completion and explore the horizons of her desire. Completion is to be recaptured through mastery of a code, for already her dream, though planted by Satan, generates a symbolic language which faithfully articulates the fantasies consequent on the partial return of the repressed.

It is my contention that Eve, as Woman, in *Paradise Lost* represents a genuine attempt to depict a female psychology, and that this attempt succeeds not least when read through contemporary psychoanalysis. However, Milton's insight functions as an ultimately disturbing force in his poem, for Eve becomes a subversive sub-text which plays against the phallo-centric master codes of the patriarchal epic. Her presence may be repressed at points but it cannot be ignored in its return.

Historically it is unavoidable that Eve should present this problem. For Milton, Woman is real in time and flesh but to be repressed if the myth of justification is to be preserved. I have already pointed out that Milton was something of a heretic, believing that 'the wiser should govern the less wise, whether male or female'.[12] *Paradise Lost* may be seen as a manifesto of marriage as affective bonding.[13] But, while it is ultimately pointless to condemn Milton for misogyny, there is still force in the statement that 'he and the creatures of his imagination constitute the misogynistic essence of what Gertrude Stein called "patriarchal poetry"'.[14] Milton was writing a revolutionary doctrine in a text which involved the re-creation through re-reading of the very texts which had been used by his enemies to justify their power. Eve is caught up awkwardly in this process for, while at times she is faithfully portrayed as a subject, at others she becomes the object of the new relations being set up in Milton's text as a product of the seventeenth century. Women, having come to the fore in almost unprecedented ways during the high days of the English revolution, were now slipping into the niche inscribed for them in the formation of the bourgeois household. The discomfort of Eve in the text is a signifier of contradiction. The break in Milton's text is representative of the rift in the historical development of women in seventeenth-century England.

I should now like to consider Eve more fully as Woman, as the dominant signifier in a sub-code. Here are three of the numerous passages in *Paradise Lost* which make use of female imagery:

> by him first
> Men also, and by his suggestion taught,
> Ransacked the centre, and with impious hands
> Rifled the bowels of their mother earth
> For treasures better hid.
>
> (i.684–8)

> These passed, if any pass, the void profound
> Of unessential night receives him next
> Wide gaping, and with utter loss of being
> Threatens him, plunged in that abortive gulf.
>
> (ii.438–41)

> Into this wild abyss,
> The womb of nature and perhaps her grave,
> Of neither sea, nor shore, nor air, nor fire,
> But all these in their pregnant causes mixed
> Confusedly, and which thus must ever fight,
> Unless the almighty maker them ordain
> His dark materials to create more worlds,
> Into this wild abyss the wary fiend
> Stood on the brink of hell and looked a while.
>
> (ii.910–18)

In the first of these passages Milton sees the earth as a mother, incestuously assaulted and fragmented by her children, just as Sin is raped by her son and wounded by the children of that enforced incest. She does not resist, but her wound carries the threat; she contains it within herself. The 'sulphurous pit' of *King Lear*, iv.vi, has grown out of benevolent Eden. In the examples drawn from book ii of *Paradise Lost* Satan sees nature as a womb, but it is the place not only of generation but also of unmaking. The terrible void whence we came and into which we return unforms us and is imaged as female. The female signifies here the active threat of mutilation and disintegration; she is the destroying goddess Kali not just the reminder of castration. Similar ideas may be found in *Paradise Lost* at v.180–4 and 294–302, and ix.1000–4, but in the first two instances the female earth is seen in the innocent, unfallen sense as a creatress. Space, the unconstituted itself, is generally seen as female; Woman as a sub-code threatens by its presence the forms and wholes articulated by the master code. Woman is the necessary Other for the master code's dialectic of identification. At least she is a silent interrogator which enables the master code to contain, as Absence, the codes it denies or represses through dominance.

In his rather unsatisfactory work on Nietzsche's style Derrida points out that

> There is no such thing as the essence of woman because woman averts, she is averted of herself. Out of the depths, she engulfs and distorts all vestige of essentiality of identity, of property. And the philosophical discourse, blinded, founders on these shoals and is hurled down these depthless depths to its ruin.[15]

This is the 'abortive gulf' of the blind poet's discourse: the threat that is assigned to Woman in the patriarchal myth. Milton conceals the threat in scattered metaphors, but he cannot conceal it in the body of Eve, social being in paradisal conversation, the body which at times averts the reflection it is doomed to bear. Nietzsche himself understood this other possibility quite well it seems:

> All the world is agreed that they [women] are to be brought up as ignorant as possible of erotic matters, and that one has to imbue their souls with a profound sense of shame in such matters until the merest suggestion of such things triggers the most extreme impatience and flight. The 'honour' of women really comes into play only here: what else would one not forgive them? But here they are supposed to remain ignorant even in their hearts; they are supposed to have neither eyes nor ears, nor words nor thoughts for this – their 'evil'; and mere knowledge is considered evil. And then to be hurled, as by a gruesome lightning bolt, into reality and knowledge, by marriage – precisely by the man they love and esteem most! To catch love and shame in one contradiction and to be forced to experience at the same time delight, surrender, duty, pity, terror, and who knows what else, in the face of the unexpected neighborliness of the god and beast!
>
> Thus a psychic knot has been tied that may have no equal. . . .

Afterward the same deep silence as before. Often a silence directed at herself, too. She closes her eyes to herself. . . .

Women easily experience their husbands as a question mark concerning their honour, and their children as an apology or atonement.[16]

In spite of the misogynism of Satanic cosmology, Woman can be the signifier which refuses its signified as surely as if she had said 'no' to him in bed.

Julia Kristeva has pointed out that, 'For a long time, a major semiotic practice of Western society (courtly poetry) attributed to the *Other* (woman) a primary structural role'.[17] This is quite true. The social absentee became the central presence of a signifying chain which reversed the hierarchies that generated it. The poetry was a sort of carnival where gender, not class, misruled. By the seventeenth century, though, the so-called 'feminisation of discourse' inscribed on the social formation a sentimentalised view of woman which neutralises the threat of the Other by pacifying its inevitable intrusions into the male world.[18] In *Paradise Lost*, a text on the cusp of the development, the Other, Eve, Woman, maintains its dissolving threat and structures, in its absence, the master code, while intruding to subvert that code in the role of destroyer and thief – a role which is assigned by the master code itself.

Incest is a narcissistic sin and mutilation is its penalty. Satan gradually loses his bright form while Eve plucks the fruit to gain, as she herself admits, 'what wants in female sex' (ix.821–2) – to recomplete herself after her loss of integrity and enforced 'incest'. She is caught in a contradiction of the patriarchal law. I wish to suppress the sub-argument concerning the precise correspondence between the relationships of Adam and Eve and Satan and Sin here. More to the point, the 'incest' on which the relationship is founded seems to cause a syntactic disturbance in Milton's verse:

> So hand in hand they passed, the lovliest pair
> That ever since in love's embraces met,
> Adam the goodliest man of men since born
> His sons, the fairest of her daughters Eve.
>
> (iv.321–4)

Try as I might I cannot agree with Fowler that this is the 'syntax of ordinary prose'.[19] There is surely a sort of synecdoche here which disposes of the tangled kinship order in a puff of rhetorical smoke. Milton's aporia reminds me amusingly of Lévi-Strauss's dictum that 'incest is bad grammar' and more seriously of the paradoxical logic found in Dante's 'figlia del tuo figlio'[20] and the hideous distortion of Sin's outcry,

> O Father, what intends thy hand, she cried,
> Against thy only son? What fury, O son,
> Possesses thee to bend that mortal dart
> Against thy father's head?
>
> (ii.727–30)

'I must now turn / Those notes to tragic', says Milton (ix.4–5). The transition is from epic to that tragic experience that was mapped out by Nietzsche. The birth of tragedy is the birth of man. When the dithyramb is over, the chorus stand about conscious of the loss they have suffered, their separation from Dionysus, the return of the cold and measuring hand of Apollo: 'As soon as this everyday reality re-enters consciousness it is experienced as such with nausea: an ascetic will-negating mood is the fruit of these states'.[21] The fruit of the Fall sounds suspiciously like the Protestant ethic. For Eve the ecstasy of transgression is the recompletion of herself, the recapturing of the moment at the pool. For Adam it is different: 'From his slack hand the garland wreathed for Eve / Down dropped'. The revels are over. Eve is the presence of Dionysus in the poem but Adam has been too much with Apollo. The garland is his last, unconscious tribute to the maenad in Eve, the disturbing reveller whose dance must end in the nausea of ashes in the mouth and an intensified consciousness of lack.

Eve then, poses a threat to *Paradise Lost* both in terms of our recognition of her as a woman inserted into a text whose master codes deny the possibility of such a being and as the Other, the dark presence which disturbs the master signifier of the phallo-centric discourse. Eve is encoded into the poem as if she were its unconscious – what Lacan calls in real life 'that chapter of my history that is marked by a blank or occupied by a falsehood: it is the censored chapter'.[22] Milton did not tell lies but he could leave blanks. The blanks may be filled just as the analyst fills the blanks in the subject's life-text by reading 'the traces that are inevitably preserved by the linking of the adulterated chapter to the chapters surrounding it'.[23] It is these traces in the text, the play of signification under and around the master code, which have been the subject of my analysis. What of Milton himself, for his text is itself the re-encoding of a code? The Woman that disturbs our reading of the explicit purpose of justification, the gap which hinders us in our pursuit of Milton's declared concern, is a function of his own rewriting, of his inscribing on a new world the myths of the old. Milton the arch-influence, the 'precious bane' of eighteenth-century poetry, is himself engaged in a sweeping clinamen, a dazzling misprision of the Judaeo-Christian myth with which he wrestled. By understanding he re-created, and in his creation are to be found, especially through Eve, the signs of his time and the traces of his struggle with a powerful pre(-)text.

NOTES

1. All quotations from *Paradise Lost* are taken from *The Poems of John Milton*, ed. J. Carey and A. Fowler (London: Longman, 1968).
2. C. Brooks, 'Eve's Awakening', in A. Rudrum (ed.), *Milton: Modern Judgements* (London: Macmillan, 1968) p. 176.
3. J. Lacan, 'The Mirror Stage as Formative of the Function of the I as Revealed in Psychoanalytic Experience' in *Ecrits, a Selection*, tr. A. Sheridan (London: Tavistock, 1977) p. 2.
4. Quoted in J. Halkett, *Milton and the Idea of Matrimony* (New Haven, Conn.: Yale University Press, 1970) p. 44.
5. T. Gataker, *Marriage Duties Briefly Couch'd Together* (1620), quoted in S. Findley and E. Hobby, 'Seventeenth Century Women's Autobiography', in F. Baker *et al.* (eds), *1642: Literature and Power in the Seventeenth Century* (Colchester: University of Essex, 1981) p. 12.
6. It is significant that the majority of examples which Milton gives in the simile which follows these lines are concerned with sexuality.
7. See K. Millett, *Sexual Politics* (Harmondsworth: Penguin, 1971) pp. 53–4.
8. Ibid., p. 54.
9. See S. Freud, *The Interpretation of Dreams* (Harmondsworth: Penguin, 1976) pp. 374–7 and 516–19.
10. H. Cixous, 'The Laugh of the Medusa', in E. Marks and I. de Courtivron (eds), *New French Feminisms* (Brighton: Harvester, 1981) p. 258.
11. J. Culler, *On Deconstruction* (New York: Routledge and Kegan Paul, 1982) p. 173.

12. For Milton's views on marriage and their context see C. Hill, *Milton and the English Revolution* (London: Faber and Faber, 1977) pp. 117–45.
13. On this see Halkett, *Milton and the Idea of Matrimony*; L. Stone, *The Family, Sex and Marriage in England 1500–1800* (Harmondsworth: Penguin, 1977), and cf. M. Foucault, *A History of Sexuality*, vol. I (Harmondsworth: Penguin, 1979).
14. S. M. Gilbert, 'Patriarchal Poetry and Women Readers', *PMLA*, 93 (1978) 368.
15. J. Derrida, *Spurs* (Chicago: University of Chicago Press, 1978) p. 51.
16. F. Nietzsche. *The Gay Science*, tr. W. Kaufmann (New York: Random House, 1974) pp. 127–8.
17. J. Kristeva, 'The Bounded Text', in *Desire in Language*, ed. L. S. Roudiez (Oxford: Basil Blackwell 1980) p. 49.
18. See J. H. Hagstrum, *Sex and Sensibility* (Chicago: University of Chicago Press, 1980).
19. *The Poems of John Milton*, p. 632n.
20. Dante, *Paradiso* (Milan 1949) xxxiii.1.
21. F. Nietzsche, *The Birth of Tragedy*, in *Basic Writings*, tr. W. Kaufmann (New York: Random House, 1968) p. 57.
22. J. Lacan, 'The Function and Field of Speech and Language in Psychoanalysis', *Ecrits*, p. 50.
23. Ibid.

Select Bibliography

Compiled by MARY SHAKESHAFT

CRITICAL STUDIES

Clark, Sandra, *The Elizabethan Pamphleteers: Popular Moralistic Pamphlets 1580–1640* (London: Athlone Press, 1983). Aims to show the variety of reading popular with the Elizabethans and Jacobeans. Analyses with copious quotation pamphlets about rogues and prisons, news and social satire, while placing the writers in their context and discussing their conventions of subject and style.

Davies, Stevie, *The Idea of Woman in Renaissance Literature: The Feminine Reclaimed* (Brighton: Harvester, 1986). Shows how the image of the feminine was rediscovered and used to create a system of values critical of the prevailing social and religious ones. Sections on Spenser, Shakespeare and Milton.

Dodsworth, Martin, *Hamlet Closely Observed* (London: Athlone Press, 1985). A very helpful book for students, taking them carefully through the text and also familiarising them with major critical controversies. While Dodsworth focuses particularly on the question of the code of honour in the play, he raises many more issues and invites readers to think for themselves and find their own answers.

Dollimore, Jonathan, and Sinfield, Alan (eds), *Political Shakespeare: New Essays in Cultural Materialism* (Manchester: Manchester University Press, 1985). After a brief introductory section explaining how the writers are defining cultural materialism, the book is divided into two sections. The first, 'Recovering History', has contributions by Stephen Greenblatt and Leonard Tennenhouse (among others) examining a representative group of plays in the light of current thinking about the Renaissance view of the state, authority, colonialism, the law and the role of women. The second part discusses the representation of

Shakespeare today on stage, in film and in examination papers.

Drakakis, John (ed.), *Alternative Shakespeares* (London: Methuen, 1985). A challenging collection of essays by a number of recent critics, including Terence Hawkes, Catherine Belsey, and Jonathan Dollimore and Alan Sinfield. They question some of the assumptions of earlier criticism in the light of post-structuralist and feminist theory. *Measure for Measure*, as in *Political Shakespeare* proves as usual to be a fruitful play for any critic of whatever school.

Eagleton, Terry, *William Shakespeare* (Oxford: Basil Blackwell, 1986). This brief and readable book in the lively 'Rereading Literature' series raises questions about language, law, value and nature in a range of Shakespeare's plays, which are often unexpectedly grouped, enabling the author to make illuminating comparisons. The study is sometimes curiously old-fashioned in the way it makes Shakespeare reflect back the author's own predilections.

Elam, Keir, *Shakespeare's Universe of Discourse: Language-Games in the Comedies* (Cambridge: Cambridge University Press, 1984). A detailed, technical analysis of the self-conscious use of language, especially in the comedies, in which *Love's Labour's Lost* is seen as a key text. The author uses recent linguistic theory to discuss games, performances, signs and figures and sees language not as something to be lifted off the surface of the play as 'style', but as 'discourse', forming the real substance of the play.

French, Marilyn, *Shakespeare's Division of Experience* (London: Jonathan Cape, 1982). A significant work in the growing body of feminist criticism of Shakespeare. Marilyn French studies the texts in chronological order to prove that Shakespeare was not only always aware of the need for balance of the masculine and feminine but also moving steadily towards integration, because the assimilation of these qualities 'make[s] this life richer, make[s] it, at its worst, bearable'.

Frye, Northrop, *The Great Code: The Bible and Literature* (London: Routledge and Kegan Paul, 1982). A study of the influence of the Bible on English literature, with illuminating comments on language, myth, metaphor and typology, and some stimulating remarks on literary criticism.

Goldberg, Jonathan, *Voice Terminal Echo: Postmodernism and English Renaissance Texts* (London: Methuen, 1986). Draws upon Derrida and Lacan in discussing Spenser, Shakespeare, Herbert, Marvell and Milton. Includes a lengthy reading of Marvell's 'Nymph

Complaining for the Death of her Faun' and a chapter on Shakespeare's characterisation.

Greenblatt, Stephen, *Renaissance Self-fashioning, from More to Shakespeare* (Chicago: University of Chicago Press, 1980). Analyses the way in which an increase in self-consciousness in the period became part of the literary art of the writers, demanding a complex response from its readers.

McGinn, Donald J., *Thomas Nashe* (Boston, Mass.: Twayne, 1981). After a brief biographical sketch has ten chapters on Nashe's major prose works, the last chapter attempting to summarise his achievement. Concludes that we should look at Nashe as 'a sort of sixteenth century Henry L. Mencken with all of that American journalist's love of words'.

Mack, Maynard, and Lord, George de Forest (eds), *Poetic Traditions of the English Renaissance* (New Haven, Conn.: Yale University Press, 1982). A volume in honour of the great Renaissance scholar Louis L. Martz. Contains sixteen essays on the historical, theoretical and technical aspects of the work of Spenser, Sidney, Daniel, Shakespeare, Jonson, Donne, Herbert, Marvell, Milton and Dryden. Contributors include Helen Gardner, Alvin Kernan, Cleanth Brooks and George K. Hunter.

Martines, Lauro, *Society and History in English Renaissance Verse* (Oxford: Basil Blackwell, 1985). A book by a historian who pleads for a breakdown of excessive specialisation and a new attempt to describe the social history of high culture.

Norbrook, David, *Poetry and Politics in the English Renaissance* (London: Routledge and Kegan Paul, 1984). Attempts a systematic reinterpretation of Renaissance critical history which involves looking at the prophetic poets of the late Middle Ages and looks forward to Shelley. Considers Spenser (especially *The Shepheardes Calender*), Sidney, Fulke Greville, Jonson and the Spenserians and ends with a consideration of Milton's early work. Refreshing to find some rather neglected writers given serious consideration.

Parry, Graham, *Seventeenth Century Poetry: The Social Context* (London: Hutchinson, 1985). Interested primarily in the effect the poets aimed to have on their readers and examines in detail poems by Donne, Herrick, Milton, Herbert, Crashaw, Vaughan and Traherne.

Patrides, C. A. (ed.) *George Herbert: The Critical Heritage* (London: Routledge and Kegan Paul, 1983). A valuable addition to this useful series, following the usual format but also giving musical settings and eighteenth-century adaptations.

Ratcliffe, Stephen, *Campion: On Song* (London: Routledge and Kegan Paul, 1981). Full study of the major poet–composer of the period, analysing Campion's syntax, phonetic structure and prosody as well as his music.

Ricks, Christopher (ed.), *The Sphere History of English Literature*, vol. II (London: Sphere Books, 1986). Deals with the poetry and prose of the period 1540–1674 and reflects the current interest in the poetry of Ben Jonson and the work of Thomas Campion.

Rivers, Isabel, *Classical and Christian Ideas in English Renaissance Poetry* (London: George Allen and Unwin, 1979). Extremely useful book for students. Each chapter is divided into three parts: an introductory account of ideas, origins, transmission and use; a collection of extracts from original sources and from English poetry 1580–1670; and suggestions for secondary reading.

Shepherd, Simon, *Amazons and Warrior Women: Varieties of Feminism in Seventeenth Century Drama* (Brighton: Harvester, 1981). Strictly speaking on the drama of the period, but has insights which could be useful in considering other writings. Chapters on warrior maids, roaring girls, witty women and virgin martyrs. The last chapter is provocatively entitled 'Beating up Men'.

Seelig, Sharon Cadman, *The Shadow of Eternity: Belief and Structure in Herbert, Vaughan and Traherne* (Lexington: University of Kentucky Press, 1981). Deals with the theory of correspondences/analogies between the physical world and the spiritual. Close and perceptive reading of texts.

Slights, Camille Wells, *The Casuistical Tradition in Shakespeare, Donne, Herbert, and Milton* (Princeton: Princeton University Press, 1981). After two chapters on the tradition of casuistry and the method by which it was expressed, proceeds to an interesting discussion of cases of conscience in Shakespearean tragedy and to show how Donne used the tradition. Herbert's treatment of it in *The Temple* is followed by an analysis of Milton's 'Hero of Conscience'.

Tennenhouse, Leonard, *Power on Display: The Politics of Shakespeare's Genres* (London: Methuen, 1986). Tennenhouse uses cultural materials such as public speeches, parliamentary debates, books on marriage and on royalty to analyse each of the genres of Shakespeare's work in terms of its formal representation of power, particularly masculine power, in the period. Chapters have intriguing headings such as 'Staging Carnival: Comedy and the Politics of the Aristocratic Body' and 'The Theatre of Punishment: Jacobean Tragedy and the Politics of Misogyny'.

Wayne, Don E., *'Penshurst': The Semiotics of Place and the Poetics of History* (London: Methuen, 1985). Interesting and detailed comparison between Jonson's poem and Sidney's home and the ideologies they embody.

Zunder, William, *The Poetry of John Donne: Literature and Culture in the Elizabethan and Jacobean Period* (Brighton: Harvester, 1982). Considers Donne's poems in their historical context, examining whether they are representative of the attitudes and values of the time. Emphasises Donne as radically departing from traditional views. Devotes a chapter each to the Satires, the love poems, the verse letters, the 'Anniversaries' and the divine poems.

Index

Althusser, Louis, 138
Anacreon, 129
Ancrene Riwle, 55
Aristotle, 164
Arthur, King of Britain, 11
Auden, W. H., 44

Bacon, Francis, 41, 108
Bacon, Nicholas, 170
Bakhtin, Mikhail, 143
Barnes, Barnabe, 121
Barthes, Roland, 3, 26, 32, 120–1, 127
Baxter, Richard, 46
Beattie, William, 57
Beaumont, Francis, 185–7, 190, 196
Bedford, Countess of, 92, 111
Bell, Robert, 171
Belsey, Catherine, 108, 115
Benjamin, Walter, 120
Berkeley, William, 189
Bible, Authorised Version of, 1–7
Bishops' Bible, 4
Black, J. B., 164
Boccaccio, 138, 144
Bodin, Jean, 89
Boklund, Gunner, 155
Boleyn, Anne, 169
Book of Common Prayer, 2, 44–56
Border ballads, 57–76
Bothwell, Earl of, 172
Brittainy, Duke of, 174
Brooke, Rupert, 3
Brooks, Cleanth, 215
Buchan, David, 59, 66
Buckhurst, Lord, 158
Bush, Douglas, 1
Byron, George Gordon, Lord, 136

Camden, William, 179
Campion, Thomas, 139
Carew, Thomas, 133–4, 139, 141
Carey, John, 107, 112

Carter, Angela, 96
Cassa, Giovanni della, 139
Catesby, Robert, 180
Catullus, 129, 138
Chambers, R. W., 55
Chapman, George, 178
Charles I, 87
Charles II, 189–90
Chaucer, Geoffrey, 10, 101, 138; works of, 14, 101
Child, F. J., 73
Christian IV (of Denmark), 180
Cixous, Hélène, 48
Cleland, John, 147
Cleveland, John, 133–4
Cobham, Lord, 180
Cocteau, Jean, 146
Coleridge, Samuel Taylor, 97
Constable, Henry, 126
Cosin, John, 48
Coverdale, Miles, 47, 53
Cranmer, Thomas, 44, 47–8, 53, 170
Cromwell, Oliver, 46, 188–9
Cromwell, Richard, 188
Cuffe, Henry, 178

Daniel, Samuel, 153
Dante, 103, 127, 223
Darnley, Lord, 170, 172–3, 176
Davies, W. R., 20
Dekker, Thomas, 27, 30–1
Denmark, Anne of, 88, 92, 195
Derrida, Jacques, 3, 136, 221
Devonshire, Duchess of, 153, 159
Devonshire, Earl of, 152, 154, 157, 168
Dollimore, Jonathan, 100
Donne, Ann, 89–90
Donne, John, 1, 9, 119, 124, 127, 132, 135; works of, 78–115
Donwald (of Scotland), 181
'Dover Beach', 114

231